Love First

"A no-nonsense approach to how to save someone you love from the ravages of addiction disease."
—William Cope Moyers,
author of *Broken: My Story of Addiction and Redemption*

"*Love First* provides the most detailed account yet of how intervention works. A significant contribution to intervention literature. An empowering antidote to the disease of addiction."
—William L. White,
author of *Slaying the Dragon:*
The History of Addiction Treatment and Recovery in America

"I am truly excited about the book *Love First*. Families and loved ones who read this look at intervention will find the keys to begin the process of recovery."
—John T. Schwarzlose,
president, Betty Ford Center

"A convincing new approach to intervention that puts love and respect first."
—Jack Canfield,
coauthor, Chicken Soup for the Soul Series®

Love First

A Family's Guide to Intervention

SECOND EDITION

Jeff Jay and Debra Jay

with a foreword by George McGovern

HAZELDEN

Hazelden
Center City, Minnesota 55012
hazelden.org

Library of Congress Cataloging-in-Publication Data

Jay, Jeff, 1954–
    Love first : a family's guide to intervention / Jeff Jay and Debra Jay ; with a foreword by
    George McGovern. — 2nd ed.
        p.   cm.
    Includes bibliographical references and index.
    ISBN 978-1-59285-661-9 (softcover)
    1. Alcoholics—Family relationships.   2. Drug addicts—Family relationships.   3.
    Alcoholics—Rehabilitation.   4. Drug addicts—Rehabilitation.   I. Jay, Debra, 1954–   II.
Title.
    HV5132.J39 2008
    362.29′286—dc22

                                                                                    2008028507

Author's note
All the stories in this book are based on actual experiences. The names and details have been
changed to protect the privacy of the people involved. In some cases, composites have been
created.

The Twelve Steps are reprinted with permission of Alcoholics Anonymous World Services,
Inc. (AAWS). Permission to reprint the Twelve Steps does not mean that AAWS has reviewed
or approved the contents of this publication, or that AAWS necessarily agrees with the views
expressed herein. AA is a program of recovery from alcoholism only—use of the Twelve Steps
in connection with programs and activities that are patterned after AA, but that address other
problems, does not imply otherwise.

The Alcoholics Anonymous Preamble (on page 235) is reprinted with permission of the A.A.
Grapevine, Inc.

The quiz "Is a Family Member Chemically Dependent?" reprinted with permission of Substance
Abuse Community Council of Grosse Pointe from the pamphlet *How Do I Know? Where Do
I Go?*

The quiz "Signs of Alcoholism and Drug Abuse in Older People" reprinted from the pamphlet
How to Talk to an Older Person Who Has a Problem with Alcohol or Medications, published by
Hazelden. Reprinted by permission of Hazelden.

The quiz "Are You Troubled by Someone's Drinking?" from "Are You Troubled by Someone's
Drinking?" copyright 1980, by Al-Anon Family Group Headquarters, Inc. Reprinted by permission of Al-Anon Family Group Headquarters, Inc.

12   5 4 3

Cover design by David Spohn
Interior design and typesetting by BookMobile Design and Publishing Services

In memory of
Pauline Ann Eisele
and
Robert Janiga Jay
who live on in our hearts

Contents

Foreword

If one of my family members were an alcohol or other drug addict and were not seeking help to deal with his or her addiction, I would call Jeff and Debra Jay and say, "Help." I know them as admired and treasured friends. But I also know them as professionals with knowledge and experience, both wide and deep, of the complicated, treacherous, and costly disease of alcoholism, as well as of other addictions. I share the view of these authors that alcoholism is the most serious and destructive of our public health problems. My knowledge of and insight about the estimated twenty million alcoholics and two million other addicts in the United States were sketchy and limited prior to the death of my daughter Terry to alcoholism at Christmastime in 1994. That sad loss of a most promising and engaging young woman whom I loved deeply forced me to delve into the struggles and possible emancipation of addicts.

One of the most important and critical steps in the rescue of an alcoholic is the intervention. This is the well-planned, carefully structured process in which family members join in lovingly but firmly confronting the alcoholic with his or her illness and the necessity of beginning treatment. Frequently the addict's close friends or employer is involved in the intervention.

The Jays have carefully assembled the step-by-step process of constructing and carrying out a loving and effective intervention. In their lives and work, the authors have encountered many of the myths related to alcoholics and other addicts, some of them deeply ingrained in the minds of intelligent people. They patiently and convincingly refute each of these myths. They discuss the excuses frequently used by the addict to account for his or her need for alcohol or other drugs and why he or she does not need treatment.

Perhaps more to the point is the manner in which the Jays work through the mistaken views frequently held by an addict's family. During the years of Terry's drinking, with its frequently sad results, she did seek help in treatment, counseling, and Alcoholics Anonymous programs. But we were repeatedly told by well-meaning, supposedly informed friends that we would have to wait until Terry really "hit bottom." The trouble is that when she "hit bottom," she died.

Intervention is a way of erecting a "bottom" before such a tragedy occurs. This point is persuasively made by these authors. The pages that follow are going to save many addicts and their families from years of suffering, loss, and sorrow. This is a tough-love book that underscores the importance of love. It is a life-saving manual for those who would live and love so that others might live.

George McGovern
American Embassy, Rome
March 8, 2000

(George McGovern is a former U.S. senator and a 1972 presidential nominee. He is now the U.S. ambassador to the United Nations Agencies on Food and Agriculture in Rome. He is the author of *Terry: My Daughter's Life-and-Death Struggle with Alcoholism.*)

Preface

When working on the first edition of *Love First*, we had a singular vision: Write a book real people can use. We wanted families, friends, and co-workers to pick up the book, read it, and carry out loving, effective interventions. We wanted to answer questions, give clear direction, and lay out a workable plan. We wrote our ideas on hundreds of index cards and began sorting and arranging them into something that made sense.

Every day we began by staring at a blank page on the computer screen, asking ourselves: "What one core truth do we write about today?" The answers didn't always come easily. We learned that finding answers required viewing the questions through the eyes of those who loved someone suffering from addiction.

When *Love First* was published, our greatest hope—that it would offer help to thousands of families—was dashed when we learned the book wasn't available in most bookstores. Our editor, in response to our bewilderment, said: "Welcome to the heartbreak of publishing."

But over time, an amazing thing happened. Slowly but surely, word of mouth spread about a little Hazelden publication that talked about intervention as an act of love. It began to appear in more and more bookstores. Even *The Oprah Winfrey Show* called, and Debra appeared several times.

Then something unexpected occurred. We began getting emails from families across the United States and from countries as far away as India and Africa, all writing to tell us their stories: how they used *Love First* to get a friend or a family member into recovery. Each story is a gift, and we treasure them all.

Just the other day, we received a beautiful email from a woman who used *Love First* to help her friend. She titled it "My experience in an intervention today":

> Dear Debra and Jeff,
>
> Your remarkable book *Love First* guided us through the process of preparing for an intervention, which brought us to the end of this day feeling as though we are in a state of grace.
>
> Thank you for reassuring us that we would feel terrified, questioning whether we were interfering or genuinely helping. Thank you for gently removing roadblocks we kept tossing in our own path, as we imagined the most devastating outcome.
>
> Throughout your book, you encouraged us to persevere. We trusted you. We made a commitment to loving our friend enough to take the risk. We set a date, we had a practice, and we issued the invitation to our alcoholic friend. We were all in our circle, letters in hand, at 9:00 a.m. today.
>
> Along with a flood of tears from our friend and her husband (who was not alerted in advance of the intervention), we read our letters aloud with love and compassion. Their relief was palpable. They thanked us with genuine appreciation.
>
> Thank you for your wisdom, guidance, and inspiration that gave us the courage to take this leap of faith.
>
> After the intervention, the alcoholic's children thanked those who intervened on their mom, sharing that they had secretly

hoped their mom's friends would reach out and help her and, possibly, save her life.

Eight years after the first publication, we began writing a second edition to *Love First*, updating it in several ways. In recent years, science has made great strides in learning how addicted brains are different. This information helps us understand more clearly why alcoholics and addicts behave the way they do, and why intervention is necessary.

We expanded the chapters on adolescents and older adults. We added new information on intervening without leverage or when alcoholics aren't experiencing many consequences. We included a chapter on executive-style intervention. Co-occurring disorders are examined along with alternative ways to intervene when psychiatric issues complicate the process.

The resources section is expanded, including how to find excellent treatment even when finances are limited. We've updated the tools section, making it easier to record information while planning an intervention. Bits and pieces of new information have been added throughout the book, much of it originating from readers' suggestions.

We hope the new edition of *Love First* helps you help someone you love, and we hope you will share your story.

Acknowledgments

The information in this book comes out of work with hundreds of alcoholics and drug addicts and the people who love them. Their struggles, courage, successes, and setbacks bring depth and relevance to this book. We thank each of these brave and wonderful souls for all they have taught us. A special thank-you to the three women who generously allowed us to reprint the letters they wrote from the interventions in their families.

We are particularly grateful to our editor Richard Solly for his invaluable insights, guidance, and encouragement. We greatly appreciate and thank George McGovern for writing the foreword to this book and for the many opportunities his support has given us. We'd also like to thank the following people for their much-needed contributions: Jerry Boriskin, Ph.D.; Michael Castranova; Carol Colleran; Robert Karp, M.D.; Lori Forseth Koneczny; Robert Niven, M.D.; and Becky Post. We thank our proofreader Nancy Solak for her good work and her good nature.

We'd like to thank our friends and family who have encouraged and supported us: Sara Jay Bayer; Arnie Eisele; Patricia Hitchcock; Philippe and Marta Malouf; Beth Loew; Fran

Kovac; Corbett Reynolds; Carlyn Erickson; Greg and Chris Dodds; Nan Reynolds, R.N., M.S.W.; George Mann, M.D.; Jeffrey and Joy Spragens; George Ritchie, M.D.; and Mel Schulstadt.

We would also like to acknowledge a debt of gratitude to the late Vern Johnson, D.D., the father of modern intervention, and to the many people whose work in the field of addictions has contributed to the base of knowledge from which this book emanates.

We thank our editors—Karen Chernyaev and April Dahl—for their insights and keen observations, contributing much expertise to the second edition of *Love First*.

Note to the Reader

Intervention is the most effective technique that families can use to help a loved one suffering from chemical dependency. It is also the most ignored. But just as CPR is often the first lifesaving step in helping a heart attack victim, intervention is the most powerful step that a family can take to initiate the recovery process.

There are many common misconceptions about intervention. Some think it is an emotional ambush or an uncaring attack. But *Love First* demonstrates that intervention is a carefully planned process founded on love and honesty. Many people have heard about tough love where tough comes first; this book puts love first.

Through our work in intervention, we have found that love is a powerful force when confronting addiction. In the past, expressions of love were delegated to a few brief sentences during an intervention. We've learned that when we expand the role of love, it is love, rather than toughness, that first breaks through denial.

In this book, we have written about intervention in the real way that families experience it. We have organized the information in a step-by-step fashion, we guide you through every nuance of the process, and we answer the many questions that families ask. If someone you care about is suffering from alcohol or other drug problems, this book will clearly explain how to use love and honesty to give your addicted loved one the chance to reach out for help. Read this book thoroughly and share it with others who love the alcoholic.

A Word about Terms We Use

Addiction is the same disease regardless of the drug used. Our society commonly differentiates mood-altering drugs by placing them in three major categories: alcohol, prescription drugs, and illegal drugs. Inhalants can be added to this list, but are substances not usually categorized as drugs. They are ordinary household solvents and substances that produce a high when sniffed. We describe addiction to these various drugs in different ways: alcoholism, drug addiction, and chemical dependency. All three words describe the same disease and are interchangeable. While detox needs can vary depending upon the drug, the recovery process is the same regardless of the drug of choice. Though illegal drugs get the most attention from the media, alcoholism is the number one drug problem in the United States, and addiction to mood-altering prescription drugs is a rapidly growing problem.

As you read this book, you will notice that we freely interchange the words *alcoholic, addict,* and *chemically dependent*. When we use the term alcoholic, we are talking about all addicted people regardless of their drug of choice. When we use the terms addict or chemically dependent, we are referring to people addicted to alcohol in addition to other drugs. Inhalants also are included when we use these terms.

Chemical dependency is an equal opportunity disease. It does not discriminate on the basis of race, age, education, economics, or sex. Keep in mind that addiction happens to both men and women, and to convey this, we have alternated the use of the pronouns *he* and *she*.

Section 1

*Insights into Alcoholism
and Other Drug Addictions*

Love First

Mother Teresa wrote, "There is more hunger for love and appreciation in this world than for bread." She wasn't the only one to understand the power of this deep human yearning. The great religious figures, philosophers, and psychologists have all identified this driving force within the human spirit. It is the basis for the Golden Rule: "Do unto others what you would have them do unto you."

Alcoholics and addicts crave the approval of their families and friends. Outwardly, they may act as if they don't need anyone, but this is a deception. Alcoholics push others away to protect the addiction and to hide their shame—not because they've stopped caring. In fact, it is by giving alcoholics what they *really* want—love, appreciation, and respect—that we can persuade them that accepting treatment is the right thing to do.

People who are addicted have lost all hope, all faith, all belief that they can survive without alcohol or other drugs. These substances are not just stress relievers or a crutch, but life itself. Without the drink or the pills or the powder, they cannot imagine survival. The drug is the oxygen that fills their lungs, the blood that rushes through their veins, the spirit that inhabits their souls. You are going to take that away? It's no wonder addicts fight for the drug like a man fighting for his life. It is their life. They can't see beyond it.

Love restores lost hope. When the most important people in an alcoholic's life come together with a sincere and honest outpouring of love, they ignite a profound emotional shift that signals a new solution. For the first time, all involved— including the addict—see the problem not as a failure but as an illness that can respond to professional care. Loved ones bring with them a promise that the real person, whom they have loved dearly, can be set free and delivered from this sickness.

On the following pages, we lay out a plan to transform love's power into a course of action we call intervention. Intervention gives love direction. It's a love armed with knowledge. It's a love that doesn't depend upon gratitude or thanks. It's a love that asks friends and family to demonstrate integrity and honor, by making the hard decision to do what is right, not what is easy.

During an intervention, love is best described as *divine energy*: the capacity to work with compassion and strength. Loved ones reveal truth to the addicted person in such a way that he will hear the message and say yes to treatment, while keeping the door open to all relationships. Intervention is first about achieving sobriety, but in the end, it is about restoring family and friendship. Alcohol and drugs have taken loved ones away, and family members want them back.

Some still advocate toughness as a means to an end in intervention, but not all means are acceptable. The goal is to preserve dignity—both the addict's and the family's. Regardless of how severe the addiction, addicts can still be approached with love and respect, even when setting boundaries and presenting bottom lines. The means used to reach a goal speak to the future. Is the family furthering the damage or setting the course for the path to healing? Love is more powerful than brute force. It also requires more from everyone involved.

Sister Wendy Beckett in her book on prayer speaks of love as reverence. Reverence, she says, allows us complete acceptance of another person, wanting only good for her. When we accept our alcoholics and addicts, not for their addiction, but for their struggles in the face of an all-consuming adversity, and by remembering who they truly are when they are healthy and whole, then we can find it within ourselves to search for a way to set them free.

When we intervene on the disease of addiction, we use love as a means to an end, because it is the means—not the end— that defines who we are and where this journey will take our family.

What Does It Take to Get
an Alcoholic or Addict to Accept Help?

"I don't know much about this problem, but one thing I know is that you can't help an alcoholic until he's ready for help." As interventionists, we've heard this statement hundreds of times. We've even heard it from recovering alcoholics and addicts, counselors and doctors. Most of us have heard it from people we know, and maybe we've said it ourselves. It's the most unchallenged myth about addiction and the one that stops us from responding to a deadly and destructive disease. It leaves us standing at the sidelines while addiction runs through our families like a freight train.

When we say, "One thing I know is that you can't help an alcoholic until he's ready for help," what we're silently thinking is: "Therefore, there's nothing you or I or anybody else can do about this problem." This is simply not true.

Take a look at what happens when we challenge this myth with a well-placed question: "If alcoholics and addicts won't accept help until they're ready, what will it take to get them ready?" When we ask ourselves this question—*What will it take?*—we change the way we think about the problem and, in turn, change how we approach the problem. Can we remain resigned to the idea that there is nothing anybody can do, or does this question propel us to search out an answer? As James Allen reminds us in his book *As a Man Thinketh*, "Let a man radically alter his thoughts, and he will be astonished at the rapid transformation it will effect in the material conditions of his life."

Alcoholics and addicts who get help "on their own" do so not because they see the light, but because they feel the heat. Something comes along that shakes them up so sufficiently, they'd rather accept help than continue drinking and drugging. We call this shake-up intervention. Most intervention is an unorganized, grueling jumble of personal tragedy for the alcoholic and the family—divorce, job loss, financial ruin, domestic violence, child neglect, jail, cirrhosis, insanity, and, ultimately, death. Something tragic intervenes before the alcoholic or addict seeks recovery. Intervention, however, can be an organized, loving act performed by friends and family. One type of intervention takes years and years of suffering; the other, a few weeks of planning.

The reasoning behind the widely repeated phrase *hitting bottom* is that we must wait for negative consequences to overrun the alcoholic's or addict's life before he will accept help. Prior to the development of intervention techniques in the 1960s by Dr. Vernon Johnson, families knew of no other recourse than to wait for the alcoholic to hit bottom. But hitting bottom comes with a big price tag. The destruction of the family is one price many people pay. Hitting bottom can also mean jail, insanity, or death. Intervention is a way of *raising the bottom*. Intervening with love first helps an addicted loved one find recovery without going through years of affliction and loss. The family, too, is saved from heartbreak and pain that can endure for decades.

The fact that you have this book in your hands means you

are probably ready to make a commitment for positive change. Roll up your sleeves and learn what needs to be done. You will be amazed at how things come together. As Napoleon Hill, researcher and writer on the philosophy of American achievement, discovered while observing successful people, "The moment you commit and quit holding back, all sorts of unforeseen incidents, meetings, and material assistance will rise up to help you. The simple act of commitment is a powerful magnet for help."

So trust the process, and take one step at a time. If, along the way, someone says, "You can't help an alcoholic until he's ready to accept help," politely ask what he or she thinks it'll take to get the alcoholic ready to accept help.

Are You Barking Up the Wrong Tree?

Just about everybody we talk to tells us they've tried everything to help the alcoholic and nothing works. But let's ask ourselves, what do they really mean when they say they've tried everything? Probably, *everything* means things such as reasoning, pleading, begging, rescuing, arguing, threatening, cajoling, bribing, ignoring, reprimanding, or punishing. Many of us have spent tremendous energy without making an inch of progress, because these efforts don't work—at least not for long.

So what's the problem? First of all, most of us were never taught how to help someone suffering from alcoholism or other drug addictions. Turn on the television or pick up a newspaper. We'll see stories about drunken drivers, drug arrests, kids shooting heroin; but we rarely, if ever, see accurate, worthwhile information that prepares us to help our relative or friend. We ask our children to "just say no," but we don't teach them what to do if they marry an alcoholic or if their best friend becomes an addict. As a society, we focus on the problems of addiction but ignore solutions for the family. We have to change that, because chemically dependent folks aren't from another planet but from our families, our neighborhoods, our world. They are our friends and relatives. With the right information, we can make a huge difference.

Not long ago, we were at a grant-writing workshop in Lansing, Michigan. The instructor looked around the room and said, "You people who are working with alcoholics and addicts will have a tough time getting grants because people have no sympathy for alcoholics." He went on to explain that if we wanted financial support for our work, we needed to put a twist on what we do, such as helping children of alcoholics, preventing kids from using drugs, stopping drunken driving. Say anything, but don't say you want to help alcoholics. This illustrates the prevalent attitude we see throughout our country. We turn our backs on alcoholics and addicts and, when we do so, we turn our backs on the people who love them.

Is it any wonder that families are left empty-handed when it comes to coping with this disease? Renowned individuals step forward to educate us about breast cancer, AIDS, heart disease, diabetes, and Alzheimer's disease. But stop and listen for a word or two of sensible advice on how families can help an alcoholic, and we'll hear very little. We're left to our own devices, dreaming up ways to solve this problem on our own, randomly pulling ideas out of thin air. If one thing doesn't work, we try another. When that doesn't work, we come up with something else. We hope and pray the next thing works, but we end up frustrated again and again. It's no wonder we've come to the conclusion that nothing can be done. We're trapped in a catch-22: No one is teaching us the right approach, yet no one can expect us to know the right approach unless someone teaches it to us.

When You and the Alcoholic Are Speaking Different Languages

How many hours have we spent talking to our cherished loved one, trying to prevent him from sliding further into the quagmire of addiction? How did it feel when we saw that our best efforts were backfiring? Did a good intention look more like World War III? Alcoholics undoubtedly come out ahead, and we walk away scratching our heads, trying to figure out what went wrong. Talking sense to an alcoholic is one of the most frustrating things we will ever do.

We probably don't realize that the alcoholic is speaking a different language than we are. To us, alcohol is the obvious problem and sobriety is the logical solution. If the alcoholic would listen, we know he would put the bottle down forever. Of course, it rarely works that way. To the alcoholic, alcohol is not the problem; it's the solution. The problem is anybody or anything that gets in the way of his consumption of alcohol. We're talking about alcohol as the problem; he's talking about us as the problem. See the problem?

To illustrate this point, consider Jeff's story. At twenty-six years old, Jeff was already in the latest stage of alcoholism. He couldn't hold down a job, eat solid food, or go more than four hours without a drink. He was living in a San Francisco city park when he couldn't panhandle enough money for a room in a flophouse. He was bleeding internally and couldn't walk more than a short distance because of a nerve disorder, called neuropathy, caused by the toxic effects of alcohol. In the face of all this evidence, Jeff still didn't think he had an alcohol problem; he thought he had a cash flow problem. He wasn't thinking about recovery; he was thinking about suicide. Although his family tried many times to convince him to stop drinking, he didn't have the foggiest idea what they were so worked up about. He argued and saw them as the problem. Subsequently, he moved as far away from his family as he could. Jeff, another faceless alcoholic, almost died in the streets. It was only after his family learned how to speak to him differently that Jeff had a moment of clarity and accepted help.

As Dr. Vernon Johnson, the father of intervention, explains in his book *I'll Quit Tomorrow*, "The reason alcoholics are unable to perceive what is happening to them is understandable. . . . For many reasons, they are progressively unable to keep track of their own behavior and begin to lose contact with their emotions. . . . Alcoholics don't know what is happening inside of them."

The solution for addiction cannot come from a mind controlled by alcohol or other drugs. It must come from an outside source. Because we are the people who clearly see the problem, it is our job to bring a moment of enlightenment to the alcoholic. But first, we need to learn a language the alcoholic will understand.

When Keeping You Off Balance
Is a Good Thing for an Alcoholic or Addict

How many times have we approached an alcoholic with our concerns, only to be blamed for everything? Suddenly, we're defending ourselves, and the drinking problem gets lost in the shuffle. Almost every family dealing with an alcoholic can relate to the blame game. Alcoholics and addicts use the blame game to deflect unwanted attention. It's a very effective technique. While we are busy defending ourselves, the alcoholic is making her getaway. Keeping us off balance is a good thing for an alcoholic.

The alcoholic will do anything to keep us off his back. *Promise them anything* is one of his defenses. Alcoholics are very adept at convincing people they can handle the problem on their own, and we've probably been through this many times by now. The addict tells us that he'll change, and we hope with all our heart that this time he keeps his promise. However, because of his addiction, he's lost his ability to consistently keep promises.

"I'll stop using the hard stuff," the alcoholic may announce. She vows to drink wine instead of hard liquor, or says she'll drink beer rather than smoke pot. She's switching to something that is perceived as less harmful and, therefore, less problematic. There's a catch, of course. Switching to wine doesn't work, because alcohol is alcohol regardless of how it is delivered into the body. Here is the formula for alcohol content: one ounce of 86 proof liquor = twelve ounces of beer = four ounces of wine. Each delivers the same amount of alcohol, so switching from one to the other is nothing but a shell game.

If the drug of choice is marijuana, cocaine, or some other illegal drug, the addict may appease us by promising to drink alcohol instead. Again, everybody is relieved because their treasured loved one is finally off drugs. However, it's all chemistry to the brain. The brain doesn't say, "Oh, this is alcohol, a legal drug. Since we're not doing illegal drugs, we're no longer addicted." When an addict switches one drug for another, it's called *switched addiction*. An addicted person cannot use any mood-altering substances, including alcohol, without eventually running into problems.

Another popular promise the alcoholic makes is: "I'll cut back." Most alcoholics, unless they're in the latest stages of addiction, are capable of cutting back for periods of time. In the early and middle stages of addiction, the alcoholic doesn't lose complete control over his alcohol or other drug use. Instead he has periodic loss of control. An alcoholic, for example, may successfully cut back to two beers a day for a month. Then, one day, he can't stop at two beers and drinks ten. This is a symptom of alcoholism, but the alcoholic will contend that the month of responsible drinking proves he has control when he sets his mind to it. He dismisses the day (or week or month) of overdrinking as inconsequential. Or the alcoholic drinks secretly, while telling family and friends that he's successfully cut down. Regardless of what the alcoholic says, as long as alcohol is entering his bloodstream, he will eventually lose control over the drug. As the addiction progresses, he experiences increased loss of control. Cutting back is never more than an unreliable, temporary fix for an alcoholic.

A highly publicized account of an alcoholic's attempt to control her drinking is the story of Audrey Kishline. Audrey decided that she wouldn't accept the label "alcoholic" and set out to prove that she and other problem drinkers could learn to imbibe socially. She championed a movement called Moderation Management, which espoused the belief that problem drinkers didn't have to give up alcohol and, in 1995, published a self-help book extolling controlled drinking as an alternative to abstinence. She became a media sensation with guest appearances on *Oprah, Dateline NBC, Good Morning America, ABC World News Tonight, Leeza, The Late, Late Show with Tom Snyder* as well as coverage in magazines and newspapers. She spoke enthusiastically about her personal success as a controlled drinker. Nevertheless, five years later, driving 60 mph in the wrong direction on a freeway, she caused a head-on collision that instantly killed a father and his twelve-year-old-daughter. Audrey's blood alcohol content was three times the legal limit. Now released from prison, she admits that soon after founding Moderation Management, she lost control of her drinking and then hid the truth from her television audiences and members of Moderation Management. She admits to consuming four to eight drinks daily.

Some alcoholics take it a step further. Finding themselves in big trouble, they take other measures to reconcile with their families. Not wanting to admit alcoholism, they make this common pledge: "I can prove I'm not an alcoholic. I'm going on the wagon." For the same reasons discussed above, people who are chemically dependent can be very successful at abstaining for varying lengths of time. Let us tell you the story of a man who came to us for help.

Bill began by telling us about the many wonderful years he and his wife have had together. However, near retirement, his wife's alcoholism had progressed to the point of destroying their relationship. He convinced her to visit a marriage counselor who rightly said that the relationship problems couldn't be dealt with as long as alcohol was still in the picture. The wife vigorously denied having an alcohol problem. The marriage counselor suggested something to the wife that made perfect sense to the untrained ear, but nonetheless was misguided and ill advised: "If you're not an alcoholic, prove it to us by not taking a single drink for an entire year." With that, the wife left the counselor's office and obliged him by abstaining for twelve months. On the one-year anniversary of her abstinence pledge, she opened up a bottle of wine and drank until she was inebriated. She proceeded to get drunk every day thereafter.

What happened here? First of all, the counselor didn't understand the concept of periodic loss of control—that only end-stage alcoholics have total loss of control over their drinking. His suggestion to go on the wagon implied that if the wife successfully stopped drinking for a twelve-month period, she wasn't an alcoholic. Contrarily, an alcohol and drug counselor would tell you that going on the wagon is a symptom of a drinking problem. It's called an *attempt to control*. Nonaddicted people don't strive to control their drinking, because they haven't lost control in the first place.

The wife, desperate to prove she wasn't addicted, sacrificed alcohol for one year. Once the year was up, she felt she had her retribution and a well-deserved freedom from future accusations. Then she did what she'd been waiting to do all year—opened a bottle of wine, started drinking, and never looked back.

The husband, Bill, is once again living with an intoxicated wife, who reminds him that she stopped drinking for the required amount of time and proved she wasn't alcoholic. The husband is now in a worse position than before he sought help. In this case, doing something was worse than doing nothing. The professional advice came from a marriage counselor who didn't have sufficient knowledge about treating chemical dependency.

Be aware of why alcoholics make promises. The nature of addiction forces alcoholics and addicts to engineer escape routes whenever they feel threatened. Many of their promises are escapes. Remember, the alcoholic is protecting access to "his solution"—alcohol or other mood-altering drugs—while keeping us, "his problem," at bay. The more educated we become, the less likely it is we'll be persuaded by the alcoholic's diversions.

What Science Has Learned about the Genetics of Addiction

We often hear people blame their loved one's alcoholism on low self-esteem, stressful lifestyles, or marital problems. While all these may be reasons why people drink, they aren't reasons why people become alcoholic. If we look at people's drinking patterns, we'll probably see that they drink for different reasons at different times: beer is part of the fun with friends on weekends; scotch relieves stress after work; wine reduces inhibitions during a romantic date; martinis feel sophisticated at a fancy party. Which of these reasons—having fun, relieving stress, reducing inhibitions, feeling sophisticated—causes alcoholism? None of them, of course. Reasons for drinking can't cause addiction. If they could, everyone who drank for those reasons would be at high risk for alcoholism.

Dr. Robert Karp, program director for genetics in the National Institute on Alcohol Abuse and Alcoholism's Division of Basic Research, explains that alcoholism is one of the most complex diseases we know and a great challenge for scientists. Although researchers are making progress, Dr. Karp says that science must develop new methods to meet the demands of studying the disease.

Dr. Karp goes on to say that there is an overwhelming

amount of evidence that alcoholism is inherited. This evidence has been gleaned through decades of adoption and twin studies that ask the question: "Does alcoholism run in families because children *learn* to become alcoholic; do they *inherit* genes that cause alcoholism; or *both?*" These studies consistently come to the same conclusion: Alcoholism is an inherited disease, not a learned behavior.

Alcoholism and other addictions are attributed to multiple genes interacting with the environment. A person must consume mood-altering substances before triggering the disease. Making it even more complicated, the genetic makeup can vary from family to family and individual to individual. Although we have not yet identified the full range of genes responsible for alcoholism, in 2004, after taking samples of DNA from people in treatment centers and from their families, researchers at Washington University School of Medicine have isolated a gene variant that increases risk for alcoholism. In 2006, another gene variant, called SNCA (alpha-synuclein), was found to influence whether a person craves alcohol. Researchers at Indiana University School of Medicine report that this discovery supports the belief that there are subsets of alcoholics. Some addicted people may be genetically wired to have stronger cravings. While the SNCA gene doesn't directly cause addiction, it might be a reason some people are highly attracted to alcohol. Consequently, this gene variant prompts patterns of drinking that can then activate genes that are responsible for alcoholism.

Researcher Tatiana M. Foroud, Ph.D., speaking on the ongoing exploration into the genetics of addiction, says, "Alcoholism is a complex disorder and we are identifying pieces of the puzzle that help us to understand why some individuals develop alcohol dependence and others do not."

Twin Studies

Twin studies separate genetics from environment by focusing on the differences between identical and fraternal twins: Identical twins have identical genes and fraternal twins have some of the same genes. If alcoholism is genetic, then identical twins should be equally predisposed to alcoholism because their genes are identical. In other words, if one identical twin is alcoholic, then the other is likely to be alcoholic. If one is nonalcoholic, then the other is likely to be nonalcoholic. Fraternal twin pairs should exhibit more differences in their predispositions to alcoholism because each twin has a different genetic makeup. In other words, more fraternal twin pairs will have one alcoholic twin and one nonalcoholic twin than will identical twin pairs.

If the influence is environmental, however, the probability that a pair of twins will match each other's predisposition to alcoholism will not change based on whether they are identical or fraternal twins. The probability of a match will be determined solely by the similarity of environments, not by the similarity of genes. So identical and fraternal twin pairs should show equal rates of matching each others' predispositions to alcoholism if each pair lives in the same environment.

After studying twins for decades, researchers found that differences exist between identical and fraternal twins. Identical twin pairs are much more likely to match each other in their predisposition for alcoholism than fraternal twins. Pairs of fraternal twins are more likely to differ in their tendency to be alcoholic, with one twin being alcoholic while the other is not. This indicates that genes, not environment, determine alcoholism. It's inherited, not learned.

Researchers have also used twin studies to determine if addiction to other mood-altering drugs is genetic. The outcomes show that vulnerability for abusing marijuana, sedatives, heroin and other opiates, and hallucinogens is highly heritable. Some studies show different susceptibilities for different drugs. Dr. Ming Tsung, a researcher at Harvard, reports that "the genetic influence for abuse was greater for heroin than for any other drug." Researchers also find that abusing one type of drug is related to an increased vulnerability to every other type of addictive drug.

Adoption Studies

Adoption studies are another way researchers have separated genetics from environmental influences when studying alcoholism. Since the 1920s, researchers have studied people born of alcoholic parents but adopted at infancy into nonalcoholic homes. These studies may be the most effective at separating nature from nurture, genetics from environment. If environmental factors are responsible for alcoholism, adoptees born of alcoholic parents who grew up in nonalcoholic homes should show low rates of alcoholism. If genetics are responsible, adoptees will have high rates of alcoholism regardless of their nonalcoholic upbringing. Researchers have found that adoptees born of alcoholics but raised by nonalcoholic parents are four times more likely to become alcoholic than adoptees whose biological and adoptive parents are nonalcoholic.

Animal Studies

Animal studies are also used to research the genetics of alcoholism. Scientists have genetically altered rats to develop a strain of *alcohol-preferring* rats and a strain of rats that avoid alcohol. Alcohol-preferring rats will choose alcohol over water.

Alcohol-avoiding rats will not drink alcohol even when deprived of water. When alcohol-preferring rats are bred, their offspring prefer alcohol, too. When alcohol-avoiding rats are bred, their offspring avoid alcohol. This indicates that a low or high preference for alcohol is heritable. The American Psychological Association reports in the *APA Monitor* that "other trait models [using rats and mice] developed by researchers include . . . strains that sleep for a long time after drinking; strains that sleep a short time after drinking; strains that develop severe alcohol withdrawal symptoms after chronic alcohol exposure; and strains that develop mild withdrawal symptoms." Behavioral scientists say that the ability to breed animals to exhibit specific traits proves that these traits are genetically influenced.

In 2007, scientists supported by the National Institute on Alcohol Abuse and Alcoholism (NIAAA) and the U.S. Army, reported finding a gene variant in mice, known as Grm 7, which contributes to alcohol consumption. Mice that possess this gene drink more alcohol. "This is a noteworthy contribution, particularly since identifying genes that predispose to alcohol-related behaviors is such an arduous task," says NIAAA Director Ting-Kai Li, M.D.

More than sixty years of research consistently finds that the modeling of parental behavior does not account for the transmission of alcoholism. Children do not become alcoholic by watching the behavior of an alcoholic parent; they become alcoholic because they are genetically predisposed to the disease. But genetics alone don't account for alcoholism. A person must drink alcohol or take other drugs to activate the disease. For this reason, the National Institute on Alcohol Abuse and Alcoholism recommends that people in alcoholic families abstain from alcohol use. Of course, if family members don't know alcoholism runs in their family, they can't make an informed decision about whether or not to use alcohol. For this reason, hiding information about family alcoholism from children puts them at greater risk for becoming alcoholic. Honest communication and education about the disease of alcoholism help children make informed decisions about drinking. A child of an alcoholic parent has a 50 percent chance of inheriting the genetic components of the disease. The only reliable way to prevent alcoholism is to choose not to drink.

Animal, twin, and adoption studies consistently establish addiction as a genetic disease. Understanding addiction as a disease is not a new idea, however. In 1877, *Scientific American* published an article titled "Inebriety as a Disease." The article states: "Science . . . draws a broad distinction between drunkenness as a vice and drunkenness as a disease. The man who drinks for pleasure, it holds, may look for benefit in the counsels of others or in his own strength of will; but he who drinks because he cannot help it, being led by an irresistible impulse, is a sick man, and needs not a temperance pledge but a physician."

The Addicted Brain

Addicted brains are different from nonaddicted brains. While genes determine a brain's vulnerability to addiction, alcohol and other drugs have a direct impact on the brain's anatomy and function.

Scientists can now study brains of living alcoholics and addicts using sophisticated brain imaging techniques. CT (computed tomography) scans create cross-sectional images that map out brain structure. PET (positron emission tomography) scans use radioactive material to record how brains function. MRIs (magnetic resonance imaging) use radio frequency to provide images of brain anatomy. Functional MRIs create movies that show both anatomy and function. Not long ago, science's only option was to autopsy cadavers of alcoholics, most of whom had died while living on the streets. They didn't know if changes to these brains were due to addiction or malnutrition. They had no means of observing brains learning, engaged in tasks, or making decisions.

As family members, we are often astonished at some of the decisions alcoholics and addicts make. We wonder why they don't get their act together and begin behaving responsibly. But it only takes one look at the brains of alcoholics and addicts to understand that something is very wrong. A healthy brain is smooth and full, but the addicted brain is so severely atrophied that it resembles Swiss cheese. Neuroscientist and psychiatrist Dr. Daniel Amen says these brains are less active, less healthy, and shriveled in appearance and have an overall toxic look, as if acid had been poured over them. Dr. Amen has found that "cocaine and methamphetamine abuse appear as multiple small holes across the cortical surface; heroin abuse appears as marked decreased activity across the whole cortical surface; heavy marijuana abuse shows decreased activity in the temporal lobes and heavy alcohol abuse shows marked decreased activity throughout the brain." These alterations to the brain translate into downgrades in the brain's capacity to function.

Brain imaging shows that alcohol compromises the brain system responsible for problem solving, memory, arranging things in order, and doing multiple tasks simultaneously. It also causes premature aging of the brain. Extensive shrinkage occurs in the cortex of the frontal lobe, an area of the brain known as the seat of higher intellectual functions. Shrinkage is also found in deeper regions associated with memory, balance, and coordination. Overall, alcoholic brains appear atrophied and are smaller and lighter than nonalcoholic brains.

Researchers at the University of Southern California studied the brains of alcoholic women between the ages of eighteen and twenty-five and found that the brains were about 11 percent smaller than women of the same age who didn't drink or drank lightly. Their brains functioned differently, too. Significant abnormalities were apparent in areas responsible for working with information, such as making sense of a lecture, following directions, or doing math. After abstaining from alcohol for six months, the abnormal thinking processes hadn't improved. Just because someone has stopped drinking, brain function doesn't immediately return to normal. Other studies have demonstrated that repairing the brain can require a year or two of sobriety, and some damage may be permanent.

Drug addiction can degrade a brain's ability to make good decisions. A healthy prefrontal cortex considers risks versus benefits when making decisions. People with addicted brains, however, make choices without considering harm or punishment. Benefits are valued too highly while risks are undervalued. Consequently, decisions are based on immediate gratification and without regard for future consequences. When decision-making functions are corrupted in this way, addicts fail to learn from past mistakes and don't shift strategies when things are going wrong. Families often see this as willful bad behavior or lack of maturity, when it is actually a symptom of a damaged brain.

Cocaine and methamphetamine use can inhibit the building of communication networks between brain cells, blocking the addict's capacity to learn new things. Research suggests that resulting cognitive impairment persists well into sobriety. Some researchers speculate that for those who use cocaine or meth in large amounts over prolonged periods, the damage could be irreversible. These serious and lasting consequences speak to the importance of intervening early.

If a woman drinks the same amount of alcohol over the same length of time as a man, her brain will be more damaged than his. Female drinkers develop brain shrinkage and memory loss sooner than male drinkers. The shrinkage is indicative of the death of brain cells, according to researchers at the National Institute on Alcohol Abuse and Alcoholism (NIAAA). This may increase the likelihood of cognitive decline and dementia with age. Brain areas most affected are those responsible for processing information during our daily lives: differentiating between good and bad, better and best; determining consequences of our decisions and predicting outcomes of our actions; moderating social behaviors; and working toward defined goals.

Until quite recently, it was believed that brains of young people were more resilient to the negative effects of alcohol and other drugs. New research technology reveals a different story: Alcohol and other drugs are more damaging to young brains than to adult brains. Researchers Drs. Susan Tapert and Sandra Brown from the University of California, San Diego, found that repeated exposure to alcohol during adolescence leads to long-lasting deficits in cognitive abilities, including learning and memory.

Further studies show that heavy drinking or drug use during the teenage years results in lower scores on tests of attention and memory when young drinkers reach their mid-twenties. These deficits affect abilities necessary for successfully navigating the challenges of adolescence and for transitioning into adulthood. According to recent studies, impairments originate from changes in brain function. Because the adolescent brain continues to develop until age twenty-five, alcohol and other drug abuse during this time in a young person's life can alter the course of brain development, causing impairment in learning, attention, and memory. By doing so, the young brain can become permanently damaged, affecting both behavior and brain function into adulthood.

According to Peter M. Monti, professor of medical sciences and director of the Center for Alcohol and Addiction Studies at Brown University, "The adolescent brain is often referred to as 'plastic' because it is built to acquire information, adapt, and learn. Alcohol, however, can disrupt the adolescent brain's ability to learn life skills. So, not only can heavy drinking during this time get the adolescent into trouble through behavior such as risk taking or drinking and driving, but it can also make the brain less able to learn important life skills that can help one avoid trouble as an adult."

The lesson for families is that we can't expect an addicted loved one to think like a nonaddicted person. The brain's functioning is changed. By intervening on the disease and getting our addict into treatment, we can halt the drug's damaging effects and begin the healing process.

Eleven Misconceptions about Chemical Dependency

There is much misinformation circulating about addiction, but not enough space here to discuss each myth in detail. Below are the eleven most common myths, each one followed with a synopsis of why it is not true. Most of us have accepted many of these myths as fact:

1. *An alcoholic or addict must be ready for help before he can be helped.* We've already addressed this myth in the first section. A recent survey conducted by Hazelden found that 70 percent of its patients sought help after a friend, family member, employer, or co-worker intervened.

2. *You're not alcoholic if you don't drink in the morning or daily.* Patterns of alcohol or drug use can vary widely from person to person. While one alcoholic may drink every day, another may drink only on weekends or binge drink once every few months. It is not when or how much someone drinks, but what happens when she drinks that will inform us if she has an addiction.

3. *You're not alcoholic if you have a good job and never miss a day of work.* When someone has a problem with addiction, he's out to prove to himself and to others that he is not addicted. Since one of the commonly accepted signs of addiction is absenteeism from the job, alcoholics often diligently go to work. It's usually

in the latest stages of the disease when some can no longer hold down a job.

4. *Illegal drugs are more dangerous to the human body than alcohol.* Although illegal drugs are quite damaging, alcohol is the most dangerous drug to the human body. It affects virtually every organ of the body, including all areas of the brain Although some studies reveal health benefits of drinking alcohol, those benefits exist when alcohol is used in very small amounts and only for certain populations. For many people, the risks outweigh the benefits. Other studies contradict the well-publicized findings about significant reported benefits, explaining that they may be related to diet, not alcohol consumption.

5. *Illegal drugs are the biggest addiction problem in our country.* Addiction to alcohol far outweighs the volume of problems associated with addiction to illegal drugs. Death from alcohol claims 100,000 people per year in the United States while drug-related deaths are approximately one-fifth that amount. Alcohol abuse costs U.S. businesses $80 billion per year as compared to $60 billion for all other drugs. Approximately eighty-seven million people in the United States are related to or living with an alcoholic, whereas about fifteen million are related to or living with a drug addict.

6. *Addiction is the result of a lack of willpower.* Chemical dependency is a complex disease that affects a person physically, mentally, emotionally, and spiritually. Willpower is not an effective therapy for this disease any more than it would be for cancer, diabetes, or heart disease. Addiction happens at a physical and psychological place that is beyond the reach of the will.

7. *A recovering cocaine (heroin, marijuana, speed, Valium) addict can still drink alcohol.* Alcohol is a mood-altering drug; therefore, no chemically dependent person can use alcohol and be in recovery from addiction. If a cocaine addict, for example, uses alcohol, it may set off cravings that will lead him back to cocaine use. If his use of alcohol continues, he will begin to show alcohol problems. This is called a switched addiction.

8. *An alcoholic can use Valium if she follows the doctor's directions.*
   A chemically dependent person should not use any addictive,
   mood-altering drugs even when prescribed by a doctor, except
   when absolutely necessary. Use of Valium or other mood-
   altering drugs on a regular basis activates addiction. Alcoholics
   may need a pain medication if, for instance, they are in acute
   pain or going into surgery, but nonaddictive drugs or drug-free
   techniques are usually recommended for long-term medical
   needs. Many doctors and dentists are now using Toradol or a
   combination of ibuprofen and extra-strength Tylenol as effective
   alternatives to narcotics. Ask your doctor about these options. If
   pain is chronic, consult with a pain management clinic that uses
   opiate-free methods. Many doctors haven't been educated in the
   mechanisms of addiction; thus they believe recovering people
   can continue to use mood-altering medications by just following directions. (Note that mood-elevating medications, such as
   Prozac, are not the same as addictive, mood-altering drugs.)

9. *There is no danger of becoming addicted when a doctor prescribes
   the drugs.* While prescription mood-altering drugs have an important role to play in medicine, some people using these drugs
   become addicted to them. Addiction is different from dependence. For example, dependence will happen to anyone who is
   on an opiate pain medication for a prolonged period of time.
   Tapering off the drug will necessitate going through a period of
   detoxification. But the person who becomes addicted will begin
   demonstrating drug-seeking behavior: increased intake of the
   drug, shopping multiple doctors to obtain multiple prescriptions, stealing the drug from medicine cabinets of family and
   friends, being dishonest and secretive about usage.

10. *Addiction is the addict's problem, not mine.* Addiction is a family
    disease. Every person who is chemically dependent directly af-
    fects eight other people on average. Family members exhibit an
    increase in emotional, financial, and health problems. Addiction
    costs society billions of dollars a year.

11. *Treatment doesn't work.* In the United States, for every dollar

spent on treatment, society saves four to seven dollars. Treatment dollars produce more effective results than interdiction dollars (money spent patrolling the borders for drugs) or law enforcement dollars. To get the same results we get from treatment, the dollar amounts work out like this: It takes $246 million in law enforcement or $366 million in interdiction to get the equivalent results of $34 million in treatment.

Myths and misconceptions originate from many sources. Please make a mental note that many health care providers, doctors, social workers, therapists, and psychiatrists are not trained in the field of chemical dependency. We recently read an article in one of the most respected newspapers in the country that was filled with erroneous information about addiction. A social worker told a friend of ours that her brother wouldn't need heroin if he lost weight and found a job he enjoyed. A book by a diet guru promises to cure alcoholism through nutrition. A doctor we know refers to alcoholism as a lifestyle choice. Don't grasp too quickly at the opinions presented by people who do not have proper training in the field of addiction.

Section 2

Understanding Family Responses

Good Intentions Can Take You Down the Wrong Road

We hear the word *enabling* bandied about quite a bit, but what does it really mean to us? Is it possible that we could be contributing to the problem, even when we believe we're doing everything in our power to stop the addiction?

Almost all families inadvertently enable addicted loved ones by helping them avoid the negative consequences of addiction. For alcoholics and addicts to stay comfortable in their addiction, they need the help of the very people who want them to stop drinking. Family, friends, and co-workers are uninformed recruits, who unknowingly enable the addiction. Every alcoholic and addict has an enabling network or collection of people, professionals, or institutions whose combined efforts unwittingly allow addiction to continue flourishing in the addict's life. This happens in a number of ways, including loaning money, taking over responsibilities, making up alibis, covering up or ignoring the problem, and allowing the alcoholic to manipulate them.

We must be vigilant against blaming each other for past enabling. Without proper guidance, we really can't expect otherwise from our families. People whose lives are touched by an alcoholic are trying to do the best they can with the information they have.

The other day, a friend of ours sent us a story titled "The Butterfly." The author is unknown, but it illustrates perfectly what we mean when we talk about enabling. The story begins with a man who came across a butterfly's cocoon. Fascinated, he stopped to watch as the butterfly struggled to free itself. After several hours, it appeared that the butterfly was stuck and unable to continue. Distressed by what he saw, the man decided to help. He took a pair of scissors and snipped away at the cocoon, and the butterfly emerged effortlessly.

But the butterfly's body was swollen and small, its wings were shriveled. The man waited, expecting the wings to enlarge and expand, the body to contract, and the butterfly to lift into the air. This did not happen. Unknown to the man, his act of kindness had interrupted the butterfly's natural struggle, which forces the fluids from the body into the wings, preparing the butterfly for flight. The man's good intentions crippled the butterfly.

The story ends with this reflection: "Sometimes struggles are exactly what we need in our lives. If God allowed us to go through life without any obstacles, it would cripple us. We would not be as strong as we could have been."

Like the butterfly, the alcoholic must be allowed to face his necessary struggles. When we help the alcoholic in ways that protect him from the natural consequences of his addiction, we may rob him of an opportunity to find his wings. We often hear recovering alcoholics and addicts warn, "Don't cheat an alcoholic out of his pain. It's the best friend he's got."

Intervening and helping a loved one get into treatment or a Twelve Step program isn't the same as enabling. Family members call us and say: "I've thought about intervention but I don't want to enable him." Enabling is focusing on the problem. Intervention is focusing on the solution. When we help a loved one get into treatment, we don't cripple him. We help him find his wings.

Remember, when we enable, our intentions are always good. But as the old saying goes, the road to hell is paved with good intentions. Explore examples of enabling behavior in section 6, page 274. Place a check mark next to any examples you recognize in yourself. Chances are, you'll see at least a few ways your best intentions unwittingly enabled the alcoholic. Make a commitment to stop repeating these behaviors and give the alcoholic the dignity to face his own, essential struggle.

Combine Love with Denial and You Have Innocent Enabling

When someone important to us is in trouble, we do what we can to come to her rescue. It's a normal reaction. The strength of families is often measured by their ability to rally in a time of crisis. When a loved one has more than her share of problems, we explain the breakdown in many ways: bad luck, immaturity, rebelliousness, lack of self-discipline, stress, youthful inexperience, or low self-esteem. We surely don't leap to the conclusion that addiction is the source of the problem.

And why not? Alcoholism is not a rare disease. It claims one out of ten people in the general population. That may seem startling, but stop to consider that this number doesn't even take into consideration addiction to street drugs, inhalants, or addictive prescription drugs. One out of every three Americans is living with or related to someone with an alcohol or other drug problem. Yet, addiction is usually the last thing we consider when we're trying to identify the source of a loved one's troubles.

Even if someone were to say, "You know, Kathy's drinking has been worrying me lately," we explain the drinking away with some plausible excuse. We refuse to explore the issue further or to consider any likelihood of addiction. A strong denial courses through our families. Alcoholism is an unacceptable diagnosis even in the face of much evidence. In our minds, addiction only happens to those people who are somehow less in control of their lives, less vigilant to such failings. To admit that this affliction has visited our family is unthinkable.

Another form of denial is the illusion that we have control over whether we'll become addicted to alcohol or other drugs. Many a self-confessed heavy drinker has explained away any potential problems with alcoholism by saying, "I'm not worried about getting into trouble with alcohol. I'm keeping a close eye on my drinking." The false premise behind this statement is that a drinker can spot the problem of addiction before it happens and somehow cut it off at the pass. Recently, during a telephone conversation with a friend, we heard an example of this form of denial. Our friend recounted a talk she had with her son. She told him that there is a history of alcoholism on both sides of the family, so he should be careful about his drinking. She went on to explain that, although she and his dad drink, he needn't worry because they were watching their drinking. The truth of the matter is all people who begin using alcohol or other drugs do so believing they are in control of their chemical use. This belief, however, does not change the fact that one out of eight people who choose to use mood-altering substances becomes addicted and never foresees it happening. No one who drinks chooses to be alcoholic, and no one chooses not to be.

The combination of this denial and our love for the addicted person generates a type of enabling we call *innocent enabling*. We help the alcoholic out of scrapes and messes, but we do not know that alcoholism is the issue, and we don't even have a rudimentary understanding that our helpfulness acts like fertilizer to a growing addiction.

The first time Robert, a young man we knew, got in serious

trouble as a result of his alcoholism, nobody identified alcohol as the problem. His parents' reaction is a perfect example of innocent enabling.

Robert was home from college for the holidays. His mother lent him her beautiful new car for an evening out with his old high school buddies. But Robert secretly had other plans. He stole away to a seedy old house where he could drink and find drugs. Once there, he spent hours smoking marijuana and drank six bottles of wine. By the time he left, it was three o'clock in the morning. Intoxicated and paranoid, he drove his mother's car toward home. When he saw a police car about a half-mile behind him, he kept his eyes locked on the rearview mirror, monitoring the cruiser's every move. He was so obsessed with the police, he didn't see the car stopped at a red light directly ahead of him. Robert careened into the car at forty miles per hour without ever braking.

Although nobody was injured, Robert totaled both cars. The police pulled up, checked out the scene, and drove Robert home in the squad car. He was too drunk to speak coherently, so Robert's mom and dad just sent him to bed.

The next day, Robert's parents told him he'd have to pay for some of the costs related to the accident, but they never discussed how intoxicated he was the night before. Robert was their beloved son, the college student, the young man with a future. A son with a drinking problem wasn't part of the image they held close to their hearts. The idea that he was also using illegal drugs was even less imaginable.

The policemen thought they, too, were doing Robert a favor by not taking him to jail and ticketing him for drunken driving. The people he crashed into decided not to press charges. They knew Robert had been the president of the student association at the local high school and didn't want to cause him any embarrassment. Each person, in his own way, was an innocent enabler.

What if Robert's car accident had been caused by a seizure rather than drunkenness? They would have settled only for the best of medical care. However, when someone is arrested for drunk driving, we don't call for an assessment or for treatment. If we call anybody, we call an attorney.

Innocent enabling takes on many different forms. Here are other examples:

+ A mother decides she cannot stand by while her grown son's house goes into foreclosure. She explains away her son's problems as a string of bad luck and writes a check to save the day. It never occurs to her that crack cocaine is behind all that bad luck.

+ A colleague takes on additional work to cover for a friend's absenteeism and poor performance. She knows her friend is having trouble at home and wants to help her. She has no idea that her friend's problems at home and work originate from alcoholism.

+ A daughter is suspended from school for drinking. Her parents find a half pint of vodka under her bed. They comfort themselves with the rationalization that all kids experiment, and she'll outgrow it.

People often say to us, "If only I'd seen the problem earlier, I could have done something then and things wouldn't be so bad now." None of us can solve a problem that in our minds doesn't exist. As we are reminded in the Al-Anon meditation book *Courage to Change*, "If my only way to cope with a difficult situation was to deny it, I can look back with compassion to that person who saw no better option at the time. I can forgive myself and count my blessings for having come so far since then."

Combine Reality with Fear and You Have Desperate Enabling

We round a corner and suddenly come face-to-face with reality. Denial is splayed wide open, and we can no longer ignore the truth. It is addiction after all. What do we do next? Do we rush to find the best information on addiction? Do we ask friends how they successfully helped someone in their lives? Check books out of the library? Make appointments with addiction specialists? For most of us, the answer is no. Instead, fear grips us and catapults us into the next stage: *desperate enabling*.

On average, families wait eleven years before reaching out for help, and the profile of desperate enabling takes on many shapes during this time. Once we know our beloved is indeed addicted, we work overtime to make sure we do not end up ruined by this blight. Our family's well-being is at stake. We can't face seeing one of our own ruined financially, incarcerated, or dead as a result of alcohol or other drugs.

To create a clear picture of desperate enabling, we're going to recount an extreme situation we came to know through our work with families. We received a phone call from a woman who was very concerned about her brother's drug addiction and how it was destroying her parents. She asked if she could bring her folks in to talk with us, and we met the next day. After an hour of talking, we learned some interesting things about this family.

The thirty-eight-year-old son we'll call Joe was addicted to crack cocaine and living at home with his retired parents. He moved in after losing his job and being evicted from his apartment. Mom and Dad realized drugs were behind his problems, but their son told them he wasn't ready to get help. So they naturally sought to protect him from any truly horrid consequences. By keeping a close eye on him, they reasoned, they could at least keep him safe.

After three or four months, drug dealers began showing up at their door demanding payment for Joe's debts. He had been buying crack cocaine on credit, and the drug dealers were threatening to kill Joe if he didn't pay up. The parents couldn't very well call the cops, because they'd have to confess that their son was on drugs. They said they certainly didn't want to get their son in trouble. So they paid off the large sums of money he owed. Living on a fixed income, Joe's parents knew they couldn't continue paying off drug debts, so they devised a plan. They told Joe they would give him a weekly allowance for crack cocaine and enough gas money to drive back and forth into the city to buy drugs. In return, Joe agreed not to exceed the allotted budget for his drug purchases.

Over the next couple of months, Joe's parents felt they were successfully managing Joe's drug habit. Never mind that he would be gone for three days at a time and return home looking like death. While away, he didn't sleep or eat, and his personal hygiene deteriorated. He stayed in a crack house and smoked crack around the clock. He came home only after he was so sick and broke he couldn't go on.

Undeterred, they welcomed him home, bathed him, fed him,

and put him to bed. When he got his strength back and felt better, his cravings for crack would kick in. His parents would give him more money, starting the cycle again.

Pretty soon, the allowance wasn't enough. Things started disappearing from the house. One day he came home without his car. He said it had been stolen. In truth, he traded it to his crack dealer for more crack cocaine. So they began lending him their extra car. He gave that car away, too.

Joe's father decided he needed to come out of retirement and get a job. Joe's sister told us the family home was going up for sale because her parents were terrified of drug dealers showing up and killing everyone. Joe was still getting his crack allowance every week, even though his parents were now several thousand dollars in debt. Joe's sister wanted to intervene on her brother and get him into treatment. We told her that intervention would likely succeed at motivating Joe to accept help if her parents would stop enabling Joe. This meant no more providing money. No more living at home unless he gets into recovery. Amazingly, Joe's parents did not feel they could follow through with that requirement. They held on to the illusion that they somehow had the power to save Joe from the consequences of his addiction. The reality of the magnitude of their son's problem, and their fear, kept them locked into desperate enabling.

This story is extreme, but it isn't uncommon. Desperate enabling intensifies as the addiction intensifies. As addiction progresses, enabling progresses. If we ask ourselves "Am I doing things today that five years ago I said I'd never do?" we will suddenly become aware of how far we've come/how much we've adapted. As addiction gets worse, we adjust and readjust to the problem. Our bottom line—the things we swear we'd never do—keeps receding out of a desperate need to save the addict from destroying himself.

Desperate enabling is born out of fear, and fear blocks us from moving out of this destructive pattern. In the book *You Can't Afford the Luxury of a Negative Thought*, John-Roger and Peter McWilliams write:

> Most people approach a fearful situation as though the fear were some sort of wall. . . . But the wall of fear *is not real*. It is an illusion we have been trained to treat as though it were real. . . . If fear is not a wall, what is it? It's a feeling, that's all. It will not [cannot] keep you from physically moving toward something unless you let it. It may act up and it may kick and scream and it may make your stomach feel like the butterfly cage at the zoo, but it cannot stop you. You stop you.

Our desperate enabling may lead us to unplanned and unimagined destinations. The alcoholic is more likely to stay in her addiction because she sees no compelling reason to change. As her chemical dependency progresses, she needs more and more of the drug to get the same results. Problems soar. Eventually she ends up in jail, goes insane, or dies as a result of her addiction. Loved ones who enable the alcoholic are at high risk for both physical and emotional problems. Stress can cause family members to suffer from diseases similar to those of the alcoholic.

According to Dr. Max Schneider, an internist specializing in families of alcoholics, the people around the alcoholic suffer from higher incidences of gastritis, stroke, heart disease, insomnia, respiratory problems, anxiety, and depression. Dr. Schneider warns that the risk of accidents, homicide, and suicide are much higher among families living with active addiction.

Desperate enabling causes every member of the family to suffer. Anger and disputes arise; blame is bounced from person to person; and the family unit itself is eventually damaged. Children are especially vulnerable to this phase of enabling. The adults in the family are so focused on keeping the alcoholic in line, they don't always notice what the children are going through. Parents may believe that their children are their number one concern, but the addiction has inserted itself into first place. Children's needs often go unnoticed. Honest conversations about alcoholism may never take place and, therefore, children blame themselves for the problems. Children are often put in dangerous circumstances, such as riding in a car with an intoxicated parent behind the wheel. Without a safe harbor, children are more vulnerable emotionally and physically. Adults aware of children living in danger because of a parent's addiction are duty-bound to take action. For guidelines on helping children cope with a parent's alcoholism, contact the National Association for Children of Alcoholics. Their Web site is listed in section 6.

In the third millennium, there is no reason anyone has to suffer silently as a loved one slips into chronic alcoholism. We have intervention; we have treatment for the alcoholic; and we have recovery for the family. Letting go of desperate enabling is the first step toward reaching these goals.

What Are the "Rewards" of Enabling?

Our instinct to avoid pain and to seek pleasure is a fundamental source of motivation in our lives. Of these two drives, the desire to avoid pain is the most powerful.

Not long ago, we read a story about an eighty-year-old woman who runs marathons. She never ran a mile before she was in her sixties. We asked ourselves why someone would take up such a grueling sport at such an advanced age. Maybe she found great pleasure in setting and achieving difficult goals; but it was more probable, we thought, that marathons were a way for her to avoid the pain of aging by developing a superb physical condition required for the sport. Avoiding pain is the more powerful motivator.

The same holds true for the person controlled by alcohol or other mood-altering drugs. If she feels pain when not drinking or drugging, she'll drink to avoid the pain. If the pain of addiction becomes greater than the perceived pleasure of drinking, she's more likely to choose recovery. If family and friends interfere by easing the pain of addiction, they upset the ratio between pain and pleasure in favor of staying in the addiction. Said simply, we make drinking easier than not drinking.

Of course, the alcoholic is not alone in experiencing the

pain of addiction. We, as family members, go through a gamut of difficult emotions. How do we escape our own emotional pain as our world seems to crash in around us? When addiction causes a problem, we are in pain, too; when the problem is solved, we're relieved and our pain is reduced. Our feelings of relief are a form of pleasure. Once we go through the enabling cycle a few times, we're conditioned to expect a reduction of pain and increased pleasure as a result of our enabling behaviors. Because we feel better, we mistakenly believe enabling works. Of course, because the addiction has not been treated, more problems will continue to surface. The only way we can keep up with the problems is to find more and more ways to enable. Our enabling progresses as the disease progresses, and our lives become increasingly unmanageable. Emotionally spent and exhausted, we start to feel like Alice in *Through the Looking-Glass* upon her first meeting with the Red Queen:

> "Now, Now!" cried the Queen. "Faster, Faster!" And they went so fast that at last they seemed to skim through the air, hardly touching the ground with their feet, 'til suddenly, just as Alice was getting quite exhausted, they stopped.... Alice looked around her in great surprise, "Why, I do believe we've been under this tree the whole time! Everything is just as it was! ... In our country you'd generally get to somewhere else—if you ran very fast for a long time, as we've been doing."
> "A slow sort of country!" said the Queen. "Now, *here*, you see, it takes all the running *you* can do, to keep in the same place."

When addiction is the *country* you are living in, you'll be lucky if all the running (enabling) you can do keeps you in the same place. More likely, you end up in a worse place.

We spoke with parents of a twenty-seven-year-old woman suffering from alcoholism. They were particularly inventive at solving their daughter's problem of chronic unemployment. They decided to give their daughter her inheritance early, so she'd have a small income to keep her comfortably housed, clothed, and fed, regardless of whether she worked or not. The parents believed this plan would keep their daughter safe and, knowing she was safe, they felt that everything they did for their daughter was all right. The parents experienced a reduction in pain and an increase in pleasure as a result of rescuing their daughter from the problems caused by her alcoholism. Recognize the built-in reward system of their enabling behaviors? How will they most likely respond when this short-term solution topples over with the arrival of new problems?

Ask yourself a question: Knowing, as I do now, that an alcoholic must be allowed to experience the negative consequences of addiction, will I be able to allow that to happen *even when it is causing me pain?* Don't say yes too quickly. For most of us, if we are experiencing pain, our instinctual response is to ease that pain. If putting the alcoholic back on his feet is the only way we know how to reduce our pain, we will most likely enable the alcoholic. If we want to stop enabling the disease, we must first find a better way of managing our own pain, called *detachment.* Detachment means we stop managing the alcoholic's problems.

A story commonly heard in Al-Anon, a Twelve Step support group for families and friends of alcoholics, tells about a woman married to an alcoholic husband who fell out of bed whenever he was drunk, which was most nights. Each time he fell, the wife would get up and pull him back into bed. After attending a few Al-Anon meetings, she heard about detachment. The next time her husband tumbled off the bed, she left him to lie on the cold, hard floor all night. At her next Al-Anon meeting, she proudly told the story of her successful detachment. The other members said, "But we meant to detach with love." The next time the woman's husband fell out of bed, armed with her new understanding of detaching with love, she wrapped a warm blanket around him as he slept the night on the floor.

Detachment helps us to choose to act rather than react, to begin letting go of problems that belong to someone else, and to do it all with love for the alcoholic. Detachment is the best solution for managing our pain in a way that frees us from enabling. Detachment, however, isn't always easy. We'll do well to seek the support of a Twelve Step group for families and friends of alcoholics and addicts. We can find an Al-Anon, Nar-Anon, or Families Anonymous meeting in our home area using the resources in the appendix or by looking in the local phone book.

Al-Anon's book *In All Our Affairs: Making Crisis Work for You* offers the following reflection: "Al-Anon helped me to focus my attention on what I could do about my situation instead of concentrating all my attention on what I thought the alcoholic should do. I was the one who had to take a stand."

Detachment: A New Recipe

The well-known Serenity Prayer, written by Reinhold Niebuhr in 1934, and later modified by Alcoholics Anonymous, is the perfect recipe for detachment: "God grant me the serenity to accept the things I cannot change, the courage to change the things I can, and the wisdom to know the difference."

We are encouraged to accept what we cannot change in other people, places, and things, and to recognize what we can change in ourselves. What does it take to do this? *Wisdom and courage.* And what is the result? *Serenity.* When we detach with love, we take our focus off the alcoholic and place it onto ourselves. When we focus on ourselves, we regain our power to make meaningful choices about what we do and what we don't do. By making this shift in our thinking and actions, the world around us changes. Our world becomes manageable, and we find peace.

Many times people react vehemently against the idea that they should detach from the alcoholic's problems. They are sure their lives will crumble if they don't continue holding up the alcoholic. However, focusing on the problem is one of the best ways to keep the problem alive. As long as our energy is spent managing the addiction, we are part of the problem. Detaching from the problem opens the door to solutions.

Successful CEOs and executives know this. The CEO of a Fortune 500 company told a reporter interviewing him that he never allows anyone to speak to him about problems. We wondered how this man could run a huge organization if he won't let his people speak to him about problems. His response? "If someone comes in to tell me about a problem, I send them away. I tell them to come back when they can tell me about an opportunity or solution linked to that problem. Hearing about the problem doesn't do me any good—but an opportunity, now there's an altogether different matter. Then I know we're getting somewhere."

How do we turn an alcoholic's problem into an opportunity? Imagine you have a thirty-two-year-old son who works and lives in a nearby city. His wife and kids moved out two months ago because of his drug problem. He's behind on his rent and has just received notice that in seven days they'll begin eviction proceedings. He's desperate. He calls and says he has nowhere else to go. He'll lose his job if he's homeless. The entire scenario flashes through your mind and your knee-jerk reaction is to rescue him. Why not? He's your son.

Imagine stepping back from the problem. You don't react to your son but instead ask yourself, What choices do I have here? You look for an opportunity and find it. Calmly, you explain to your son that you love him very much and want to help him. You've seen the effects drugs have on his life. You ask him if he'd be willing to accept treatment as a solution to his problems. If he says yes, help him make immediate arrangements. Suggest he call the employee assistance professional at his job to arrange admission into a drug rehab center that day. Explain that upon admission to treatment you will help him make payment arrangements with the apartment management. If he is in enough pain or has no other enablers to turn to, he'll very likely accept this offer of help.

If he refuses to seek treatment, stop trying to convince him further. Simply say, "It is your choice. If you change your mind, call me. I am willing to help, but only in the right way." By keeping your focus on yourself, rather than getting caught up in his crisis, you found an opportunity to lead your son into recovery. Even if he refuses help, you can still feel good knowing you've done the right thing. You approached him with love, offered help, resisted enabling the disease, and left the door open for him to change his mind. You made choices that gave him the best chance to reach out for recovery.

Napoleon Hill, the motivational writer who knew some of the greatest achievers in the history of our country, tells us, "It is virtually impossible not to become what you think about most. If you concentrate on something long enough, it becomes part of your psyche. . . . If you think about problems, you will find problems. If you think about solutions, you will find solutions. . . . The successful person understands this and learns to overcome them by focusing on the desirable objective, not on undesirable distractions."

If we are focused on the alcoholic, we are focused on the problem. Take our eyes off the problem, and we'll no longer be trapped in it. We put our focus on self. We resign from our job as manager of the problem and sign up for the team that creates solutions.

At this point, we can start thinking about how a crisis can give us the best ingredients for intervention. We can memorize the Serenity Prayer so we know the recipe for detachment. We focus on self and how we can change what we do. We learn what we need to know in order to do this successfully.

Are You Seeing the Addict as a Bad Person or as a Sick Person?

As we delve into a discussion about addiction, we pay close attention to what our heads tell us versus what our hearts tell us. It is not unusual to have an intellectual understanding of alcoholism as a disease, yet continue to react emotionally as if it were a moral failing or lack of personal discipline. Even professionals struggle with this, so we can't beat ourselves up over it. If we are aware of what is going on with us, we can step back and see where our responses to the alcoholic are coming from.

We can ask ourselves these questions: At this moment, am I seeing the alcoholic as a bad person (failing morally) or as a sick person (suffering from a disease)? How is my point of view coloring my reaction right now? If we're feeling angry and want to yell at the alcoholic over a broken promise, we back up and take a look at where this reaction is coming from. Can we readjust our thinking and readjust our expectations of him? Can we see that his disease blocks his ability to be reliable?

Addiction is a predictable, progressive, and chronic disease. The word *predictable* tells us there are certain symptoms we can reliably expect to see when alcoholism is present. We can organize those symptoms into a list and use that list as *diag-*

nostic criteria. The list is a tool that tells us what signs and symptoms indicate chemical dependency. The stage of addiction (early, middle, or late) is determined by the number of symptoms a person exhibits. In the earliest stages of alcoholism, the symptoms may be so few that it is difficult even for a professional to make a reliable assessment. In the latest stages, the symptoms are so numerous just about anybody could make a diagnosis of addiction.

The term *progressive* means that without treatment, the problem always gets worse. Unchecked, addiction eventually leads to incarceration, insanity, or death. Halting the progression requires abstinence. Long-term abstinence is most likely achieved when the alcoholic works a program of recovery in Alcoholics Anonymous or another Twelve Step program. The medical community may treat other physical and psychological illnesses that co-exist with the addiction, but Twelve Step recovery programs are crucial to long-term, contented sobriety.

In Finland, a study of recovering alcoholics showed that the only significant predictor of sobriety at ten years after treatment was ongoing participation in the fellowship of Alcoholics Anonymous. There is always a story about an alcoholic who put the bottle down without a recovery program and hasn't had a drink since. This happens, but rarely. Alcoholics without a program of recovery are at high risk of returning to alcohol use. In addition, an alcoholic without recovery rarely finds the quality of life or healthy relationships in her sobriety that recovering alcoholics find in a Twelve Step program.

Even if an addict is abstaining from drug use, without recovery the symptoms of the disease may continue to progress. The drug is out of the picture, but the addict behavior is not. Abstinence is only the first step. The ultimate goal of recovery is contentment, serenity, and joyous relationships. The Big Book of AA, *Alcoholics Anonymous*, states:

> A.A. does not teach us how to handle our drinking. It teaches us how to handle sobriety. I guess I always knew the way to handle my drinking was to quit. It's no great trick to stop drinking; the trick is to stay stopped. A.A. led me gently to embrace reality with open arms. And I found it beautiful! For at last, I was at peace with myself. And with others. And with God.

During the downward progression of the disease, the alcoholic will have moments of improvement. These moments can obscure the forward march of the disease from the eyes of family and friends. Look at the whole picture rather than specific points in time to identify the increasing damages caused by addiction.

The word *chronic* reminds us that there is no cure for chemical dependency. Once a person is addicted to alcohol or other mood-altering drugs, there is no going back to drinking as a nonalcoholic. The best we can do is put the disease in remission. A medical diagnosis may read like this: "Alcoholism: arrested." No amount of time without alcohol or other drugs can change this diagnosis to: "Alcoholism: cured." There is no cure. A return to drug use reactivates the disease. Recovering people explain it this way: "Once you're a pickle, you can never be a cucumber again."

People often ask us how to tell if a person is actually addicted to alcohol or other drugs. Laypeople worried about a friend or relative can ask themselves one question: Is the person experiencing repeated negative consequences in any area of his life due to alcohol or other drugs, and does he continue to drink or use anyway? If the answer is yes, the person is probably chemically dependent and would benefit from a professional assessment by an addictions counselor. For the specific symptoms and stages of alcoholism, turn to the Jellinek chart on page 300.

To learn everything we'd ever want to know about the disease of alcoholism, and actually have fun doing it, read the book *Loosening the Grip* by Jean Kinney and Gwen Leaton. A quote from the book underlies what we are striving to say: "Alcoholism—alcohol dependence—has not always been distinguished from drunkenness. Alternatively, it has been seen as a lot of drunkenness and categorized as a sin or character defect. The work of E. M. Jellinek was largely responsible for the shift from a defect to an illness model. In essence, through his research and writings, he said, 'Hey, world, you folks mislabeled this thing. You put it in the sin bin, and it really belongs in the disease pile.' How we label something is very important. It provides clues about how to feel and think, what to expect, and how to act." By understanding that addiction is a disease, not a choice, we will approach the problem differently.

Addiction isn't something the alcoholic does to us nor is it a moral failing. Many people of tremendous accomplishment succumb to this illness. Unimpeachable character is not a vaccine against chemical dependency—addiction is an equal opportunity disease. Yes, it's true that people have to choose to drink before they can become alcoholic, but we live in a society that promotes drinking. Mood-altering drugs are widely prescribed to help people sleep, calm down, cope with stress, and escape pain. Illegal drugs are readily available any place you go—even in maximum security prisons—and are considered fashionable in some social circles. When we use mood-altering drugs of any type, we can expect that a certain percentage of users will become addicted to those drugs. Once the choice to use a mood-altering drug is made, it is anybody's guess as to who will or will not become chemically dependent.

Using the Power of the Group

Believe it or not, intervention is more about us than about the alcoholic. Certainly, our motivation to intervene comes from the problem of addiction. And, yes, our goal is to deliver the alcoholic into treatment, followed by a program of recovery and a contented sobriety. But when all is said and done, intervention is about taking our eyes off the alcoholic and putting the focus on ourselves. It is about what we choose to do and not do. It is about choosing to reach out to the alcoholic with love and honesty, acting in a way that preserves the alcoholic's dignity, and moving into the solution.

To motivate an alcoholic to accept help requires a new outlook. The first thing to realize is that one-to-one confrontations with an alcoholic rarely work. Alcoholics and addicts are skillful manipulators. Dealing with alcoholism effectively—whether in the family, in a treatment center, or in Alcoholics Anonymous—is all about working in groups. The power of the group can triumph over the power of addiction. One-to-one, an alcoholic can manipulate even a well-trained addictions counselor, but not an educated group. Groups are the driving force behind intervention.

In recovery circles we always will hear people refer to the

power of the group. The first word of the Twelve Steps is *we.* It is common to talk in terms of *the we of recovery.*

The next section of this book will teach you how to work in a group, how to think in terms of *we.* Approaching the alcoholic one-to-one saps all your power. There are a few exceptions to this rule, but we'll leave that discussion for later, in section 4.

Remember that intervention is a process, not an event. It teaches us a new way of dealing with chemical dependency and asks us to consistently integrate what we've learned into our lives, not just during the hour or so it takes to do an intervention. Make a commitment to the process of intervention, not just to a one-time event.

One of the first questions people ask us when talking about intervention is, "How successful is it?" Statistically, success ranges between 80 and 85 percent—if we define success as motivating the alcoholic to accept help. However, we believe all interventions, correctly done, are successful. Four primary reasons make every intervention a success: (1) the family is united through education and open communication; (2) the addicted person hears how much her family loves her; (3) the family members have an opportunity to explain how the addiction has affected them; and (4) the addict learns that the family will support recovery but not addiction.

The fact that the family has finally come together as a group, learned about the disease of chemical dependency, and perhaps for the first time talked about the problem and its solution makes intervention successful. Although individual family members may have known about the addiction for years, intervention is often the first organized attempt by the entire family to work toward a remedy.

Another reason for success is that during the intervention,

the alcoholic hears in very specific terms how much he is loved. Most of us will live and die and never experience a time when the people we care about come together in one room, at one time, to tell us how much they love us and why. Take a moment to imagine that experience. Close your eyes. Picture a pleasant room with a circle of chairs. Think of the people closest to you sitting in those chairs. Now, go around the circle listening to each person reveal to you how much he or she loves you. Hear them describe the special qualities they cherish in you and the memories of you they hold dear to their hearts. Be still and notice how you feel as you visualize this experience. As you can imagine, this is an overwhelming emotional encounter for an alcoholic who hasn't felt lovable in a very long time.

Yet another reason for success is that the alcoholic finally hears how her addiction has affected those people who love her. There is no anger, there is no blame, only honesty and love. Even if the alcoholic refuses the help offered to her, these words from her family and friends will resonate in her mind for a long time. She can't forget them. This will profoundly affect her future drinking.

Finally, the alcoholic learns that the people closest to him no longer intend to enable the disease; but instead, each person has made a commitment to support only recovery. He is told that everyone in the group is willing to help him get into recovery, but no one is willing to help him stay sick. Accomplishing this much is a huge success. After laying down these ground rules, many a "failed" intervention turns itself around in a few days, weeks, or months, once the alcoholic reflects on his situation and decides to reach out for help after all.

Intervention is not a complicated process, but it does require planning and preparation. If we want the best results, we follow the directions to the letter and don't cut corners. As Norman

Vincent Peale tells us in *The Power of Positive Thinking*, "It is not enough to know what to do about difficulties. We must also know how to do that which should be done."

One last word before we move on to the next section. If an alcoholic's behavior is endangering a child, including an unborn child, or setting up dangerous situations such as drunken driving or domestic violence, the alcoholic relinquishes the right to choose. Although we cannot control an alcoholic's actions, we do need to control how we respond to those actions. Take the necessary steps to safeguard defenseless victims, even if that means calling the police.

Not too long ago, a man who learned his wife had taken their three-year-old son on a drug deal and then smoked crack cocaine in the car while the child was in the back seat contacted us. This man rightly went to court to request suspension of the mother's visitation rights. In another case, a woman called us to initiate an intervention after her husband drove drunk with their daughter and son in the car. She said, "I've put up with a lot due to his drinking, but I promised myself I'd draw the line if he ever put our children's lives in jeopardy." She successfully intervened on her husband's alcoholism, but if he hadn't accepted help, she was prepared to ask him to move out of the house as a way of protecting their children. Addiction increasingly diminishes the addict's ability to make responsible decisions. Take swift and appropriate action if poor decisions on the part of the addict are endangering others or himself.

Section 3

Preparing for an Intervention

Building a Team

Dante once wrote, "A mighty flame followeth a tiny spark." You are about to do a powerful thing. You are getting ready to pick up the phone to call the people closest to the alcoholic and ask them if they are willing to learn about something that could save the alcoholic's life. With every call you make, you ignite a spark.

Building a team gives you the best possible chance of defeating addiction. Your success depends on the help of a well-selected group of three to ten individuals working together. Intervention requires a team of people, because it's the power of the group that defeats addiction.

Selecting a team for an intervention starts with making a list of all the significant people in the alcoholic's life. These are people the alcoholic loves, respects, depends upon, needs, likes, and admires. You'll find names for your list among relatives, friends, co-workers, employers, clergy, teachers, and medical professionals. Turn to "Building a Team" in section 6 and use the worksheet to write down everyone who comes to mind. Don't edit anyone out just yet, and don't start making phone calls. Right now, you are creating a preliminary list.

You'll use it to select your final team. Only then will you begin contacting people.

As you fill out the list, begin with relatives. Then write down friends. Finally, add other important people such as employer, co-workers, neighbors, clergy, doctors. Not all of these people will necessarily participate in the intervention, but get their names on the list. You may use their help in other ways besides attending the intervention.

Don't exclude them from your list because they live far away. If you're thinking, "Oh, Jack can't make it. He lives eight hundred miles away and has a demanding work schedule and three kids." Let people decide for themselves. We've found that people go to great lengths to help a loved one. In one case we worked on, every family member and close friend of the alcoholic lived in a different state except for the parents. When the alcoholic's parents started contacting people, each sibling and friend they asked to participate said yes. Everybody took time off work, arranged for child care, and made airline reservations. When the alcoholic walked into his parents' house at the time of the intervention and took one look at all the people assembled in the living room, he knew why they were there. Before anyone said a word, he announced, "Okay, I'll go." The alcoholic, so strongly affected by seeing his friends and family from all over the country in one room, realized there was only one reason for them to be gathered together— his alcoholism. Don't underestimate what people will do to help someone they love.

But be prepared. When you first call people to discuss the possibility of intervention, you may get a mixed reaction. Some people may be very enthusiastic, others somewhat reluctant, and still others may be fiercely opposed. Meet everybody at their starting point. Before you pick up the phone, mentally give each person permission to express his or her feelings *even if they're different from your own.* Each person has had unique experiences with the alcoholic, and it's not uncommon for family members to feel angry or fed up. The idea of an intervention may not be welcomed with open arms. That's all right. Don't try to talk people out of how they feel. Let people have their feelings. Listen to them. Have empathy. Put your agenda aside long enough to hear what they have to say. They'll give you valuable information about the toll addiction has taken on them. How they feel gives you a starting point.

Set realistic goals for yourself before you begin building your team. Before you place a call, ask yourself, "What do I want to accomplish with this first conversation?" Businesspeople often say that the only goal they have for their first meeting with a new client is getting the second meeting. Start by setting up realistic goals for yourself. For instance, consider asking relatives and friends to agree to learn about intervention. This is a comfortable first step for most people. Your first conversation might begin with something like this: "I see things getting much worse with Johnny, and I'm very worried about him. I've been learning how we might help him in a way we've never tried before. It's called family intervention, and it's done with a great deal of love and care. Would you be willing to learn a little bit more about intervention with me? Maybe we'll find it's something we want to do and maybe not. But I don't think we can lose by taking a look."

If the person you're asking launches into all the reasons why Johnny is beyond help, don't interrupt. Let her express her frustration. All of her previous experiences tell her that Johnny is a hopeless case. Once she's finished saying what she needs to say, you can empathize: "I know how frustrating this is and how Johnny has repeatedly disappointed us, but

I thought it wouldn't hurt to find out a little more. As much as I've been angry with him, I love Johnny and I know you do, too. Would you be willing to join me just to look into it?" Even the person most fed up with Johnny is likely to agree to that much. She doesn't have to believe Johnny can be helped or that intervention works; she just has to agree to learn about it. That is a successful first step.

Approaching people about intervention can be stressful and emotional. You don't know how people are going to react to the idea—or to you. Fearing a negative reaction can sometimes be enough to keep you from asking at all. Initially, call people you think will support you. Get them on your team first. Then call relatives and friends who are likely to be reluctant. By naming other family members willing to learn about intervention, they may be persuaded to say yes. This is an example of how the power of the group is more effective than one individual.

If you are concerned about talking to someone who is a particularly tough prospect, one or two family members who are supportive of intervention should talk to that person with you. Keep in mind that it's okay for someone to be reluctant. Reluctance is only a starting point. It tells you the person needs more information. Don't expect him to meet you at the point where you are—respect his feelings. Remember, those feelings are coming from repeated experiences of hurt, frustration, and disappointment. You might say to him, "I don't blame you for feeling the way you do. In fact, with what you've been through with Johnny, I can't imagine you feeling differently than you do. What we're suggesting doesn't erase the past, but it might change the future for the whole family as well as for Johnny. Will you agree to a first step and learn about it with us?"

Sometimes the first step needs to be small and easy. The more convenient and the less arduous the request, the more likely people will agree to it. Consider a variety of options. Obviously, you can ask family members to read this book. It's a handy and inexpensive choice. You can even find the book in your library. But what if reading a book is more of a commitment than some are willing to make? Find an easier first step. Over the years, we have developed an informative Web site that is easy to navigate and offers a tremendous amount of free information. You can give people the link, www.lovefirst.net, and ask them to take a look. Many people decide to read the book after examining the Web site. If people show interest in a complete education on intervention, but still prefer not to read, we've taped a video workshop that's available online. Everyone on your team can watch it on a home computer. Go to www.interventionworkshop.com to view sample videos and to learn more. Another option is hiring a professional interventionist for a consultation. If team members live in different cities, the meeting can take place on a conference call. The interventionist provides education, assesses the problems and needs of the addict based on family information, and answers questions. A consultation typically lasts from one to three hours, depending on the needs of the family. At the end of a consultation, most families have a good idea of how they want to proceed.

If a relative or friend still doesn't want to participate, respect her wishes. Don't force the issue. Stay on good terms with her, letting her know that the door is always open.

As you build your team, one person's reluctance to participate shouldn't stop you in your tracks. Things have a way of falling into place if you keep moving forward. As comedian

Gracie Allen once said, "Never place a period where God has placed a comma." Keep moving ahead, even if you feel like you've hit a brick wall. Brick walls often turn out to be nothing more than mist—you can't see past them, but if you keep walking, you get through them easily enough.

A Few Things to Consider
before Picking Up the Phone

You may already know who will be on your intervention team, but before you begin making phone calls, be sure each person you plan to ask is appropriate for the intervention. Use the following guidelines to screen each person on your list.

Exclude anybody on your list who is actively chemically dependent. A practicing alcoholic or addict is rarely included on a team intervening on another addict or alcoholic. He may sabotage the intervention. He can turn against the team in the middle of the intervention, become angry and defensive, or minimize or rationalize the alcoholic's problems. However, there are extenuating circumstances. Sometimes a chemically dependent family member is crucial to the success of the intervention. Including such a person is tricky and this is a time when you want to consult with a professional. In more than one intervention we've facilitated, an addicted team member agrees to get treatment after going through the training process. In one case, a father with a drinking problem told his crack-addicted son during the intervention, "I know I have a problem, too. I am not only asking you to accept help; I am making a commitment to go into treatment myself." In other cases, an alcoholic team member has a less severe problem and sees the person being intervened on as the "real alcoholic." But because they've done a lot of drinking together, we ask them to acknowledge their drinking history. All members of the intervention team will write a letter to the alcoholic. In this case, the letter could begin by discussing the past: "Johnny, we've done a lot of drinking together over the years and had a lot of fun. But those days are gone. Alcohol is no longer your friend. I see it hurting you and that hurts me."

Many times family members worry about their nonalcoholic drinking histories with the alcoholic. They fear the alcoholic will say, "Hey, how can you say anything to me? I've seen you do your share of drinking." A history of social drinking with the alcoholic is not a problem and should not keep anyone from participating *as long as they are not chemically dependent themselves.* We'll discuss this issue in more detail later in the book. For now, cross off your list any person with an active alcohol or drug problem, unless that person is a necessary figure in the intervention process and then talk with a professional before proceeding.

Next, consider whether anybody on your list is likely to tell the alcoholic about the intervention ahead of time. Some people think they're doing the alcoholic a favor by warning him about the intervention. If someone on your list is incapable of keeping it a secret, don't ask that person to be on the team. If an alcoholic learns about the intervention, the intervention will likely fail. By notifying the alcoholic in advance, his natural reaction is to build defenses that protect the disease and keep you out. Again, if a person is vital to the team, but can't keep a secret, don't inform him about the intervention until about twenty-four hours before it is held. This requires rapid training and, again, a professional interventionist is best equipped to handle this difficult situation.

A few years ago, we facilitated an intervention that had all of the elements for success. The key people were all in attendance: the wife, mother, father, sisters, brother, a favorite uncle, the best friend, and the boss. We had a letter from the family doctor recommending treatment for alcoholism. Everything was beautifully planned, and everyone was highly prepared. The alcoholic showed up on time, sat down, and listened to everybody. The intervention went without a hitch—until we asked the alcoholic to accept help. Instead of agreeing, he unemotionally announced to the group that he did not need help, thanked everybody for expressing their opinions, stood up, and calmly walked out. We were stunned. We quickly learned the reason behind the calculated and cold response. His wife, in a fit of rage, had told him about the intervention a week before it took place. He had seven days to think and plan. He hardened himself against his family and friends. All the love expressed during the intervention had little effect on him. The intervention was doomed before it began, because the alcoholic knew he was going to walk out before he arrived. Explain to each person why the alcoholic can't be told.

The last thing to consider is whether anyone on your list is strongly disliked by the alcoholic. If so, they should not participate. We use love to reach the alcoholic. If the alcoholic feels disdain for a particular person, there's no love to work with. Many people in the family probably have had arguments with the alcoholic and resentments build up. There may be sibling rivalries. But the alcoholic still loves these people regardless of the problems. What we're concerned about is deep-seated resentment or conflict that goes way beyond disagreements or bickering. If the alcoholic has such a potent dislike for somebody, that person is not appropriate for the intervention team.

Again, sometimes there are extenuating circumstances. The parents of a heroin addict contacted us to plan an intervention. The addict's sister had been so angry, she hadn't spoken to him in two years. We didn't think intervention was the appropriate setting for a reunion between the two, but we did feel she should have a presence. Her brother needed to hear she was involved and that she cared. Down deep, he loved her even though they were estranged. The family agreed that she would not attend but would write a letter. She asked her mother to read the letter during the intervention. She began the letter by writing, "Even though I stopped talking with you, I never stopped loving you. I just didn't know what else to do."

During the planning stages of another intervention, we were told that the alcoholic "hated" her brother-in-law. Our first response was to say that he couldn't participate, but the situation was complicated. We learned that the alcoholic had never told her sister how much she disliked her husband. The consensus was that opening this can of worms before the intervention would cause a serious rift in the family, and the sister of the alcoholic might refuse to attend the intervention if her husband were excluded.

After discussing this problem thoroughly, we settled on a compromise. We included the brother-in-law in the intervention but placed him in a chair slightly out of the alcoholic's direct view. We minimized his potentially negative impact by sandwiching his involvement between two people for whom the alcoholic had great respect and love. We diplomatically suggested he keep his letter to the alcoholic short, and we edited the letter for anything that could trigger anger. In the end, the strained relationship did not disrupt the intervention, and the alcoholic agreed to treatment. There are times when things are not black and white, and we need to make judgment calls. Take time to problem solve and you'll find workable solutions.

Involving Doctors and Other Professionals

Before you talk to a doctor about your plans for intervention, get your family and friends on board. Work with your team while you decide how, and if, to contact the addicted person's doctor. Use the following guidelines to help you make your decisions.

A letter from a doctor recommending treatment can be a powerful tool during an intervention. It is particularly helpful if the addict is using prescription mood-altering drugs, since she may falsely believe she can't be addicted to a drug prescribed by a doctor. In this case, the addict may be "shopping docs," or going to numerous doctors for the same drug. Contact the addict's primary physician and let him know about the drug problem. Before you call the doctor, gather as much information as you can. Find out the types of drugs being used, how many doctors are prescribing, and the drug-related behaviors you've witnessed. The more information, the better.

When talking one-to-one, doctors may advise alcoholic patients to quit drinking, but alcoholics cannot quit so easily. The physician might say, "You have the beginnings of cirrhosis. This is a serious life-threatening condition, and if you continue drinking you'll die." The alcoholic, truly shaken by the news, tells the doctor he's had it with booze, and that he'll quit drinking immediately. But the next day he's drinking again. He truly meant to quit, but his disease of alcoholism is more powerful than his fear of death. A doctor talking to an alcoholic one-to-one usually doesn't get very far, but in the context of an intervention, a doctor's recommendation can be powerful.

Alcohol is the most damaging drug to the human body. It affects all organs. In a report to the National Institute on Alcohol Abuse and Alcoholism at the National Institutes of Health, it was estimated that 30 percent of patients in hospitals have alcohol-related illnesses, and that alcoholism is as common as coronary disease among the elderly. Yet many doctors have difficulty diagnosing alcoholism. According to a 1992 study published in the *Journal of Studies on Alcohol*, doctors with special training in addictions failed to identify 65 to 84 percent of their patients with alcohol-related problems. In a 1998 study, the National Center on Addiction and Substance Abuse at Columbia University (CASA) found that only 1 percent of primary care physicians identified alcoholism when presented with classic symptoms of alcohol addiction in an older woman. Families are often frustrated when their loved ones come home with a glowing report of physical health from a family practitioner, knowing alcoholism was overlooked.

In some cases, doctors fear that questions about alcohol use will offend their patients, so they gloss over the issue or ignore it completely. Other times, an illness caused by the toxic effects of alcohol is treated but the alcoholism is not. For example, chronic alcoholism can cause certain heart problems. A doctor may prescribe heart medication for a patient with arrhythmia or other abnormalities without ever assessing the patient for alcoholism.

Sometimes a doctor's personal relationship with alcohol interferes with her ability to diagnose alcohol problems in others. One out of ten doctors is a daily drinker. Doctors using alcohol every day may not be as concerned about patients who are abusing alcohol. A doctor is apt to view drinking patterns similar to her own as normal. If the doctor is a heavy drinker, she may find the alcoholic's drinking less of a concern than does the family.

Every so often, we come across doctors treating alcoholism with Valium or similar drugs. We recently worked with a sixty-five-year-old alcoholic woman whose doctor did just that. It didn't take the woman long before she was mixing Valium with large amounts of alcohol—a deadly combination. Valium is not a treatment for alcoholism; it's a switched addiction. A doctor making these kinds of recommendations may be a big hit with the alcoholic, but not with the family.

Many doctors are not knowledgeable in the area of chemical dependency. In four years of medical school, doctors may get as little as two hours of education on the number one problem in America. If your attempt to work with a doctor fails, it may be that he is unprepared to deal with chemical dependency. Consult with a doctor who is an addictionist and a member of the American Society of Addiction Medicine (ASAM). These doctors have completed special education in the area of chemical dependency. If your addicted loved one is seen by an addictionist, it's more likely the doctor will be supportive of the intervention process. For a referral to an ASAM-certified doctor, call 301-656-3920 and ask for the membership assistant, or send an email request to email@asam.org.

Doctors who have a good understanding of chemical dependency are often very helpful and supportive of intervention. When asked, they gladly write letters recommending treatment. Select someone from the team to read the doctor's letter during the intervention. Don't expect a doctor to attend an intervention unless she is also a close family friend.

If the family doctor isn't familiar with assessing chemical dependency, suggest he read *The Physicians' Guide to Helping Patients with Alcohol Problems*, a pamphlet published by the National Institute on Alcohol Abuse and Alcoholism. The twelve-page pamphlet is available online at www.medhelp .org/NIHlib/GF-183.html.

You can use the same guidelines as you would for doctors when asking other professionals—such as a counselor, social worker, or psychologist—to write letters for the intervention. Keep in mind, some professionals do not understand that chemical dependency is a primary disease, and they may be prone to explain it away as a symptom of another problem. You must be vigilant in your expectation that the addiction be treated as a primary disease.

While writing the first edition of this book, we learned that a relative of ours is addicted to prescription drugs. Her insurance company sent her to see a psychiatrist. Although she asked for treatment at a chemical dependency center, the psychiatrist instead directed her to a psychiatric hospital and diagnosed her with major depression. When our relative explained she wasn't depressed and had never experienced symptoms of major depression, the psychiatrist dismissed her objections. He said addiction was caused by depression. This is incorrect. Some people who are addicted are depressed, but depression doesn't cause chemical dependency. If you remember only one thing from this section, remember this: *Addiction is a primary disease, not a symptom of something else.* Other problems may coexist with the addiction—and often do—but addiction left untreated will block solving these other problems.

If a professional talks to you about addiction as a symptom of something else and wants to focus on that instead of treating the addiction, an alarm should go off in your head. If your house is burning down, you're not going to waste time talking to the firefighters about your bad plumbing. If the professional you're working with wants to focus on depression, or low self-esteem, or childhood issues while your loved one is in the throes of addiction, look for a more knowledgeable professional. Call an alcohol and drug treatment center for suggestions. They usually know the doctors, psychiatrists, psychologists, and counselors who understand chemical dependency.

Involving the Workplace

In preparing an intervention, contacting the workplace causes family members more concern and fear than any other issue. They fear the addict will be fired once the boss learns of his alcohol or other drug problem. It is more likely, however, that the company has policies supporting treatment and recovery.

Ignoring the work issue only invites the alcoholic to use his job as an ironclad reason why he can't accept help. When you are in the middle of an intervention, the alcoholic may say, "I can't go to treatment because I'll lose my job." You want to be prepared to say, "We've followed company policy and made the necessary arrangements for your medical leave. Your job will be waiting for you when you are finished with the treatment program."

A family came to us after their thirty-two-year-old alcoholic son was hospitalized for esophageal varices, a rupture of the veins along the esophagus caused by chronic drinking. The rupture led to massive bleeding and their son nearly died. A few days after his release from the hospital, he started drinking again. The family decided intervention was their last hope to save him. Before the intervention, we explained to the family that they must contact their son's workplace and arrange for a medical leave. In this particular case, the alcoholic's father was a longtime friend of the employer, and he agreed to make the phone call. We decided that if the alcoholic used work as an objection to treatment, the father could explain he had talked to the boss and made all necessary arrangements for a medical leave. As we predicted, the son used his job as an objection to treatment. We turned to the father, expecting him to speak, but found out he hadn't called his son's boss after all. We had no way to refute the alcoholic's objection. Seeing all was lost, the father reached for the phone and called the boss right there and then. He explained that the family was in the middle of doing an intervention on the son. The boss replied, "It's about time. Tell him he'll keep his job, but I don't want to see him back here until after he completes treatment." With that news, the son changed his mind and went to treatment immediately.

Calling the addict's boss directly may not be appropriate for everyone. There are a few other ways you can approach the workplace. Many companies provide an employee assistance program, or EAP. Call the workplace for the telephone number of the EAP. You do not have to say who you are or why you want the number. When you talk to the EAP, ask if your conversation will be kept confidential. Once you know confidentiality will be maintained, explain that you are planning an intervention on a relative who is an employee, and you need to know the company's policies regarding medical leave for chemical dependency treatment. The EAP will give you guidelines to follow. By following the company's policies, you'll protect the alcoholic's employment status and strengthen your position during the intervention.

Some families worry that a company may support treatment but fire the alcoholic later. Addiction is a problem most companies face and firing people who are in recovery is not common practice. Businesses invest huge sums of money to train their employees—whether you're in the mailroom or the boardroom. Employee turnover is costly. It's smarter to help employees solve problems than to fire them. Even if an employer did try to fire someone for addiction, the Americans with Disabilities Act prohibits discrimination against people seeking help for chemical dependency. An alcoholic is more likely to get fired if she doesn't seek treatment. No law will prevent an employer from firing someone who is missing work or performing poorly due to the use of alcohol or other drugs.

If you are dealing with a company or small business that does not have an EAP, contact a co-worker of the alcoholic. This person can tell you about company policy or the best person to contact for information. Or you can call the human resources department anonymously and ask them about the procedures for taking a medical leave. Keep in mind that human resources personnel are not bound by confidentiality, so if you choose to identify the alcoholic by name they may pass the information on to management. Some families contact the addict's boss directly if he is known to be fair and supportive.

If you decide you cannot contact the workplace under any circumstances, you will be at a disadvantage during the intervention. You can minimize the disadvantage by scheduling the intervention early in the weekend—Friday afternoon (only if she's sober) or Saturday morning. If the alcoholic says he can't go into treatment because of work, ask him to check in for a three-day assessment and detox on Saturday, Sunday, and Monday. Monday will count as a sick day, and the attending physician will write a doctor's excuse to give to the boss. Once detox is complete, the alcoholic can be transferred to an evening outpatient program so he can work during the day.

This is appropriate for people who need a short medical detox and who don't need the extra support of an inpatient program. You should discuss this plan with the treatment center staff. A fallback plan is better than no plan, but you'll always have a stronger hand if the workplace issues are resolved before the intervention.

One family we worked with called the addict's boss about the intervention even though they didn't know how he would react. Knowing how sick their son was, they decided his life was more important than his job. His dad said, "We figured the worst case would be that he'd have to find another job. But if he lost his life, there'd be no second chance." During the conversation, the boss told the dad that he already knew there was a problem and agreed to write a letter of support that the family could read during the intervention. That letter from the boss was a powerful tool for the family. If you can get a letter from the alcoholic's employer, you're almost guaranteed the alcoholic will agree to treatment.

We've also worked with families who decide not to contact the workplace, and they take a risk, too. When a job issue is left hanging unresolved, plan for the alcoholic to use it as an opportunity to avoid treatment. It's best to take the time to investigate your options. Not all companies have clear-cut policies or EAPs. If you investigate the workplace and find little or no guidance, you'll have to evaluate your situation and make a decision based on the best judgment of the intervention team as a whole.

Finalizing Your Team

Everyone on the intervention team should be trained and prepared before the intervention. Latecomers will not be prepared unless you bring them up to speed; it is far easier and more expedient if you finalize your team before you begin planning and rehearsing the intervention.

A good rule of thumb is to have at least three people on your team and no more than ten. If you have fewer than three, you no longer have a group. For all purposes, it's a one-on-one confrontation with the alcoholic, which works only in rare circumstances. If you have more than ten people, the intervention takes too long and can cause sensory overload for the alcoholic. We don't want to lose the alcoholic by talking his ear off. Strike a balance. More is not always better.

Of course, there are always exceptions to every rule. We've worked with large, close-knit families with as many as fifteen team members. Each person involved was significant and couldn't be left out. We compromised by asking each person to shorten the intervention letters. By doing so, we didn't overwhelm the alcoholic with an overly long intervention.

Sometimes a friend or relative would like to attend the intervention but cannot. She may have health problems, live too far away, or have important plans that conflict with the date of the intervention. Whatever the reason, a person can participate by writing a letter and asking another family member to read it during the intervention. We do this frequently, and it works very well. Sometimes we put the person on the phone to read the letter directly to the addicted person. While you're building your team, tell someone who can't attend that she can still participate. She will still need to learn about intervention along with the rest of the team.

Sometimes a person you really want on your team doesn't want to get involved. He may be uncomfortable with the idea of intervention. We've found that many people mistakenly believe intervention is about beating up on the addict. The media has been known to misrepresent intervention, and word of mouth has carried the wrong message far and wide. Many times, when people learn that our goal is to preserve the addict's dignity and approach him with love, they change their minds and agree to participate. Sometimes they just need more information.

If you have a family member who remains reluctant, yet is very important to the success of the intervention, ask the person to participate in the planning and rehearsal stages before making a final decision. Going through the rehearsal is exactly like doing the intervention except the addict is not present. Having this full experience changes many people's idea about intervention, and they decide to join the team. But if they remain unwilling, then they should not be pushed to get involved. While it is reasonable to ask people to learn about intervention before making a decision, in the end they must make up their own minds. Anyone attending an intervention under duress weakens the intervention process.

One last word about your team: if a member can't attend

the rehearsal, she shouldn't attend the intervention. Under rare circumstances we've made exceptions. Once, a wife was coming in from out of town with her alcoholic husband in tow and couldn't attend the rehearsal without tipping him off. Delayed flights, weather problems, and last-minute emergencies have kept people from attending rehearsals. But most can get to a phone long enough to go over the rehearsal with the rest of the family or get up to speed by talking with the interventionist. Whatever the situation, rehearsal is not optional. Everyone needs to be prepared.

Becoming Aware of the Influence of the Group

Everyone who comes to an intervention has some degree of influence with the alcoholic. Past arguments and disagreements aside, these are people the alcoholic loves and respects most in his life.

Many people discount the power of their influence. We hear people say things like, "You don't know Frank. He's not about to listen to anybody." After all, this has been their experience. They've tried to talk to him—begged, pleaded, and bargained—but the alcoholic remained unmoved.

Being part of a group, each person's influence is more powerful than if they stood alone. A person who appears to have very little clout may have tremendous influence in an intervention. A recent experience of ours is a perfect example. As we were conducting an intervention and letters were being read, the alcoholic wasn't showing any signs of emotion. His fourteen-year-old daughter was slated to read her letter last. When her turn came, she paused and said nothing for what seemed like an eternity. In the silence that filled the room, all of our hearts raced faster. Finally, she looked at her father with tears in her eyes and a wonderful smile. She said, "Daddy, I love you so much!" Instantly, the man's eyes filled with tears, and he began to cry openly. The room was choked with emotion. Then his daughter cried, "I just want my daddy back." Everyone started to sob, and our man of stone melted before the plea of his young daughter. She ran into his arms and hugged him. He immediately promised to get the help he needed. Never underestimate the influence of love.

Later, as you begin working on your letters, consider the effect of each person's influence when deciding which order to read the letters in. Ending the intervention with a letter read by someone possessing extraordinary emotional influence, such as a child or an aging parent, can have a powerful impact.

We've heard it said that ultimately it is grace that breaks through an alcoholic's denial. We can't predict at what moment or with what word we will touch the alcoholic's heart. Our job is to be an instrument of love. We can never know in advance how things will work out, but we can do our best.

Understanding the Role of Leverage

Some people in the alcoholic's life carry enough weight or leverage to dispense consequences if the alcoholic chooses to continue drinking. Leverage is never a threat or a punishment. Rather, it is the refusal to continue enabling the alcoholic.

A boss has leverage over an employee. She can stipulate that the alcoholic go to treatment to keep his job. If the boss is present at the intervention, she may never have to spell out the consequences of job loss to the alcoholic. The boss's presence alone speaks volumes. The alcoholic may say, "So I guess I have to go along with this treatment if I want to keep my job."

If the boss doesn't attend, but writes a letter to be read at the intervention, he might say, "Maria, you're an important part of our team. We value you. But you need to accept help for your alcoholism before you return to work. We're here to support you in that decision." Sometimes the boss includes personal disclosure: "I have a sister in recovery. I understand this is a disease."

If Maria doesn't go to treatment, she must accept responsibility for losing her job. She made the decision that led to her dismissal. The alcoholic always has a choice, but some choices come with negative consequences. Using leverage causes adversity in the alcoholic's life. Bill Wilson, co-founder of Alcoholics Anonymous, wrote: "Someone once remarked that pain is the touchstone of spiritual progress. How heartily we of Alcoholics Anonymous can agree with him, for we know that the pains of alcoholism had to come before sobriety, and emotional turmoil before serenity."

A spouse has leverage, because she can choose to ask for a separation or divorce. A wife might say to her husband: "Jack, your alcoholism has taken a terrible toll on our marriage and our children. My choice is to save our marriage. I love you. But if you won't accept help for yourself, I am prepared to put the welfare of our children first. I can't continue to raise our beautiful children in an alcoholic household. If you choose alcohol as the most important relationship in your life, I cannot stand by you under those circumstances."

Parents supporting or housing adult children have leverage. We've worked with parents who support their alcoholic offspring in grand style—paying their rent or mortgage, buying a condominium or house for them, covering car payments and insurance, bankrolling one failed business venture after another, and providing spending money. No self-respecting alcoholic would give up so much just to get sober. Think of it this way: if your refrigerator, freezer, and cupboards are plumb full of food, why would you bother grocery shopping? If an alcoholic has all his addiction needs covered, why bother getting sober?

Parents use their leverage when they tell an adult child she will be financially cut off if she chooses alcohol and other drugs over treatment. This is very difficult for parents, because playing the role of caretaker is comfortable and natural. Even if the alcoholic is forty-two years old, the parents may emotionally react as if she were a child. There is an implicit agreement between the parents and the alcoholic: The parents will continue to act as caretakers as long as the alcoholic continues to act irresponsibly, and the alcoholic will continue to act irresponsibly as long as the parents continue to take care of him. Using leverage puts an end to that agreement and sets up a new expectation: "We love you, and it's time for you to take on adult responsibilities."

Leverage can come from sources outside the family. For example, if the alcoholic is arrested for driving under the influence, the court may mandate treatment. We recently had a call from a mother who was unable to control her seventeen-year-old daughter. The girl had been in trouble with the police and was skipping school. She was addicted to illegal drugs and running off with a twenty-four-year-old boyfriend who supplied her with drugs. The girl was on probation so we advised the mother to contact the probation officer and bring the girl into court. The judge offered her an alternative to juvenile detention: treatment. The daughter quickly agreed. The boyfriend disappeared when he learned the parents weren't afraid to use the criminal justice system.

Sometimes leverage is based on relationships. Here are some examples: An adult daughter tells her addicted mother she won't bring her family home for the holidays because of the pills and drinking. An alcoholic grandmother is informed she can no longer babysit the grandchildren. A best friend refuses to bail his alcoholic buddy out of jail again, lend him money, or listen to his drunken tales of woe.

Three daughters shop and go to lunch with their mother every Saturday. It is the highlight of the mother's week. During an intervention, they were prepared to tell their mother that there would be no more Saturday lunches if she didn't accept treatment. Sometimes leverage is redefining the relationship.

Again, this is not a punishment. It is saying, "If you choose to stay sick, I will no longer pretend everything is all right. Your alcoholism causes me to suffer, too. I need to start taking care of myself."

The alcoholic instinctively knows who in the room has leverage. We have seen alcoholics size up a situation in a matter of seconds and, calculating the sum of the leverage in the room, readily agree to help. If it is possible for you to involve someone who has heavy leverage, you are well advised to do so.

When a doctor, lawyer, or mental health professional has a chemical dependency problem, families resist intervening. They fear ruining their loved one's professional reputation; they worry about interfering with the income the person is generating; they don't think they have any leverage and worry that they have minimal influence over the high achiever in the family. Yet allowing addiction to progress is far more risky and can irreversibly damage careers. These professions come with grave responsibilities, and mistakes can be tragic.

There are organizations designed to help impaired professionals while protecting their confidentiality and their professions. These organizations are called diversion programs, monitoring organizations, or peer assistance programs. A relative, friend, colleague, client, or patient can report the problem confidentially. The matter is not taken to the licensing board. The monitoring organization will investigate, conduct an assessment, make recommendations, and monitor the recovery process. If the impaired professional stays sober for a designated period of time, her record at the monitoring agency is erased. This protects professional reputations and careers. Some families use monitoring programs as leverage. If the alcoholic refuses treatment, contacting the monitoring organization is the bottom line. If your loved one's profession requires that she be licensed or is in professional school, you can find help through a professional organization in most cases. Martha Burkett, the program administrator of the Lawyers and Judges Assistance Program in Michigan, assures family, friends, and colleagues:

> If you are fearful that a call to the Lawyers and Judges Assistance Program (LJAP) will result in a report to an employer, the Attorney Discipline Board, the Attorney Grievance Commission, or anyone else, please lay those fears to rest. All inquiries to the program are handled with utmost discretion. The LJAP wants to help lawyers and judges get the treatment and support they need and to ensure their ability to practice their chosen profession while on the path to recovery. Similarly, the LJAP supports law students in anticipation of review by the State Bar Standing Committee on Character and Fitness, prior to admission to the bar. All contact with the LJAP is completely confidential. Our policy is based on federal confidentiality guidelines, which prohibit disclosure about program participants to anyone without prior written consent.

If you are intervening on someone living off a trust fund, the money can make it easier for the alcoholic to say no, and you may believe you have no leverage. Consult with the trust officers. They have a fiduciary responsibility to curtail funds when money is contributing to a major problem in the person's life. During an intervention on a twenty-eight-year-old with a trust income that exceeded $100,000 a month, the trust officer reduced the twenty-eight-year-old's income to $60,000 a month when he refused treatment. For most of us, that still sounds like a small fortune, but it wasn't for him. The reduction meant he couldn't afford his house, his yacht, his airplane, and continue to live in the style to which he was accustomed. He decided treatment was a better option.

There are ways to create emotional leverage. Speak of the alcoholic's long-standing reputation with family, friends, and colleagues and about how addiction is taking away her good name. Talk about treatment and recovery as a course of action that will reclaim her standing as a fine and trustworthy person. When discussing the disease, talk about how addiction erodes character because it changes the brain and diminishes the human spirit.

Almost all addicts suffer from *grandiosity*—an inflated ego used as a defense against feelings of inferiority, shame, and inadequacy. Sometimes, especially when we have no apparent leverage, we appeal to grandiosity as a way to get them to accept help. For instance, we might choose a treatment center that has cachet or star quality. Of course, we also make sure these centers have rock solid recovery programs. The prestige of a treatment center can feed into an addict's grandiosity and result in a successful intervention. Additionally, most centers offer patient aid for those with financial limitations.

When you have no leverage, get creative. A few years ago, we helped intervene on a retired father. The team had no leverage, but one of the team members was quite wealthy and owned a private jet. When the father found out the jet was waiting to fly him to treatment, he readily agreed to go. Most of us can't afford private jets, but if we can spring for first-class seats, it might be the little extra that convinces the alcoholic. Sometimes the knowledge that he can have a drink or two on the plane is enough.

Another time, we worked with parents of a fifty-year-old addict. They told us that they had no leverage over their son. However, they had been frugal throughout their lives and amassed a sizable nest egg. We found our leverage. The parents decided to put their son's inheritance in a trust with the stipulation that he would receive funds only if he was in recovery.

We'll talk more about this when we discuss bottom lines. For now, take an inventory of your team's leverage. Turn to the planner in section 6.

What Do You Need to Know?

Members of an intervention team need to work together. Everyone should read or listen to the same training information. By doing so, the team can seamlessly discuss what they are learning, find answers to questions, and settle differing opinions. If everybody is getting information from a different source, sharing information can be clumsy and confusing.

If your team is using this book as a guide, become familiar with section 6. You will find a planner to help you compile and organize information and a checklist to keep you on track. We've compiled brainstorming ideas to give you a head start when it comes to deliberating on possible objections, writing letters to the alcoholic, and evaluating treatment centers. We offer suggestions on the best recovery books, support groups, and Web sites. If your entire team uses this section, the group will move ahead in an organized and focused fashion.

Begin by asking everyone on the team to read this book cover to cover. Most of us are procrastinators at heart, so set a finish date. Then meet to discuss the necessary steps for preparing your intervention. If people are scattered across the country, set up a conference call. Go online to find free or low-cost conferencing services.

During your meeting, select a detail person. For this role, choose someone who is an organizer, someone who is willing to act as a liaison among team members. The detail person's two most important jobs are to keep communications flowing and to compile information. Important tools are the planner and the checklist in section 6. The detail person should serve the team rather than manage it.

During your pre-intervention meeting, collect information. Using the planner, fill in as much information as you can. If the team doesn't have all the facts, ask for volunteers who can find the answers. Present newly gathered information to the detail person.

List tasks that need to be completed and ask for volunteers. As each person completes a task, the detail person checks it off the checklist. Information should eventually find its way to the detail person so nothing gets lost in the shuffle. Record everything in the planner; don't rely on memory.

Think of intervention as a project—perhaps the most important project you'll ever work on. Intervention isn't complicated, but it requires knowledge and careful preparation. We've had calls from families telling us they're going to intervene on a loved one the next day. They don't know how to do it and have made no preparations. They plan to wing it. That's a failed intervention in the making. Always start by learning what you need to know. Then plan and prepare.

The most important thing your team can do is work together and stay on track. Everyone participates in preparation and planning. Don't take shortcuts. Put in the work, so you'll be in the best position for success.

Using the Planner

When you begin an important project, what's the first thing you do? Plan, of course. Even baking a cake requires a plan. Every recipe is, after all, a plan. You're given a list of ingredients and the exact quantities you'll need. If you toss the recipe aside and throw a random amount of flour, sugar, water, eggs, and oil in a pan and bake your cake at whatever temperature you feel like using, you won't win any blue ribbons at the state fair. Without a plan, you'll most likely end up with a flop.

Intervention success comes with careful planning. There is a specific recipe to follow, and the planner in the tools section helps you assemble the ingredients you'll need. Once you've selected your intervention team, start by listing names, phone numbers, and email addresses in the planner. This gives you a one-stop resource when you have to sit down and call team members. It's the small annoyances, like not finding a telephone number when you need it, that create frustrations at a time when nerves are already frayed.

Continue to use the planner, step-by-step, just as you would follow a recipe. The planner asks you for the dates and times of the intervention and the rehearsal. Work with your team to set a schedule. This may require some juggling, but unless something is very important, most people can make reasonable adjustments in their schedules. Once you set dates and times, you are going to plan by working backward from your intervention date. If your date and time for the intervention is October 3 at 10:00 a.m., all of your planning starts at that point and works backward: "We'll assemble at Mom and Dad's house at 9:00 on the morning of the intervention, giving us an hour before everything begins. We'll rehearse on October 2 at 6:00. We'll set our admission time at the treatment center for October 3 at 11:30." Having a date, time, and location for the intervention sets all wheels in motion.

Next, determine financial details. This has everything to do with how you proceed in locating treatment for the alcoholic. If the alcoholic has health insurance, the insurance company often dictates which facility it will cover and what steps you must take. In other words, you must follow its rules or it may not cover the cost of treatment.

Once upon a time, treatment centers could be very helpful when investigating insurance coverage. They could look up a policy and give you details on copays, average number of days covered, and pre-certification requirements. Things have changed. There are almost an infinite number of different policies, and coverage isn't uniform. This causes a great deal of uncertainty. Before the intervention, most treatment centers can't offer much more than: "We have pretty good luck (bad luck) with that insurance carrier. It depends on your particular benefit. We'll just have to see."

Don't rely on written policy guidelines when determining the number of days the insurance company will cover. It is not unusual for a policy to say it will cover thirty days of inpatient treatment and then certify only seven days. Most insurance companies use medical necessity as the criterion for determining the length of inpatient treatment. This means that once the alcoholic or addict is physically stable—detoxed from the drug—the insurance company will no longer pay for inpatient treatment. Alcoholics and addicts requiring more treatment are often denied further coverage. Families are sometimes left to believe it was the treatment center's decision to discharge the patient, not the insurance company's refusal to pay.

If you have access to the alcoholic's insurance card, call the number on the back of the card and ask two questions: (1) What inpatient treatment centers are in network? (2) What does the benefit cover if we go out of network? This will help you decide on a treatment location. If the insurance carrier tells you that the addicted person must be pre-certified to qualify for benefits, call the treatment center. Most are capable of pre-certifying the addicted person when he arrives to treatment after the intervention.

Treatment centers employ people whose only job is to negotiate with insurance companies, HMOs, and managed health care organizations. They try to get the best reimbursement possible, but most insurance carriers authorize only a few days at a time. Treatment centers are forced to call every two or three days, trying to extend the authorization. Keep in mind that because of the variability and uncertainty of insurance coverage, we can't give you definitive guidance. We can only make suggestions. Each case is different. It is highly probable that you will have to pay privately for part or all of the treatment stay. If finances are tight, refer to the resources section for low-cost options. If you have a health savings plan, check with your employer, who helped you set up the plan, about how to access funds for treatment.

A family we worked with was furious when their thirty-nine-year-old son, suffering from late-stage alcoholism, was discharged after six days of inpatient care. Unknowingly, the family blamed the treatment center for discharging him too soon. After all, the insurance carrier had assured them that the policy included thirty days of coverage. With some investigation, we learned the insurance company declined to pay after six days. The treatment center appealed the decision, but the insurance company denied the appeal. The alcoholic was discharged from treatment and, as predicted by the treatment staff and his family, drank soon after his release. If you are willing to pick up where the insurance carrier leaves off, make arrangements with the admissions staff in advance.

If the alcoholic does not have insurance, explore your options. If you decide to pay for treatment privately, ask about discounts for private payment. In addition, inquire about patient aid. Many treatment centers raise funds to help pay a percentage of the costs for people without insurance or financial means. If there is no family money available for treatment, look for other funding sources. Call a local treatment center for suggestions. They may know of agencies in your local area that can help.

Once you've narrowed down your treatment center choices, ask the staff about admissions policies. They will explain what you need to do before the alcoholic can be admitted. The admissions staff might ask for the alcoholic to call for a pre-intake interview. Do not assume the person you are speaking with is familiar with intervention. Explain that you are planning an intervention and that it's impossible to ask the alcoholic to call the treatment center. Suggest that a family member provide pre-intake information. As a group, your team can compile facts essential to the pre-intake interview and record them in the planner. Each team member has seen different parts of the alcoholic's life, so use the collective experiences of the group. By completing this section of the planner, you should be able to answer all of the pre-intake questions.

Get in the habit of using the planner from the beginning. Laying the groundwork prepares you for each step to come. As Plato wrote in the *New Republic,* "The beginning is the most important part of the work."

Keeping Tabs on Your Progress

You will always know what you've done and what you haven't done by faithfully using the checklist in the tools section. The checklist is an indispensable tool for the detail person, but every member of the team should monitor the progress of the intervention preparations.

Many of us think we can rely on our memories, but intervention requires attending to too many details. Consider planning a wedding without a checklist. If you get 95 percent of the details right, it won't be of much comfort as you try to explain why there are no flowers because you forgot to confirm the order with the florist. Although planning an intervention isn't as complicated as planning a wedding, every little detail is important. If the addict agrees to treatment and no one packed a suitcase, the time it takes to pack the suitcase could give the addict enough time to think up a reason not to go.

The checklist can be used as a resource for assigning tasks. Read through the tasks with the entire team. The detail person can write the name of the responsible person next to each task on the checklist. Team members can place an asterisk next to the tasks for which they volunteered. Some things on the checklist are completed by everyone on the team, such as writing a letter to the alcoholic and identifying objections the alcoholic may use to avoid going to treatment. As team members complete tasks, they should contact the detail person so he or she can check them off the master list.

When the team assembles for the rehearsal, begin by reviewing the checklist. If anything has not been done, this is your last chance. If there are problems, now's the time to straighten them out. The only tasks left unchecked should be ones that don't pertain to your intervention, such as making airline reservations when the treatment center is local.

The checklist gives you bare-bones information, and this book provides the fat. Your success materializes from your preparation, not from half-measures and a wish for good luck. As Thomas Jefferson noted, "I find the harder I work, the more luck I seem to have."

Calling Treatment Centers and Asking Questions

Treatment centers are not created equal, so ask questions. Most people do not know what to look for when shopping for a treatment center and often make random choices. Choose programs that treat addiction as a primary disease and use the Twelve Steps of Alcoholics Anonymous. These programs are considered the most effective.

If you stumble across someone who claims to have found the cure or a new way to treat the problem no one else has thought of before, be wary. People who come up with overly simple answers to complex problems make exciting promises, but upon closer examination, they don't have the experience or research to back it up. Quick fixes and easy promises lead to disappointments.

Talk to people who are active in Alcoholics Anonymous and Al-Anon. They can often give recommendations based on personal experiences with treatment centers. Use recommendations as a starting point. Since treatment centers can change over time, it is important to also research each center for yourself.

Make an educated decision by evaluating treatment centers using the questions in the tools section. Make sure you talk with a qualified staff member. Ask to speak with someone who is familiar with the workings of the treatment program. Sometimes people working in admissions are very knowledgeable and other times they have a limited experience with the clinical aspects of the program and cannot provide detailed information. Remember, you are the customer. Expect clear information about the services before you buy them.

Take the time to research treatment centers. If an insurance company gives you only one choice, research it anyway. If you think it's a bad choice, search for a place that you can afford to pay for privately. It's difficult to get an alcoholic or addict into treatment in the first place. Once you do, you want them to have the best treatment possible.

Choosing a Date and Time

As you choose a date for the intervention, turn your attention to what works for the alcoholic. Selecting the right day, time, and place can determine the success of an intervention. By intervening at the wrong time, the intervention can fail.

The first and perhaps most important consideration is selecting a time when the addicted person is most likely to be sober. With this goal in mind, we usually schedule interventions early in the morning, shortly after the alcoholic awakens. If an alcoholic is not sober for the intervention, it's difficult to reach him emotionally. Alcohol and other drugs block emotional intimacy and alter moods. While a person is high, the drug dominates his feelings and reactions. When an alcoholic is even slightly inebriated during an intervention, he is more influenced by the drug than by his family, often forcing loved ones to depend more on leverage than influence.

Sometimes the family will tell us the alcoholic is never sober. This is certainly true of alcoholics who drink around the clock to keep withdrawal symptoms at bay. In these circumstances, the alcoholic may get up every few hours during the night to drink. Also, those addicted to opiates or prescription medications may be high most of the time. If this is what you are facing, select a time the person will have the least amount of alcohol in her system. She'll never be alcohol-free. Try to catch her when she's drinking her first eye-opener of the morning. When we've intervened on round-the-clock drinkers, we've had to let them take a drink or two before treatment so they don't go into withdrawal. This is a situation when you should consider working with a professional.

Another strategy is to choose a location where the alcoholic is unlikely to drink. For example, we did an intervention on an alcoholic who drank all the time except when he was visiting his mother. He never touched a drop at his mother's house. The family planned a three-day visit with the mother over Memorial Day weekend. That Sunday morning we held the intervention. The alcoholic was cold sober and receptive to the family's expressions of love. He cried as everyone read letters to him, and he agreed to go into treatment. Another time, we intervened at the alcoholic's workplace because she was most likely to be sober on the job. A supportive boss agreed to hold a confidential intervention in an unused conference room.

If your loved one is using drugs other than alcohol, it can be difficult to know when he's intoxicated. Again, early in the morning is usually the best time to intervene. Afternoons and evenings are times when addicts are most likely to be high. If the drug is crack cocaine, the pattern is often binge use—using large quantities of the drug for a given period of time followed by a period of abstinence. Crack addicts run out of money, exhaust themselves, become physically ill from lack of sleep and food—all of which will force them to stop using crack long enough to recuperate. In these cases, be flexible enough to intervene when the addict is coming off a binge. Make sure he's not using alcohol to come down from the crack at the time of the intervention.

If the drug is heroin or other opiates, the addict usually has the drug in her system all the time. Marijuana use is harder to predict. The pattern of use can vary widely, as with that of alcohol. Some marijuana addicts light up as soon as they open their eyes in the morning. If that's the case, look for opportunities when the addict won't be smoking pot. That may be during a holiday at the folks' house or a time when he's expecting to get together with nieces and nephews. You have to be creative in these situations.

Once they've made the decision to intervene, families usually want to move ahead quickly. But don't sacrifice smart planning for speed. If you believe the alcoholic or addict is in immediate danger of hurting herself or someone else, by all means move as quickly as possible. We've done interventions twenty-four hours after first being contacted by a family. If you need to move this quickly, contact a professional interventionist right away. You simply cannot properly prepare for an intervention in a day or two without using a professional. Most families working on their own take at least two weeks to get ready.

We've had many calls from people wanting to intervene on an alcoholic or addict when he's on the wagon. Don't intervene on someone who is abstaining at the moment, because he'll say, "Hey, I'm sober. I'm not drinking. I don't need help." How can you refute that objection? He has to be drinking or using again before you intervene.

Occasionally families want to intervene right before an important function or celebration. If you are planning to ask a father, for instance, to miss his daughter's wedding to go into treatment, you'll probably lose the battle. Of course, there are exceptions. We once intervened on a man just before his cousin's wedding. The cousin wrote a letter for the intervention saying the best wedding present the alcoholic could give him was to go into treatment. If you believe the alcoholic is in danger, don't let anything stand in your way of moving quickly. However, if you feel it is reasonable to wait a few days or a week, let the alcoholic attend the big event before the intervention.

Choosing a Place

Besides dates and times, there are guidelines to follow when selecting a location for an intervention. Choose someplace other than the addict's home. When you hold the intervention in a neutral location, such as a relative's house or a private room in the workplace, the addict is not as empowered as he is on his own turf. When choosing someone's home, select from family members or friends the alcoholic holds in high regard. The addict is naturally going to be on his best behavior in such an environment. Never intervene on an addict in a public place, such as a restaurant.

When you've selected a location, be sure you devise a plausible reason for the alcoholic to show up for the intervention. Remember, she must not know she's going to be intervened upon. Intervention is a bit like a surprise party. If the birthday girl is tipped off beforehand or doesn't show up at all, your surprise party goes bust. When selecting a location, think of ways to get the alcoholic there. Families do this in a variety of ways.

One family, intervening on their grandmother, invited her to an early afternoon birthday celebration for her adult grandson. After successfully intervening on the grandmother, they cut the cake and sang "Happy Birthday." Another family asked an addicted uncle to show up early Sunday morning to babysit his nephews. They knew he'd show up sober and on time. A boss summoned an alcoholic employee for a meeting, and when he arrived his entire family was present. In another case, a man set up a golf date with his alcoholic brother, their father, and the alcoholic's best friend. He arranged for everyone to meet at the dad's house first. An addict needing money will usually show up if he thinks he's getting a financial bailout. In most cases, parents, grandparents, or best friends have enough influence to successfully summon the alcoholic for a visit.

Evaluate the relationships in your family and decide what will work best to get the addict to the intervention site. Make these decisions as a team. If possible, arrange for someone to drive the alcoholic to the intervention location. Do what you can to ensure that the alcoholic shows up.

There are times when it is impossible to get alcoholics to go anywhere, and you'll have to use their home for the intervention. If an alcoholic lives with someone else, such as a spouse or a roommate, that person is key in making these arrangements. They know the alcoholic's day-to-day habits. Before the intervention, everybody other than the person who lives with the alcoholic meets at another location. A parking lot or landmark close to the alcoholic's home works well. Once everyone has arrived, drive to the alcoholic's house caravan-style. This way, everybody arrives at the same time and walks into the house together. Have a cell phone with you so the alcoholic's spouse or roommate can contact you with last-minute directions. Maybe you need to wait a little longer before arriving because the alcoholic is in the shower.

If the alcoholic lives alone, make a surprise visit or have a family member call ahead to say she's stopping by. One family used an addict's eviction as a reason to show up at his apartment. They called and asked if they could help him move his furniture into storage. The family arrived, successfully intervened, drove him to treatment, and then returned to the apartment to move his belongings, just as they'd promised.

What if the addict is living on the street, in his car, or in a flophouse? In one case, a good friend found the alcoholic living out of his car and invited him home for dinner. Another homeless addict would only respond to his grandmother, so a sister found him and told him the grandmother wanted to see him right away. He got in the sister's car and went with her to the grandmother's house where the rest of the family was waiting.

Sometimes, when the addict is homeless, we set up a small mobile intervention team. It might be a group of three or four people who carry a lot of influence with the addict. The mobile team is trained and ready to take action when opportunity presents itself. This requires flexibility. The mobile team meets the addict wherever she might be. If she's in jail, they show up at the precinct. If she's living in a flophouse, they contact her there. They may even track down her car and try to catch her sleeping in it. When they do locate her, they proceed with the intervention just as they would in any other setting.

When somebody is homeless, the family may have less influence and leverage. But again, we've seen success stories in the most extreme circumstances, so we discourage anyone from labeling an addicted person as hopeless. The co-author of this book is a perfect example. His dad found him in a rundown flophouse on the day Jeff was planning to commit suicide. The family intervened, got him into treatment, and Jeff's been sober ever since.

It's always a good idea to get input from the entire group

before you choose the date, time, and location for the intervention. The more ideas you generate, the better. There's always a chance the alcoholic won't show up. If this happens, don't fret. Put your heads together and come up with another plan. Remember, intervention is a process, not an event.

Selecting a Chairperson

The chairperson is a combination of host, guide, and spokesperson during an intervention. Select a relative, friend, or colleague who is highly respected by the alcoholic. This is a person the alcoholic would not want to disappoint. It might be someone he'd likely turn to in his hour of need. Most families know right away who the chairperson should be.

The chairperson isn't always the one who is emotionally closest to the alcoholic. Close emotional relationships often are the most tumultuous. Anyone experiencing a stormy relationship with the alcoholic won't be appropriate as chairperson.

We worked with a woman who intervened on a husband who was incorrigible, unemployed, and had a girlfriend on the side. He didn't seem to care about the marriage, and the wife had little influence or leverage. What made all the difference was selecting the alcoholic's father as the chairperson. The father commanded great respect from all his children. The mere idea of disappointing his father was unimaginable. The alcoholic, greeted by his father at the door, was receptive during the intervention and agreed to accept help. Going against his father's wishes was a more painful idea to him than going to treatment.

Another family asked a seventy-five-year-old uncle to be the chairperson. He didn't have the closest relationship to the addict, but the addict was most likely to respond to him in a positive and respectful manner. Yet another family chose an older sister who'd been in recovery herself for several years. Another selected a brother who'd always been steady and calm in his dealings with the alcoholic. Other good choices may include a friend, mentor, pastor, priest, or rabbi. Select the person who best fits the profile for chairperson.

Prior to the intervention, everyone writes a letter to the alcoholic, which we'll discuss later in this section. Although team members might offer a warm and brief greeting when the alcoholic arrives, once the intervention begins, no one says anything other than what is written in her letter, except the chairperson. If someone briefly goes off script, promptly return to the letters. When being read to, the alcoholic is inclined to sit and listen rather than initiate a debate.

The chairperson greets the alcoholic, seats the alcoholic, makes an opening statement, asks the team to read their letters, answers any objections, asks the alcoholic to accept help, and makes the closing remarks. If other people on the team are going to answer specific objections, make this decision during the rehearsal. There are circumstances when a chairperson may decide to open up a group discussion, usually when the alcoholic is highly resistant even after all objections have been answered and bottom lines read. This is a judgment call. The chairperson should feel confident that the team will stay on message and respond without anger. Later in the book, we've provided a script for the chairperson to use as a guide. We will prepare the chairperson for any number of responses from the alcoholic, but alcoholics typically do not act out during interventions.

The team must never get into a free-for-all debate with the alcoholic. If you do this, the alcoholic will take the power away from the group and the intervention will fail. Team members read their letters and rarely say anything else. The chairperson is the singular voice for everything that needs to be said. Hearing one constant voice disarms the alcoholic and makes it difficult for him to bait or manipulate the group. If the alcoholic challenges someone in the group, that person usually doesn't respond—the chairperson does. If you have the urge to speak up during the intervention, don't. Trust your chairperson to do her job. If the chairperson thinks you need to respond, she will invite you to say something. Arguing with the alcoholic hasn't worked in the past. Don't be tempted to fall into old patterns during the intervention.

If the alcoholic has alienated everybody in his life, and there's no one who can fill the role of chairperson, use a professional interventionist. If you are unable to locate an interventionist, ask a clergyperson or chemical dependency counselor. Unless they are trained in intervention, they'll need to go through this book with the rest of the team.

Do You Need a Professional Interventionist?

Before intervention techniques existed, families were powerless in the face of addiction. They had no option but to watch the alcoholic spiral downward out of control. Then, in the 1960s, a minister named Dr. Vernon Johnson and his congregation developed a way families could intervene on an addicted loved one. Intervention techniques were designed for families and were not part of the professional world. Since that time, a new profession sprung up based on Dr. Johnson's work—the interventionist.

Since intervention became professionalized, there has been an ongoing debate among addiction specialists whether families should proceed without a professional interventionist present. We believe that many families who take the time to educate themselves, follow all the guidelines, and thoroughly prepare for an intervention do not need to hire a professional. We've had conversations with many families who have competently performed interventions without an interventionist. In his book *Intervention*, Johnson writes, "Anyone who sincerely wants to help, can help. Chances are you're quite capable of doing an intervention without the assistance of a qualified professional. However, if you feel the need for such assistance, you should seek it."

Many families prefer to have an interventionist present. They feel more comfortable working with a professional; other families feel confident proceeding without one. You should make the decision based on the feelings of your team as a whole.

Alcoholics and addicts may be facing problems that go beyond chemical dependency, making intervention more complicated. In these cases, a professional interventionist should be present for the rehearsal and the intervention. Dr. Johnson described four special circumstances when families should consider using a professional: (1) there is a history of mental illness; (2) behavior has been abusive or violent; (3) there has been a long-lasting, deep depression; or (4) you suspect illicit or prescription drugs are being used, but you can't verify which drugs.

In addition, we would suggest seven more reasons to hire a professional:

1. The alcoholic had previous treatments followed by relapse
2. Evidence of serious emotional problems or brain damage
3. Suicide attempts or threats of suicide
4. A history of physical or psychological trauma
5. The addicted person is suffering from chronic pain
6. There's evidence of a cross-addiction such as gambling or sex addiction
7. Family relationships have greatly deteriorated with the alcoholic and no one is appropriate for the chairperson role

If none of the above special circumstances fit your situation but you feel more comfortable working with a professional, call a local treatment center for a referral. If there are no treatment centers in your home area, call the Hazelden Foundation at 800-257-7810. They maintain a roster of interventionists who travel nationally to facilitate interventions. Other nationally known treatment centers can also make referrals.

Choosing Inpatient
over Outpatient Treatment

Following an intervention, we prefer to send alcoholics and addicts to inpatient treatment programs. During the intervention, the family breaks through denial and the alcoholic sees the light—but only for a short time. The disease will take control again and denial will spring back into place. Residential programs offer a greater level of support than outpatient programs.

All alcoholics experience anger while in treatment, but after an intervention, anger may rise up faster and with more intensity. When this happens, we want alcoholics in a residential program staffed by counselors ready to pick up where the family left off. Breaking through denial and helping the alcoholic work through anger are two important tasks of the clinical team.

Since the onset of managed care, many insurance policies pay only for outpatient treatment. They certify the lowest level of care and reassess the alcoholic's needs at that point. How would we respond if a woman with breast cancer first was treated at the lowest level of care? Would it be acceptable to deny her surgery until she first failed at radiation? Certainly not. The same holds true for chemical dependency. Start with the support of a more intensive treatment program and move to less intensive care when the alcoholic is ready. When an alcoholic fails in treatment and starts drinking again, it's not easy for a family to convince him to go back into treatment. With each relapse, there is a risk of losing a loved one.

In 1991, MEDSTAT, a company that specializes in health services research, completed a study of three million people. Among other things, they studied people who entered treatment for chemical dependency and documented what percentage relapsed within the first year. MEDSTAT found there was a direct correlation between the rate of relapse and the length of stay in an inpatient treatment setting. Alcoholics who stayed in treatment longer had a lower rate of relapse. Forty-eight percent of the people who received one to seven days of treatment relapsed, whereas only 21 percent relapsed after twenty-two to thirty days of treatment.

We offer a list of treatment centers in the back of the book. They all have excellent reputations, base their treatment programs on the Twelve Steps of Alcoholics Anonymous, employ certified alcohol and drug counselors, and offer family programs. Evaluate these centers for yourself using the questions in the tools section and determine which offers the best program for your loved one.

If inpatient treatment isn't possible, make an appointment at an outpatient program for the day of the intervention. A counselor will do an assessment of the addict's needs and make treatment recommendations. Ask the addict to follow all recommendations. If a spouse or roommate is worried the addict may return home and lash out in anger, arrange for one or two people from the intervention team to spend the night. Or spend the night at a relative or friend's house. Refuse to engage in debates or arguments.

Finding Low-Cost or No-Cost Treatment

It doesn't do any good to intervene on an alcoholic and then have nowhere to go for treatment. If the alcoholic doesn't have insurance and has little or no money for treatment, there are several options. With a few phone calls, most people find public funding or a low-cost or no-cost treatment program. Keep in mind as you begin making phone calls that employees at state agencies and publicly funded treatment centers often are overworked and have very little time to talk. Prepare your questions before you call, stay focused on getting the information you need, and be brief. If the person you're talking with can't help you, ask her to refer you to someone else.

Funding for treatment is often available at the local, county, and state levels, but policies can vary. Some agencies require the addict to call personally, come in for an evaluation, and wait a week or two before funding is granted. If you come up against similar policies, you can call treatment centers and ask if they know of programs that treat people with no funding. Or you can ask the addict to make the required call to the agency at the end of the intervention and have someone from the intervention team accompany him to the evaluation.

A friend told us about her cousin who was dying of alcoholism. Insurance covered a one-week stay at a treatment center, then discharged her. She went to a few Alcoholics Anonymous meetings, but started drinking again. She was in the latest stages of alcoholism and needed more than a week of intensive treatment, but she had no money. We called around to different treatment centers throughout the alcoholic's home state. Eventually we were referred to a state-funded center that provided the alcoholic with three months of treatment at no cost.

The Salvation Army provides treatment programs in many cities throughout the country. Some of the centers accept people on a first-come, first-served basis only, and beds aren't guaranteed or reserved. Call your local center about their admissions policies to see if they will fit your needs.

Low-Cost Recovery Programs

There are recovery programs around the country that provide impressive care—some in beautiful settings—at a very low cost. You may have to buy an airline ticket, but this is a worthwhile option if you have limited financial resources. We've listed quality low-cost facilities in the resources section.

Not all alcoholics and addicts go to treatment. Many get sober by going directly into Alcoholics Anonymous or Narcotics Anonymous. Treatment prepares people for recovery, but recovery happens in the Twelve Step groups of Alcoholics Anonymous and Narcotics Anonymous. Some people need the initial support of treatment to give them a good running start at sobriety. But if you find yourself in the position of having absolutely no treatment options available to you, you can ask the alcoholic to go to Alcoholics Anonymous or Narcotics

Anonymous. At the end of the intervention, say, "We'd like you to go to Alcoholics Anonymous (Narcotics Anonymous), get an Alcoholics Anonymous (Narcotics Anonymous) sponsor, and work the Twelve Steps." Call Alcoholics Anonymous and request a schedule of local meetings so you can give it to the alcoholic after the intervention. There is no fee, just a voluntary donation of a dollar or two at meetings.

Families often say, "She'll never go to Alcoholics Anonymous. She hates Alcoholics Anonymous." Most alcoholics, walking through the doors of Alcoholics Anonymous for the first time, feel the same. But after working a good program of recovery, they learn to love it. If the alcoholic objects, remind her that it's not about liking Alcoholics Anonymous; it's about needing it.

How many meetings a week are necessary? A good rule of thumb is to ask the alcoholic to go to the same number of meetings as the number of days he drinks every week. If he drinks every day, go to a meeting every day. Recovering alcoholics often recommend beginning with ninety meetings in ninety days. We'd suggest no less than four meetings per week for someone new to recovery.

Family members should not attend Alcoholics Anonymous meetings with the alcoholic but attend a Twelve Step program for families. Often Al-Anon, Nar-Anon, or Families Anonymous meetings are scheduled at the same time and same place, but in different rooms from Alcoholics Anonymous and Narcotics Anonymous meetings.

Writing a Letter to
Your Addicted Loved One

During an intervention, emotions can run high. For this reason, each person writes a letter to the alcoholic to read during the intervention. Letters prevent you from exploding into spontaneous anger or freezing up at the last moment.

When you begin your letter, try to keep the length between one-half page and two pages. This doesn't mean squeezing three pages into two by using a tiny font size on your computer. Your letters should be double-spaced and no longer than two pages. Be selective about what you write. The alcoholic knows what you're talking about without hearing every single detail.

Think of your letter as having three main parts. First, begin with a message of love. The alcoholic needs to hear you speak from your heart. This may be the most important part of the letter. It's not enough to say "I love you" or "You're my best friend." Use the "who, what, where, when, how, and why" rule that journalists follow. The *who* is the alcoholic, but *what* about the alcoholic do you love or cherish? Talk about memories. *Where* you were when it happened, and *how* you felt. Tell him *why* you love him. List special qualities he possesses and things you miss about him since he became addicted. Be specific and speak with sincerity.

If the alcoholic helped you when you were facing a tough time, tell her how much that meant to you. A mother once told her son, "When your father died, you were there for me. You came over every day to keep me company, to fix things around the house, to give me a shoulder to cry on. If it hadn't been for you, I don't know how I would have gotten through that time."

A brother told his sister, "When I went through my divorce, you were there to keep me going. My world was falling apart, and it was your strength and optimism that got me through. Today I'm here for you." Accepting help can be difficult. If you can remind the alcoholic of a time when she helped you, it may be easier for her to take the help you are offering now.

Has your relationship with the alcoholic been strained for so long you don't have much good to say about him? A wife once told us, "How can I write about loving him? I hate him!" We reminded her that you only feel "hate" when you still care about someone. When you don't care, you feel nothing. We suggested she reflect on all the reasons she married him in the first place and write about those. If your relationship with the addict hasn't been the best lately, think back to a time when it was better.

The second section of the letter addresses the addiction. When you write this part of the letter, you must be vigilant against anger, judgment, and blame seeping in between the lines. No matter how angry you are with the alcoholic, leave the anger outside the door when you come in to do an intervention.

When you write your firsthand experience, be specific. A good example comes from a letter a woman wrote to her husband:

Three Saturdays ago, you started drinking around noon. It was beer at first, but then you switched to Jack Daniels. Your mood changed. You ended up yelling loudly at the kids, and you cussed at me. You took off in the car. I heard your tires screech as you pulled out. Little Darrell went into his bedroom and cried after you left. I worried all night that you'd kill yourself or someone else driving while intoxicated. I was so afraid. Every time the phone rang, I thought it was the police. The next morning when you came home, I was so upset that I gathered up the kids and left. You're a good dad and husband sober, but alcohol changes you. It makes me feel like you don't love us.

Notice how the wife avoids making judgmental statements. She expresses what she witnessed and how she felt. She didn't try to tell her husband what he was thinking. She only reported what he was doing.

When reporting the facts, you don't have to be cold or unemotional. You can report how you felt at the time. That's a fact, too. But don't let judgment, blame, or resentment sneak into your letter masquerading as truth. Test yourself by asking, "Am I trying to shame the alcoholic by saying this?" Intervention is no place for settling scores.

Here is a list of words that express uncomfortable feelings. Use them to communicate what you were feeling in a given situation. None are blaming words.

Angry	Hurt	Frustrated	Bewildered
Discouraged	Insignificant	Rejected	Confused
Helpless	Insecure	Reckless	Embarrassed
Anxious	Inadequate	Lonely	Miserable
Depressed	Ashamed	Guilty	Inferior
Worried	Afraid	Apathetic	Numb

The woman writing to her husband used the words *worried*, *afraid*, and *upset*. Again, her focus was on herself. These words explained how she felt. She didn't use extreme words like *tormented*, *terrified*, and *furious*. Those words imply blame.

Avoid digging up ancient history in your letter. We suggest sticking to the last six to twelve months. Occasionally an incident that took place several years ago is important and needs to be mentioned. Or it may be that you don't have recent experiences to draw from because you've been out of touch, but you have examples from an earlier period. You might say, "We haven't seen much of each other in the last year, but I've been concerned for quite a while. I remember times when you couldn't remember conversations we had when you were drinking. I also used to worry a lot about you drinking and driving. I should have done more to help you then. This is a progressive disease. It gets worse when it's not treated. That's why I chose to be with you today." Use the most significant information available to you and use discretion when deciding what to include in your letter.

A team member who has never witnessed the alcoholic's drinking or drugging behavior can write something like this: "I've been living far away for a long time. You and I haven't seen much of each other except during holidays. But for the last three or four years, Mom has called me to share how concerned she is about your drinking. So I've been worried, too. This isn't a secret anymore. And none of us should be surprised. Alcoholism runs in our family. Uncle Art died of cirrhosis and our cousin Regina has been in recovery for five years now. I'm here today because I know alcoholism is a serious disease, and I don't want to lose you."

Those who say they've never witnessed the alcoholic's drinking often remember little things as they prepare for the intervention—slurred words during late-night phone calls, conversations the alcoholic can't recall later on, repeated requests for loans, broken promises, prescription pain pills missing from the medicine cabinet. Don't overlook the subtle ways your relative's or friend's alcoholism has shown itself to you.

Write one to three examples of your firsthand experiences with the addiction, including any failed past attempts at sobriety. When the addict has caused endless trouble, it is tempting to list everything. But an endless litany of transgressions will sound abusive. Detail is good, but being overly scrupulous is not. Keep it short.

A special note to spouses. Because yours is a uniquely intimate relationship with the alcoholic, you may have been exposed to behaviors too private to repeat during an intervention. Be discreet. Humiliating your husband or wife is unacceptable. Our first goal is to preserve the alcoholic's dignity, so keep highly personal examples out of your letter.

The third section of the letter is the closing. Repeat here how much you care and how concerned you are. Give the addict a sense of purpose and a reason to get sober. Then state your support of recovery and ask the alcoholic to accept help. This can usually be accomplished in one paragraph. Here's an example:

> Mom, I can't imagine what life would be like without you. The pain would be unbearable for me. I don't want to lose you to this disease. And your grandchildren need you. They love you so much. You play a big role in shaping their lives. If they lose you, they lose a precious gift. This disease can't be allowed to rob them of a loving relationship with their grandmother. I am committed to doing whatever it takes to help you get into recovery. I've taken the time to learn a lot about alcoholism, and I know you can get better with the help of others. In fact, you'll be amazing in recovery, because you have so much to give. Will you please accept the help we are offering you today?

A few last words on writing your letter. Begin your letter with a salutation, such as *Dear Dad* or *Dear Kathy*. End your letter by referring to your relationship, such as *Your best friend, Kay*. Stating your relationship is powerful. It may seem silly since you and the alcoholic are sitting in the same room, but it isn't. These words have a deep emotional impact.

End your letter by directly asking the alcoholic to accept help. Make it clear that you are asking him to take immediate action by including words like *today* or *now*. The entire purpose of writing your letter is ultimately to ask one question, "Will you accept the help we're offering you today?" Everyone's letter should end with a similar question.

As you write, stay in first person. Don't speak for the group, only for yourself. Instead of writing *we all love you*, write *I love you*. By using *we* instead of *I*, you dilute the emotional force of your message. Only use *we* when you specifically want to refer to the intervention group, such as in your final question, "Will you accept the help *we* are offering you today?"

We have created guidelines to follow when writing your intervention letter. By using this seven-point format, composing your letter will be simpler.

1. **Introduction:** Write a brief opening statement of love that specifically states the nature of your relationship. ("Jack, I have been very lucky to have you as my best friend for over twenty years. Not many people in this world have the good fortune to have a friend like you.")

2. **Love:** This is the longest part of the letter. Do not bring up problems related to addiction in this part of the letter. Instead, give specific reasons why you love and care about the person, remembering times when you were proud of her, when she was there for you, fun times you experienced together, examples of her best character traits. This part of the letter must be sincere,

avoiding empty flattery. If the addict's behavior has been difficult for a long time, remember back to better days. ("Carrie, I can remember back, like it was yesterday, to the day I asked you to marry me. You were so beautiful as we walked through the snow. When I looked at you, I thought my heart would burst. I'd never before known a girl like you. . . .")

3. **Reframing:** Shift from the love section to a discussion of the problem by stating your understanding of addiction as a genetic disease. Differentiate addiction from character and willpower issues. Talk about the need for professional treatment. If other people in your family have suffered from alcoholism, mention that it runs in the family. ("Michael, problems with alcohol dependence affects one out of eight people who drink, because it is a genetic, inherited disease. You didn't choose this any more than dad chose diabetes. Alcoholism runs in our family. Our great-grandfather was an alcoholic, and Aunt Kate became addicted to prescription drugs. It requires professional treatment just like any other disease.")

4. **Facts:** Provide specific, firsthand examples of problems caused by alcohol or other drugs. Don't use judgmental or angry language. Don't try to tell the addict what he was thinking. Instead, describe what you saw and how you felt. Let the facts speak for themselves. Be brief. One to three examples is sufficient, and don't dredge up things from years ago unless there is a very good reason to do so. ("Patti, alcohol is making decisions in your life I know you would never make for yourself. Last week you drove the kids to soccer practice after you'd been drinking. You're a great mom, and I don't believe you'd ever do that if there weren't a problem with alcohol. The kids have told me that sometimes you smell of beer when you pick them up from school. Two nights ago, I heard you slurring your words when you put them to bed. I see alcohol hurting you, and it's hurting them. And I hurt, too.")

5. **Commitment:** Make a personal commitment to stand by the alcoholic and help her in any way that is possible and appropriate.

("I have learned that this is a family disease. It requires that we all participate in the recovery process. I am pledging to do my part. I will attend the family program and Al-Anon. Together, we will heal and we will grow. It'll be a wonderful journey as a family.")

6. **Ask:** This is a direct request that the alcoholic immediately accepts the treatment program being offered. One team member can write a few lines about the treatment center you've selected. If the treatment center provides special programs or amenities that will be of interest to your loved one, mention them. ("Josh, we have taken the time to find the best program for you. It's a great facility in the mountains with an Outward Bound wilderness experience. It's a special program for people in your age range—young men in their teens and early twenties. We think you'll really like it. Will you accept the help we're offering you today?")

7. **Affirmation:** End on a positive note, painting a positive picture of the future. Give your loved one a reason to want to get sober. Speak of ways the addict is important to you and others. Give him a sense of purpose. Express faith in his ability to follow through and succeed. ("Dad, I need you in my life. You are my rock. I'm graduating from college next year, and Sean and I have been talking about getting married. I need you healthy to walk me down the aisle. I want you to be the best grandfather for my children. It's you I want to lean on in the tough times and celebrate with in the good times. I love you, Dad. I want you back.")

Give yourself plenty of time to write your letter. Some people write their letter one day and revise it the next. Write from the heart. During the intervention training, share letters with each other. Read them aloud during the rehearsal. Make necessary edits. Remove any language that could make the alcoholic or addict angry or defensive. Rewrite your letters to incorporate changes so they are neat and easy to read. Don't leave scribbles or notes in the margins. Always use loving, nonjudgmental honesty when talking about the problem. Throw your heart into the love section of the letter.

When your loved one goes into treatment, deliver all letters to the treatment staff. If she refuses treatment, have the interventionist, chairperson, or another appropriate team member deliver the letters to your addicted loved one at the earliest possible time. Team members should keep a copy of the letter they've written for themselves.

Letters Written for Real Interventions

Below are two letters that were read in actual interventions. Both are excellent examples of how to write an intervention letter. Changes have been made to protect the anonymity of the writers and the people being intervened on. For additional examples of real intervention letters, go to www.lovefirst.net.

The following letter was written by a college-aged granddaughter to her grandmother.

Dear Granny,

You and I have always had a special bond. We like to sit and talk about life and philosophy, and it always seems we end up solving the problems of the world. I can always count on you for anything and everything. I think you know you are like a second mother to me. I told you just the other day how much Christmastime means to me, and I thank you for providing me with so many warm memories. As far back as I can remember, every stay at your house was a joy for me. I know you always go out of your way to make things special for me.

I love you so much—it's more than love, even—you're just more important to me than you could possibly imagine. You and Granddad keep this family together; you make us whole. I am here for you today, because I want you to be healthy. While I may speak of the past, this is about the here and now—today, and our future together as a family. So please know this is not meant to hurt you, but about bringing our family together with love.

Granny, when you are sober, you are as reliable as a clock. Since there are long periods when you do not drink, I can let myself ignore the fact that you suffer from this disease and just concentrate on the good times. I always think, "Maybe she won't drink again. Maybe that last time was her last."

Last spring, when a binge landed you in the hospital, Mom, Dad, Janie, and I decided for about the third time that we were going to do something to get you help. But then you got pneumonia, and that allowed me to forget about the drinking and concentrate on other things. It is easy for me to pretend nothing is wrong—especially a week or so after a drinking binge. It is more comfortable for me to concentrate on the good stuff.

Last April, after I got back from visiting you and Granddad, my mom told me you drank again. I was so surprised and all those old feelings I push out of my mind came rushing back. They always come back when I hear about a binge. Questions run through my mind. "What made her do it this time?" "How bad was it?" "How long did it last?" "How far and where did she drive?" "Did she hurt herself?" "Is she at home or in the hospital?" "Is Granddad okay?"

You may not know this, but I usually find out when you've gone on a binge, even a small one. Mom might say, "We think Granny's drinking." It isn't a secret. Everyone knows, everyone hurts; it's on everyone's mind.

The Thursday you started drinking this last time, I remember coming home and finding you sitting in the kitchen. Granddad was doing the dishes, and you and I had a great conversation for about five minutes before I realized your laugh was a little too hearty; you were talking a little too much. The realization came upon me like a slap in the face. I actually backed away from you physically and could only respond in one-word sentences. I just wanted to get out of there and forget what I was seeing. When Mom told me you had drunk, it felt like a punch in the stomach.

I don't have many memories of witnessing your binges. Instead, what I have is a feeling that is always with me. It is a fear that nags at me, "Someday Granny is going to die of alcoholism." A lot of the time, I rely on my denial so I can go on without going crazy from that thought. A picture that stays in my head is you lying dead in a snowdrift, having passed out after a binge. I read about a woman in her forties dying that way a few years ago. The image stays with me. Granny, I don't want to have those kinds of thoughts about you.

A few days ago, I started thinking about the fact that despite this devastating, debilitating disease you've been suffering with for nearly half a century, you've accomplished so much and deserve the love and respect of so many. You're really quite amazing. It takes a strong woman to do what you have done for so long in the face of a disease that kills so many. I know you can beat this disease, but that is not accomplished alone. If it could be done alone, you would have done it by now. But no one recovers alone. It requires reaching out to others.

So will you please accept the help we are offering? The help I am asking you to take? We are together as a family, and I promise I will do my part. Please take the first step toward recovery with us today.

Love,
Miranda

A mother wrote this letter to her adopted son.

Dear Brian,
Not flesh of my flesh
Nor bone of my bone
But still miraculously my own

Don't ever forget for a single moment
You didn't grow under my heart but in it.
I am your mother, and I have a special love for you that no one else can share. You were put in my arms at five days old and came home

to family and friends who surrounded you with love. Look around this room. How lucky you are. You are still surrounded with love.

You were a blond, bright, blue-eyed little boy, anxious to excel in every way. You were such a great athlete. You ran like a gazelle. You completed your first marathon at the age of ten. I was so proud of you. Then you encouraged me to begin running races and marathons and ran along with me whenever you could.

Tennis was our family sport for a while. However, I didn't compete very well, and it took only one mother/son tournament for you to decide that maybe it was not our strength as far as competition went. But it was fun anyway, just being on the court with you.

You've always had such warmth and feeling for everything you did. You have a wonderful sense of humor. You're so bright and witty. You always made everything fun.

It was always apparent how much you loved family and enjoyed being together with everyone. Family dinners, holidays, and especially trips—you were always exuberant and full of merriment. Those were warm, fuzzy times. I remember our Winnebago trip to Colorado when you first experienced snow. You were only seven, and you began crying from the cold. Who would have thought you would become an expert skier and encourage me to improve my skiing skills? A difficult task, to say the least, but you never tired of cheering me on.

Now I watch you playing golf with your son—encouraging him, praising him, and being so patient with him. You call him "Buddy," and as you told me, "He is my buddy. He's my very best friend." You are a proud parent—you know that feeling, too.

I acknowledge that you have a disease, one that makes you powerless over alcohol and other drugs. But, in spite of it all, I know that when this disease does not consume you, you are still the warm, caring, loving young man who can do whatever he sets his mind to do.

When you come over to the house to see me, I always want to give you a kiss. When you bend forward and turn your cheek away, I know you are trying to hide the fact that you've been drinking or even doing something else. It hurts me that you try to hide the truth. It hurts me that this disease makes you pull away from me.

I know that sometimes you get behind the wheel of your car while intoxicated, and I fear for your life, your son's life, and for the lives of innocent people who are on the road driving, biking, or walking. My grandchildren—and your nieces and nephews—are on those roads in cars and on bikes. I know how unfair it is to jeopardize innocent lives. I'm worried, concerned, and, yes, even angry when I think of you possibly injuring or killing someone while drinking.

This is not the example you would want to set for your beautiful son. It hurts me terribly to see him exposed to the behaviors caused by addiction. I know this isn't the father you want to be. I've always said, "Be the kind of man whose hand your child can hold and proudly exclaim, this is my father." You are capable of being this person for your son, and he deserves nothing less. But it requires that you first seek help for yourself.

I adore you, Brian, and I promise to stand by you. I will do all I can to help you, and I ask that you embrace this promise of mine by going into treatment today. Take this opportunity to arrest this disease of addiction by making a 100 percent commitment for at least thirty days of treatment. Reclaim your life as the loving, caring, responsible, and compassionate man you are. I want you back in our family to share the wonderful times yet to come. I want my son healthy and whole, and, above all else, free to be the person you were intended to be. I love you with all my heart, Mom.

Your Bottom Line

When an intervention is well planned and executed, about 85 percent of people being asked to accept help do. But that leaves 15 percent who refuse to accept help and choose to continue drinking or using other drugs. If this happens, we present our bottom lines to the alcoholic. Bottom lines are those things we will no longer do to support the disease of addiction. They include the ways we are going to take care of ourselves.

You already are prepared to set your bottom line if you did two things earlier in the book: (1) identified ways you've enabled the alcoholic in the past; and (2) identified any leverage you may have. If you haven't yet done these things, turn back to section 2. The decision to discontinue an enabling behavior is your bottom line.

If you go to the tools section of this book, you will find examples of bottom lines. Use these examples to help you brainstorm. Once you know what your bottom line is, write it on a separate piece of paper. Bottom lines are never written on the same page as your letter. A bottom line might read something like this:

Barbara, you mean so much to me, and watching this addiction robbing you of your vitality is hurting me more than I can express. I've learned that I've been doing things—thinking I was helping you—that were only helping the addiction. I was unknowingly hurting you, too. I love you too much to continue doing that. Today, I have made a commitment to only support your recovery. For this reason, if you choose not to accept treatment, it's not all right to continue living in my house. You will have to find your own place. And I can't give you any more money. My kids—your nieces—love you, but they're confused and frightened by the addiction. Until you get help, you cannot spend time with the children. They need their aunt well and whole. Not the way it is now. It is too hard on them and me. Let's avoid all of this pain. Instead, please accept the help we're offering you today.

You can hear how much love is expressed even as the bottom line is being delivered. We aren't trying to blame or shame the alcoholic when we use leverage. This is not the tone we set in our bottom lines. We make it clear that our actions are based on our intention to support recovery and to stop supporting addiction. We also make it clear that we will no longer let the addiction take priority over the welfare of our families.

Bottom lines cause negative consequences only when addicts choose alcohol and drugs over recovery. We aren't doing these things to our addicted loved ones. They are bringing the consequences onto themselves. Do you see the difference? We are explaining what we will and will not support, and how we'll behave in the future. Alcoholics make their own choices.

Not everyone chooses to use the leverage they have, and some people have no leverage to use. Occasionally, nobody on the intervention team has leverage. We've done many interventions using only the influence of family and friends. To create *emotional leverage*, include everyone on the team whom the addict admires, respects, loves, or relies on for advice, emotional support, or companionship. The more people, the better. You want to create a powerful emotional experience. Including children adds tremendous emotional leverage. Most people have a close relationship with at least one child: daughter, son, niece, nephew, godchild, or grandchild. If a child isn't old enough to join the team (usually twelve years and older), have them draw a picture or make a thirty-second video you can play during the intervention on a laptop or iPod. This message should be about love, mentioning nothing about addiction or treatment. If an older child is unwilling to participate, ask him to attend the training and rehearsal. He may change his mind once he understands the process. If not, ask if he would write a letter and select a family member to read it for him during the intervention.

If you don't have leverage, you can still write a bottom line. Use the influence that comes with your relationship to the addicted person. Here's an example:

Dear Ginny,

You and I haven't seen much of each other lately. I just figured you were busy with your new life out in the world as a career woman. I'm getting old and not up on everything, but as your grandmother, I know a lot about the history of our family. You aren't the first to suffer from addiction, Sweetie. But to my knowledge, you are the first being given the chance to get help. We can't waste a life as wonderful as yours. I'm asking you to reconsider and take this opportunity. It may seem difficult at first, but I bet you'll find it to be one of the best things you've ever done for yourself. The quality of your future depends upon it. Won't you go with your mom and dad today, and get this good treatment?

Quite often, a resistant addict changes her mind once she hears the team's bottom lines. She sees her life crumbling before her. Going to treatment becomes a more palpable option. Some people claim treatment won't work if addicts go "against their will." Well, they're not going against their will. They are making a choice based on information they are given during the intervention. They can say yes, or they can say no.

The Hazelden Foundation conducted a twenty-five-year survey comparing success rates between people who came into treatment on their own and people who were mandated into treatment by the courts. The success rates were virtually the same for both groups. Alcoholics and addicts all suffer from denial and anger regardless of what motivated them to get help. Does a DUI or a lost job or a divorce make them more willing than an intervention? No. Everyone struggles. The clinical staff helps them work through these challenges. It's not how addicts get into treatment that counts; it's what happens once they're there.

In some states, you can petition the courts to order an addicted person into treatment. In Florida, for example, the Marchman Act allows family members or friends to go to court and ask that an alcoholic or addict be mandated into treatment. Most states will court-order minor children into treatment at a parent's request. Court orders can be very effective when the addicted person is so sick or rebellious that you have no other way of helping.

Several years ago, a family came to us with concerns about their fifteen-year-old daughter who was addicted to street drugs. Her older boyfriend was a drug dealer. He had more influence over her than did her parents. The family obtained a court order, but decided to use it only if their daughter refused help during the intervention. They hoped the influence of their relationship would carry the intervention to a successful conclusion. But that didn't happen. The daughter refused treatment and her father used the court order as a bottom line.

He said something like this: "We'd hoped you would come to this decision on your own. But we also prepared ourselves for the chance that you would not. We are your parents, and your welfare is our responsibility. For that reason, we have obtained a court order stipulating that you go to treatment. Either you go with us now, or the police will pick you up and escort you there." The girl cried, but she agreed to go with her parents.

Remember, you only share bottom lines with the alcoholic when he refuses recovery. If he agrees to go, do not read your bottom lines. Additionally, don't ever use bottom lines as a bluff. If you say it, you need to be 100 percent sure you'll follow through. If you don't follow through, you'll empower the disease, and the intervention is reduced to an exercise in futility. Test yourself sufficiently before choosing your bottom line. If a voice says, "I'll never do this," find another bottom line.

There are times for discretion when implementing bottom lines. A person may agree to treatment, but not agree to leave immediately. Don't read bottom lines when an addict has committed to a later date and has called to change her admissions appointment. Use bottom lines only if she doesn't go to treatment as promised. Have some or all of the intervention team present on the new admission day so if there is a change of mind, bottom lines can be delivered then.

If you have leverage that you don't want to use as a bottom line, explore the reasons behind your decision. If you're afraid the addict will be angry with you, maybe you need to tell yourself that it's all right for him to get angry. Some people put it in perspective this way: "I'd rather have him angry with me than dead. I'll take anger over that any day."

When writing your bottom line, place the focus on yourself. Make decisions based on what you know is ultimately right. Don't worry about the addict's reaction. Maybe she needs to go through anger before she can reach a place of change. We've heard many recovering alcoholics say, "The person I was most angry with then, I am most grateful to today."

One last thought. Always end your bottom line by repeating the same question you used in your letter: "Will you accept the help we're offering you today?" Give the alcoholic a chance to change his mind. Watch the tone of your voice when you read your bottom line. If you're seething with anger, even the most loving words can feel like bullets. Stay in a place of love. If the alcoholic says no to treatment, remember, it is the stranglehold of his disease that prevents him from reaching out for help.

Section 4

The Intervention

Listing Possible Objections and Your Answers

When intervening on someone with an alcohol or other drug problem, you are undoing all of the addict's hard work to safeguard the addiction from outside interference. As soon as the intervention begins, the alcoholic realizes that the power has shifted to the group and her old methods of manipulation and avoidance are no longer going to work. Her mind races as she looks for escape routes. When she's found one, she'll present it to you in the form of an objection. It's the team's job not to let the alcoholic slip through. Don't depend upon impromptu responses during the intervention. You must plan ahead.

Objections aren't the end of the world. When alcoholics raise objections, they are giving you an opportunity to demonstrate how thoroughly prepared you are. When you tell them that the team has already solved that problem, your seriousness becomes unmistakable. With no escape routes, alcoholics usually accept help.

Prepare for the alcoholic's objections. Involve the entire team. If you need help getting started, turn to the tools section and read sample objections. Have the team brainstorm all possibilities. The detail person can keep a list.

Next, decide how to answer each objection and determine

any action steps you need to take. For instance, if you are intervening on a mother with small children, you have to determine who will care for the children while she's in treatment. Select someone the mother knows is trustworthy and dependable. Questions may be raised about paying bills, collecting mail, mowing the lawn, taking care of the cat, or what to tell the neighbors. We usually don't bring up objections during the intervention, but wait for the alcoholic to bring them up. But some objections—such as child care—always need to be discussed during the intervention. A parent needs to know that his children will be well cared for.

Of course, if an objection is too big to overcome—a graduation, wedding, funeral, baptism, vacation—you may have to schedule the intervention after the event. If it's dangerous to delay, go ahead and intervene. Give the alcoholic permission to miss the big event by explaining that her life is more important.

Some objections are harder to answer than others because they are based on opinion rather than fact. A wedding is a fact, as is paying the bills or taking care of pets. Facts are clear-cut. Opinions, however, are a different matter. Let's imagine that the alcoholic says, "I'm not going to treatment, because I don't think I have a problem." In this case, he's using an opinion—*I don't have a problem*—to object to treatment. If the team attempts to change his opinion, they could start a power struggle that the alcoholic will probably win. If objections are based on opinions, don't try to change the alcoholic's thinking. That hasn't worked in the past, and it won't work during an intervention.

So how do we handle opinion-based objections? First keep the focus on the group, rather than on the alcoholic. Speak from the group's position, not to the alcoholic's point of view.

Let's see how this works using the example from above: "I'm not going to treatment, because I don't think I have a problem." The chairperson avoids being pulled into a debate by saying: "We've learned that people with alcohol problems are the last to know they have a problem. I think you'd agree with me when I say that none of us would choose to do this unless we truly believed alcohol is causing problems in your life. We're not asking you to determine if you have a problem. We're asking you to get a professional assessment. If you don't have a problem, they'll tell you. We've taken care of setting up the appointment. We're just asking you to find out from a professional."

Nothing the chairperson said opened the door to a power struggle between the alcoholic and the team. The alcoholic may still refuse treatment, but the integrity of the intervention is not damaged. This is important because properly executed interventions have an immense impact upon alcoholics even when they don't accept help immediately. It increases the likelihood that they will change their minds and accept help at a later date.

Let's look at another objection, one that appears to be based on fact but is really a thinly veiled opinion: "How can you say I have a problem? You've been out drinking with me plenty. At that Super Bowl party, you put away your share of beer." The alcoholic is observing some facts about a team member's drinking, but the unstated opinion is, "No one who drinks alcohol can tell me I have a problem."

We don't demand that all team members be teetotalers. By challenging someone else's drinking habits, the alcoholic is attempting to shift the focus off herself and onto someone else. If she succeeds, she'll grab the power away from the group and the intervention will fold into chaos. To deal successfully with this objection, avoid becoming defensive. Don't say, "Hey, Bob might have a few drinks, but he's never had a problem with alcohol." You are now reacting to the alcoholic by countering her opinion with your opinion, and you put her in control of what is happening in the intervention. Keep the focus on the alcoholic's problem and needs. The chairperson can respond, "Today we're talking about your drinking. We've learned that it's not about how much you drink but what happens to you when you drink."

If objections are based on personal responsibilities—money, work, kids, or pets—offer good solutions. For instance, if the alcoholic says, "I can't go to treatment because I have to take care of Rover," the chairperson says, "We thought of that. You know how well Rover and Jack's dog get along, so Jack is taking care of Rover for you." Or if the alcoholic says, "I can't afford to take time off work for treatment; I have a mortgage to pay," the chairperson says, "We thought of that. We've all chipped in to cover any cash shortage you might have so you can go to treatment and pay your bills this month. You can pay us back when you're on your feet again." If the addict says, "I can't leave my house that long," the chairperson says, "We thought of that. Sean will pick up your mail each day after work. Pat will mow your lawn, and Eileen is going to stop by to water your plants."

Answering objections based on work-related responsibilities is such a critical issue that we've devoted an entire section to the topic. We suggest you turn back to "Involving the Workplace," in section 3, for a review. Objections regarding work can give an alcoholic the best possible escape route.

Sometimes an alcoholic will hang strong to an objection. No matter how well prepared your answer is, he won't change his mind. An objection alcoholics tend to cling to is this: "Okay,

I may drink too much, but I can stop on my own and that's what I'm going to do." The chairperson may say, "Doctors do not recommend that people quit drinking on their own. Quitting cold turkey from alcohol can be dangerous. It can cause seizures or worse. Also, we've learned that long-term success requires the right kind of help. It's not the quitting you need help with. You've done that before. It's staying quit and being content sober." When the alcoholic remains steadfast to the idea of quitting on his own, the chairperson can say, "While we don't agree that this is the best way to handle the problem, it is your decision. However, if your way doesn't work, and you take another drink, we ask that you give us your word that you'll do it our way and go to treatment. Is that a deal?" Most alcoholics agree.

If an alcoholic or addict insists on quitting on her own, specify that quitting requires abstaining from all addictive drugs, including mood-altering prescription pills. Quitting alcohol doesn't mean switching to marijuana, and quitting cocaine doesn't mean switching to beer. The chairperson can say, "We've learned that using other mood-altering substances is called switched addiction. We ask that you don't switch to other drugs once you've quit."

Objections are answered by the chairperson. If there are objections that another team member needs to answer, decide that during your rehearsal. A single, consistent voice keeps order to an intervention, whereas several people talking to the alcoholic creates the impression of a free-for-all. When responding to objections, be brief. If an objection can be answered in a couple of sentences, all the better.

Since the chairperson is designated to reply to objections, he should role-play with a team member acting as the alcoholic. A team member reads each objection, and the chairperson answers. Practice the objections with the chairperson until he feels confident. To make things comfortable and natural, the chairperson shouldn't memorize answers but rather put them in his own words.

One last thought about objections. As important as it is to be prepared for them, the alcoholic or addict usually doesn't bring up many objections. While we want to be ready for every possibility, you probably won't be facing a barrage of objections during the intervention. It is more likely that the alcoholic will have just a few questions or won't object at all.

Rehearsing the Intervention

A rehearsal is necessary before doing the intervention. Everyone who plans to participate in the intervention should attend. If a team member cannot physically attend the rehearsal, ask her to participate over a speakerphone. Or she could meet with you a couple of hours before the intervention to review details of the rehearsal. No one should go into an intervention without knowing exactly what to do.

Review the checklist with the detail person and make sure all tasks are complete. Call the treatment center and confirm your appointment. Be sure all financial arrangements are set. You want everything to be in place when the alcoholic arrives at the treatment center.

The rehearsal has four segments. The first segment is to edit and rehearse the letters. Each person reads his letter aloud while the group listens carefully to both tone and content. Following are seven considerations when editing letters:

1. *Remove negative undertones.* Anger, blame, or judgment can creep into letters without our awareness. Families and friends commonly feel angry about the addiction. Sometimes it shows up in the words we use or in the way we read our letter. If

teammates hear something in a letter that sounds angry, ask its author to remove it or find another way to say it.

2. *Listen for the message of love and concern.* Do the letters communicate empathy and support? Approaching the alcoholic with love may be the most powerful force for breaking down denial while preserving the alcoholic's dignity.

3. *Make sure everyone in the group is using firsthand experiences when talking about the addiction and is refraining from repeating secondhand information.* Hearsay sounds like gossip and can trigger a defensive reaction from the alcoholic. There are rare exceptions to this rule. One example of using hearsay appropriately is when a team member lives far away and hasn't witnessed the addiction firsthand. A person might say, "You and I haven't seen each other in the last few years, so I haven't seen this problem firsthand. But it hasn't been a secret. I've known about it because there's been so much family concern."

4. *Are letters written in first-person singular, using the word I rather than we?* All intervention letters are to be written in first person. When you write your letter speak for yourself, not for the group. If your letter isn't written in first-person singular, rewrite it by replacing the word *we* with the word *I*.

5. *Eliminate redundancy.* If more than one person wrote about the family fishing trip or about Uncle Ed's alcoholism, consider revising letters so each letter tells unique family stories.

6. *Does each letter end with a request to accept help?* Make a clear and direct appeal. Without asking, alcoholics don't know what we want from them. It's a simple question: "Will you go into treatment today and accept the help we are offering you?"

7. *Do all team members have completed letters?* Help team members who are having difficulty completing their letters. If someone can't decide what to write, suggest she listen to other people's letters. This will help her come up with ideas of her own. Schedule twenty minutes for people to rewrite or finish letters.

In the second segment of the rehearsal, determine in what order you'll read the letters. The sequence can strengthen your intervention. The alcoholic will make his decision about treatment after all letters are read. For this reason, the last letter may be the most important. So ask yourselves: *Who will the alcoholic have the most difficulty saying no to?* That person should read his letter last. If the alcoholic is angry with his wife and she reads her letter last, he'll find it easy to say no. However, if his grandmother, whom he adores, reads her letter last, he's likely to say yes.

Now identify a person who commands the alcoholic's respect. This person should read her letter first. The alcoholic won't easily walk out of the intervention while someone she respects is reading a letter to him. Once the alcoholic listens to the first letter, it is highly unlikely she'll get up and leave the intervention.

Anyone who has a strained relationship with the alcoholic should read their letter between two people with strong emotional influences over the alcoholic. If the alcoholic is angry with his wife, but has a good relationship with his mother and uncle, have the wife read her letter between the two of them. The uncle and mother serve as buffers for angry reactions the alcoholic may have toward his wife.

You also might decide the order after listening to the content of all the letters. One person's letter may be more intellectual than emotional, which wouldn't be the best letter to read last but perhaps a good letter to read second. Do whatever feels right for your family. The chairperson or interventionist can listen to feedback from the team and then guide everyone to a final decision.

The third segment is to choose your seating arrangement. Sitting at a table creates a barrier between people, so avoid the dining room table and use the living room instead. Arrange furniture so everyone is turned toward the alcoholic. Seat the alcoholic on a couch between two people he loves and respects.

Seat the chairperson between the alcoholic and the door, so if the alcoholic decides to leave, the chairperson can follow him outside and ask him to return. If anyone has a troubled relationship with the alcoholic, keep that person off to the side. The person seated directly across from the alcoholic has direct eye contact throughout the intervention, so choose wisely.

The fourth segment is the dress rehearsal. Do everything exactly as you will the day of the intervention. Sit in your assigned seats. Put away cigarettes and food. Turn off telephone ringers and cell phones. Put the dog outside. Think of all possible distractions and interruptions and eliminate them.

Now begin. Everyone stays in their seats until the last letter is read. The chairperson begins by going to the door as if she were greeting the alcoholic. Another team member can play the alcoholic if this is helpful. The chairperson makes the opening statement and then everyone reads their letters. The chairperson practices what he'll say if the alcoholic accepts help, and what he'll say if he doesn't. Everyone reads their bottom lines. After the bottom lines are read, the chairperson asks again if the alcoholic will accept help. When you've finished the rehearsal, decide if any letters or statements need changes.

Set aside time to rehearse objections and answers. One person can play the alcoholic and read objections to the chairperson. Review until the chairperson feels comfortable with the answers.

You may find that reading your letter is a very emotional experience. If you become overwhelmed, stop and take a few deep breaths. Once you feel composed, start reading again. Most people find that after reading the letter at the rehearsal, they aren't as emotionally overwhelmed during the intervention. It's a good idea to have tissues available just in case.

If the location for the rehearsal is not the same as the location for the intervention, make a diagram of the room you plan to use and create a seating chart. Then rehearse the intervention as if you are at the other location. If you're using the alcoholic's house for the intervention, you might say, "Okay, we're going to meet at the church two blocks from Anita's house at 9:15 a.m. We'll drive to her house together, park, and walk to the front door as a group. Tom will answer the door. We'll all take our seats in the living room while the chairperson goes into the kitchen to greet Anita." Once you've set the scenario, begin your rehearsal.

Feelings of anxiety are normal when planning an intervention. The closer you get to the event, the greater the anxiety. Most people report that they don't sleep well the night before an intervention. Talking about your fears can help. Breathing exercises will calm you down. Here's one that can be done anywhere:

+ Sit comfortably with straight posture.
+ Inhale slowly and say to yourself *I am* . . .
+ Exhale slowly and say to yourself *relaxed.*

It also helps to plan some fun at the rehearsal. Put together a buffet of sandwiches, snacks, desserts, and nonalcoholic beverages. Eating and socializing helps everyone relax.

Some Thoughts for Intervention Day

It's the day of the intervention, and if you're like most people, your pulse is racing and your stomach is full of butterflies. The anticipation period before the intervention is more stressful than the intervention itself. Once the intervention begins and the letters are being read, your anxiety level will drop significantly.

While watching *The Oprah Winfrey Show* on television one day, we heard Oprah mention that she had participated in an intervention. She described it as one of the most loving things she had ever experienced. We think you'll probably have a similar reaction after your intervention. Intervention gives you an opportunity to be an instrument of love.

Before the intervention, renew your resolve to stick with your plan and trust the process. If this is the first time you've participated in an intervention, you won't know what to expect. You may feel as if you are jumping into an abyss with no idea where you will land. Just remember, many people have successfully taken this road before you. Even though you've never done it before, intervention is a tried-and-true way of helping someone with an alcohol or other drug problem.

Keep your focus on yourself, your team, and your plan. Don't start reacting to what the alcoholic does during the intervention. If you focus on the alcoholic rather than your plan, the intervention process will dissolve into unmanageability. If the alcoholic isn't responding as you expected, all the more reason to stick to your plan. Have faith and keep moving forward even if all appears lost. As Dr. Robert Schuller, author and pastor, reminds us: "What appears to be an end of the road may simply be a bend in the road." In many ways, intervention is an act of faith.

If the alcoholic refuses treatment, read the bottom lines. Remember, your bottom line is a way of saying, "I will not support this disease." It is a way to take care of yourself when addiction continues to assault your family. You are not being punitive. The alcoholic brings the consequences upon himself by choosing addiction over recovery. He can avoid consequences in one of two ways: (1) choosing recovery or (2) convincing people to enable his addiction again. If people stop supporting the addiction, alcoholics who refuse treatment are likely to choose recovery in the days, weeks, or months following the intervention.

Once you present your bottom line to the alcoholic, don't change your mind later on. If you do, you are empowering the disease and telling the alcoholic: "I said I wouldn't support your disease anymore, but I don't follow through with my promises. It's easier just to go along with the addiction."

Once all letters are read, give the addict a chance to talk. Sometimes a refusal turns into an agreement when the alcoholic can talk through her fears and frustrations. Although the chairperson is designated to answer objections during the intervention, be flexible when the alcoholic is speaking to the group. The right words from another team member may be very helpful.

If the alcoholic agrees to accept help, tell her how proud

you are of her. Everyone should get up from their seats and give her a hug. Get everyone on their feet and ready to go. The chairperson can move things forward by saying something like: "We have a suitcase packed for you, and it's already in the trunk. Your dad and I are driving you to the treatment center, and everyone else will follow in a separate car. We have an 11:30 appointment, so we should get going if we want to be on time." Then, lead the alcoholic outside and into the car. In most cases, the alcoholic will leave immediately or right after a quick bathroom stop.

Take care of details so the alcoholic doesn't have to stop to buy cigarettes or tie up loose ends. If you anticipate that he will need to make phone calls before leaving, have a cell phone ready for him to use in the car. Once in a while, an alcoholic will agree to treatment but demand to take a shower first. If this happens, ask him to take a ten-minute shower so you can still make the appointment on time.

If the treatment center is out of state and you have time to kill before the departure of the airplane, drive to the airport and have lunch there. Keep the conversation light and have a good time. Levity and laughter will do the alcoholic more good than a serious conversation about her problems. If the alcoholic wants a drink on the plane, let her. Many an alcoholic describes her last drink as the one she had on the way to treatment.

The power of honesty and love during an intervention brings families together whereas the dishonesty and anger of addiction rips them apart. Intervention opens communication and initiates change. Regardless what the alcoholic decides, you will know you did the best you could to make a difference.

Notes for the Chairperson

As chairperson, you set the tone for the entire team during the intervention. This is a job requiring a positive attitude. If you stay calm and avoid anger, the team will follow your lead. Remember: *Intervention is an act of love.* This thought will help you stay on track.

Your roles as chairperson include host, guide, and spokesperson. You'll greet the alcoholic, seat him, and make an opening statement. You will cue the team members to begin reading letters, you will answer objections, and, if the alcoholic refuses help, you will introduce bottom lines. Once team members read their bottom lines, you will again ask the alcoholic to accept help.

Review the sample intervention at the end of this section. Pay close attention to what the chairperson says. You'll notice that he remains calm, speaks clearly, and speaks concisely. When the alcoholic speaks, he listens and doesn't interrupt.

During the rehearsal, practice your greeting and your opening and closing statements. Use the following examples to help you decide what you might say:

Greeting: Kathy, everybody is here today because we love you very much and have some important things to share with you. Come on in and take a seat right over here.

Opening: Everyone has taken time to write you a letter. We'd like you to listen as we read our letters to you. Your grandmother would like to begin.

Closing #1: Kathy, we've taken care of everything for you. You don't have to worry about anything. Will you accept the help we're offering you today? *(Kathy agrees to treatment.)* I know I can speak for the entire group when I say we're very proud of you. *(Everyone gets up and gives hugs.)*

Closing # 2: (when treatment is accepted, but delayed) Kathy, for many reasons we would prefer you to go to treatment today, but we understand that you have a few loose ends to take care of before leaving. Will you have enough time to take care of everything today and leave tomorrow? We can certainly help. *(Kathy asks for two days.)* We know you are an honorable person. Are you giving us your solemn word that you will go to treatment on Tuesday? *(Kathy assures the team that she will.)* Let's get on the phone together and change your appointment at the treatment center. I have the contact person's name and number right here. But first, let me give you a hug. *(The team did not read bottom lines because Kathy agreed to go. If she doesn't keep her word on Tuesday, the team will deliver bottom lines.)*

Closing #3: (when treatment is refused) Kathy, we respect your right to make this decision for yourself. We've also made some decisions and hope you will respect our decisions. We love you too much to continue doing anything that supports your addiction, and we need to take care of ourselves, too, because your addiction causes us pain. We'd like to share our decisions. Your grandmother will begin. *(Everyone reads their bottom lines.)* Kathy, will you accept the help we're offering you today? *(Kathy still refuses help.)* Kathy, accepting treatment is ultimately your decision. If you change your mind, you can call any one of us for help. If you choose to stay in your addiction, we must stand by the decisions we have just shared with you.

If you feel more confident reading your remarks rather than ad-libbing, go ahead and write them down on a separate piece of paper. We've worked with several chairpersons who read their closing statements without diminishing the effectiveness of the intervention.

If the alcoholic refuses help, you can ask him why. This gives the alcoholic an opportunity to express his thoughts and feelings. By listening carefully, you may discover the reason behind his resistance. For instance, when asked, an alcoholic told his family he wouldn't go to treatment because, "No one is going to lock me up in a nuthouse." He thought he was being committed to a lockdown ward in a psychiatric hospital. The chairperson immediately pulled out a color brochure from the alcohol and drug treatment center. He showed the alcoholic pictures of the nicely decorated rooms and the beautiful campus. He assured the alcoholic that no one was planning to lock him up and explained that staying in treatment would be his choice. With his fears alleviated, the alcoholic agreed to go.

Sometimes the reasons for refusing help keep changing, and no solution is good enough. In these cases, the real reason she won't go is because she wants to drink. Every so often, letting alcoholics have a drink before leaving for treatment gives them relief and the fortitude to accept help.

If you don't know how to respond to something the alcoholic says, pause and take time to think. Rely on two considerations: (1) speak to the alcoholic from a place of love and (2) stay focused on the goal of treatment. We suggest memorizing a standard answer you can use as a safety net if you find yourself at a loss for words: "I hear what you are saying, but today we're talking about how we're going to help you with your (alcohol or drug) problem."

This simple statement is practical and a good safety net

during an intervention. It assures the alcoholic that you are listening to what he is saying while bringing the focus back to treatment. If the alcoholic tries to lure you into an argument, you can repeat the standard answer over again, regardless of what the alcoholic says to you. When you do this, you keep the focus on your message and avoid being pulled off track. Repeating this standard answer is an excellent technique for deflating an alcoholic's long-winded debate designed to deflect focus from him and onto other issues.

Sometimes an objection comes up that wasn't anticipated and must be answered by someone other than the chairperson. This happened during an intervention we facilitated on a middle-aged, divorced alcoholic. At one point the alcoholic turned to his grown children and said, "This isn't about my drinking. This is about your anger toward me because I divorced your mother." The chairperson knew she couldn't speak for the adult children in this instance, so she asked if one of them would like to reply. The oldest son responded saying, "I do have feelings about the divorce. But my concerns about your drinking started before you divorced Mom. The only reason we're here today is because we love you and want you to get help." His answer was a version of the standard answer. First he assured his father that he was listening to him, and then he brought the focus back to the alcohol problem. It's a good idea for everyone on the team to memorize the standard answer in case they have to respond to an unexpected objection.

Once the intervention begins, trust the process. If all objections have been answered and the alcoholic still refuses help, keep your team focused on bottom lines. You've put the process into motion. Stay on course.

Making Team Decisions

Intervention is not the end of the story. It's the beginning. Prepare yourself for the journey ahead. It won't always be easy. Whether the alcoholic goes into treatment or not, he will test you. At some point, he'll be difficult and unpredictable, and it won't be easy. The addiction and all the related problems didn't happen overnight, and they won't be fixed overnight.

If you find yourself thinking, "I can handle the alcoholic on my own now," you're putting yourself in a vulnerable position. Believing you don't need help from others makes you more susceptible to the alcoholic's manipulations. It's easy to get pulled into enabling the disease again, which short-circuits the recovery process. Alcoholics can manipulate one person more easily than a group of people. Therefore, after the intervention, keep using the power of the group. Maintain an interdependent relationship with your team members—a shared dependence and mutual support of one another. You need support now more than ever.

Be prepared for your loved one to attempt to persuade you to support her addiction again. She may call and tell you she's leaving treatment early. She'll ask you to pick her up. She'll convince you she doesn't need treatment anymore. We've seen many people intervene on loved ones only to turn around and "rescue" them from treatment a few days later. If you find your-self ready to do something like this, call your team members and talk it out before you take action. If the alcoholic starts asking you to do favors for her, say, "I'll have to get back to you on that." Then call your team members and, when possible, the counselor at the treatment center. Make team decisions.

Intervention puts the wheels of change into motion, and change rarely comes quietly. It may shake up your life. You've learned certain survival skills that helped you cope with the addiction in your family. These changes in your behaviors happened gradually and subconsciously. Your focus was on the alcoholic's or addict's behaviors, not on how the problem was changing you. Everyone must begin a personal recovery program. Family members must identify how the addiction has changed them, and how to begin healing themselves and their relationships. A passage from Al-Anon's *Courage to Change* expresses this well: "One of the effects of alcoholism is that many of us have devalued our talents, feelings, achievements, and desires. In Al-Anon we learn to know, appreciate, and ex-press our true selves."

Begin by attending the family program at the treatment cen-ter. Continue your recovery in Al-Anon, Nar-Anon, or Fami-lies Anonymous. These are Twelve Step groups for the family, and they are the best way for relatives and friends to embrace recovery and positive change.

Sometimes, after an intervention, the team splinters. They stop doing what they agreed to do, just like alcoholics and ad-dicts sometimes do. We can't ask our addicted loved one to do what we are not willing to do. We have no moral authority if we ask them to make changes but we refuse to do the same. It helps if the entire team agrees to a "Family and Friends

Commitment Statement." Such a statement clearly spells out the promises we are making to ourselves, to each other, and to the addicted person. Everyone signs the commitment statement and everyone gets a copy. We know alcoholics and addicts need a sense of accountability; sometimes we do, too. Look in section 6 for a sample.

Intervening on an Adolescent

No amount of alcohol or other drugs is safe for a child or adolescent. Addiction progresses more quickly in young people than it does in adults. A study by the National Institute on Alcohol Abuse and Alcoholism shows more than 40 percent of people who begin drinking before the age of fifteen become alcoholic. More than 24 percent who begin drinking at age seventeen become alcoholic. When young people wait until age twenty-one or twenty-two to drink alcohol, their risk of alcoholism drops to 10 percent.

In adolescence, we go through more physical and emotional changes in a shorter amount of time than any other period in our lives, except for birth to age three. Mood-altering substances block the development of social skills and emotional maturity. A sixteen-year-old who's been drinking for five years has the maturity of an eleven-year-old. Our children are bombarded with messages about the pleasures and benefits of drinking alcohol when they watch television and look at magazines. Yet we expect them not to drink. In her book *Deadly Persuasion*, Jean Kilbourne writes, "One of the most striking examples of advertising is the very successful and long-running campaign for Absolut Vodka. . . . Collecting Absolut ads is now a common pastime for elementary-school children, who swap them like baseball cards." She goes on to say, "What's the best way to appeal to young people? One way, of course, is to present the product as strictly for adults—as in the so-called moderation messages of the alcohol and tobacco industries. . . . Another ploy is to use cute little animals and cartoon characters like Spuds MacKenzie and the Budweiser frogs, lizards, and Dalmatians." Although alcohol presents the number one drug problem among youth, illegal drugs are easy to obtain in our communities. Children can frequently purchase them from fellow students in the corridors and classrooms of schools.

It's become fashionable among some parents to tolerate their children's marijuana use. It's wrongly thought of as a fairly benign drug that is nonaddictive and without major consequences. The reality of marijuana use is far more disturbing. Some of the consequences are

+ impaired judgment
+ high-risk behaviors
+ addiction
+ unknown additives (PCP, herbicides)
+ short-term memory loss
+ car accidents
+ reduced learning capacity
+ acute anxiety and paranoia
+ lost potential and low motivation
+ increased risk of cancer
+ increased risk for sexual activity, pregnancy, HIV infection
+ decreased testosterone levels affecting developing bodies

Brain imaging shows how marijuana changes young brains. Dr. Daniel Amen, a clinical neuroscientist and psychiatrist, has published photos of the brain of an eighteen-year-old who smoked marijuana four times a week for three years. The imaging shows significant atrophy of the brain and decreased activity in the prefrontal cortex, often referred to as the CEO of the brain. This is the seat of consciousness and is responsible for our sense of who we are. It controls our thoughts and behaviors and affects our judgment and decision-making. It's crucial for controlling impulsive behavior. Our ability to succeed in life depends upon the health of our prefrontal cortex. The temporal lobe activity of marijuana smokers is diminished, too. This region is known as the *emotional brain*. It is the seat of our passion and joy for living. When affected by marijuana or other drugs, feelings and moods become increasingly negative. The effects of marijuana on the brain can lead to anger, irritability, and anxiety and are associated with memory, attention, and motivational problems.

The adolescent brain is rapidly developing both in structure and function. Recent studies show that alcohol and other drugs change how young brains develop. Drugs can have a significant impact on the ability to learn and remember, and these changes may be permanent. Using rats as test subjects, scientists have shown how alcohol-induced impairment continues into adulthood. Dr. Aaron White, an assistant research professor in the psychiatry department at Duke University, speaking to the *New York Times*, explains the seriousness: "We definitely didn't know 5 or 10 years ago that alcohol affected the teen brain differently. Now there's a sense of urgency. It's the same place we were in when everyone realized what a bad thing it was for pregnant women to drink alcohol."

Many young people successfully hide their use of alcohol or other drugs from their parents. Other times, parents often ignore symptoms of drug use or dismiss them as typical adolescent behavior. But experiencing serious and repeated problems isn't a normal part of growing up. If you suspect an adolescent has an alcohol or other drug problem but are not sure, take the quiz "Is Our Teen Chemically Dependent?" in the tools section and review symptoms of abuse and addiction. If your child is experiencing some of these warning signs, consult with a counselor at an adolescent treatment facility.

When intervening on an adolescent, avoid presenting yourself as an authority figure. Don't preach, lecture, or use your intervention letter to express your disappointment in the child. Approach your child with respect and talk about the addiction as a family disease. Take the focus off the young person and put it on the family system. In other words, talk about addiction as *our* problem, not *your* problem. Phillip LaCourse, a limited licensed psychologist with a specialty in adolescents and addiction, explains: "Each person in the family takes responsibility for improving *themselves*. By doing so, they create a harmonious environment within the family system. Participation of the family as a whole is crucial to the adolescent's receptiveness to treatment and recovery."

Parents should not take the role of chairperson for an intervention. There's too much potential volatility. Choose someone whom the young person will listen to more openly. This might be an aunt or uncle, a coach, or a family friend. Parents often dominate an intervention by talking too much, and the adolescent shuts down. Parents need to talk less and listen more. Give the child time to talk once the letters are read. Let the chairperson respond.

An adolescent is not fully developed emotionally, which can make the intervention process more difficult. Therefore, it is important to recognize and validate the struggles she is experiencing. Focus on how alcohol and other drugs have interfered with her goals, the loss of trust in relationships, the decline in grades or athletic performance, and legal problems. Help her see that the alcohol and drugs are preventing her from being where she wants to be in her life.

By referring to addiction as a family problem, you are making a commitment to participate in the treatment process. Inform your child that everyone plans to attend the family education program and counseling sessions. Make a promise to attend Al-Anon, Nar-Anon, or Families Anonymous meetings weekly. Your example will influence your child's commitment to treatment and recovery.

If you are concerned that your child will refuse to go into treatment or try to run away, consider obtaining a court order. Most states allow parents to use the court system to order children younger than eighteen years of age into a chemical dependency treatment center. If you obtain a court order, use it as your bottom line. Proceed with the intervention without mentioning the court order. Give your child the dignity to accept help on his own. If he refuses help, use your bottom line to inform your child of the court order. We've worked with parents who've explained it like this: "It was my hope that you would choose help on your own. As your parent, I am responsible for protecting you when you are unable or unwilling to help yourself. For that reason, I have obtained a court order that mandates you into treatment. You have the choice to go to treatment on your own, but if you refuse, the police will escort you to the treatment center today."

If either parent abuses alcohol, prescription drugs, or illegal drugs, your child may ask you to answer for your behavior. You'll have to be honest with yourself about your own chemical use. If alcohol is a prerequisite for a good time, is your usual way to reduce stress, or is part of your nightly ritual, you may have to reconsider your relationship with alcohol and the message you're sending to your child. If the adolescent brings up your alcohol use during the intervention, you can say something like, "Today we're talking about *your* alcohol and marijuana problem. But I promise to be honest about my alcohol use when I talk with the treatment staff and make any changes they recommend." If you say that, however, you'd better follow through.

When looking for an adolescent treatment center, be sure it has a strong family component and uses the Twelve Step model of recovery. Look for a program that involves the adolescent in the treatment planning process, offers an aftercare program for both the child and the family, provides education and recreation programs, and involves the treatment peer group in the therapeutic process. Staff members should have credentials in addictions counseling and child development.

Contact your child's school and speak with someone in the Student Assistance Program (SAP) for a referral to an adolescent treatment center. The SAP may also offer support groups, relapse prevention programs for recovering students, and a list of young people's Alcoholics Anonymous meetings in your hometown. The tools and resources section includes a list of some youth programs we are personally familiar with.

Intervening on Someone Over Age Fifty-five

If the alcoholic is an older adult, defined as age fifty-five or older, you need additional information before proceeding with an intervention. Symptoms of alcoholism can mirror symptoms of aging. These symptoms include shakiness, frequent falls, excessive napping, depression, reduced interest in food, isolation, dizziness, confusion, memory loss, bruising, incontinence, and poor hygiene. Alcoholism is sometimes misdiagnosed as Alzheimer's disease, stroke, or Parkinson's disease.

The consequences of alcohol or other drug problems are different for older adults. Since many are retired, drive less, live away from family and friends, are financially independent, and drink alone at home, they don't experience the same kinds of consequences as a younger person. When you write your letter to the older adult, shift your thinking when looking for examples of negative consequences. A younger person may have a drunken driving arrest, threat of job loss, financial problems, or divorce. These consequences are less likely to occur in an older adult's life.

It's a good idea to contact the older adult's doctor when planning an intervention. The doctor may have no idea that his patient's health problems are symptoms of an underlying alcohol or prescription drug problem. It is not uncommon for doctors to misdiagnose or under-diagnose addiction in older adults, even though it is a significant and growing health problem. The U.S. House of Representatives Select Committee on Aging commissioned a study in the 1990s that found that 70 percent of all hospitalizations of older adults are related to alcohol or mood-altering prescription drugs. One in five hospitalized older adults has a diagnosis of alcoholism.

A doctor may unwittingly contribute to the problem by prescribing sedatives, pain pills, or tranquilizers. An older adult may mix these medications with alcohol, increasing the chance of addiction and creating a potentially deadly combination. Furthermore, doctors often don't recognize addictions in older adults because they interpret the symptoms as signs of aging. The following chart helps illustrate the confusion.

Aging	Addiction
Memory loss	Memory loss
Shaky hands	Shaky hands
Frequent naps	Frequent naps
Boredom	Boredom
Depression	Depression
Frequent falls	Frequent falls
Bruises	Bruises
Dizziness	Dizziness

Addicted older adults often have several doctors prescribing mood-altering drugs. If you have the opportunity, check prescription bottles for names of prescribing physicians and pharmacies. This will help you determine if the older adult is using multiple doctors to get more drugs and shopping at different pharmacies to avoid getting caught.

Older adults with limited budgets sometimes stop buying drugs that don't produce a high in favor of spending money on medications that are mood-altering. For example, blood pressure pills may be abandoned in favor of tranquilizers and sedatives. Ask the pharmacy for a computer printout of the prescriptions being filled to determine if this is a problem.

Ask the doctor to write a letter recommending treatment. A family member can read the letter at the intervention. Older adults usually respond favorably to the authority of the medical profession. If prescription drugs are the problem, a doctor's letter will also counteract objections such as, "I can't be addicted to these drugs because they are prescribed by my doctor."

Before contacting an older adult's physician, go back to "Involving Doctors and Other Professionals" in section 3 and review the suggestions about talking with doctors. Remember, addiction is a specialized field and most doctors do not have much education in this area. When you speak with the doctor, briefly provide clear examples of the problem. It's a good idea to write down what you want to say prior to making the phone call. In most cases, the doctor is going to respond more positively if you present precise information in a short amount of time. Be clear about what you are asking the doctor to do.

For instance, you might say: "Dr. Smith, the members of my family and I believe our seventy-nine-year-old mother, who is your patient, has an alcohol and prescription drug problem. We have found her passed out during the middle of the day. She is increasingly confused and has fallen on several occasions. We have begun monitoring her alcohol consumption by counting the bottles she throws away, and we think it's reasonable to say she drinks a pint of vodka every day. She is mixing alcohol with Valium prescribed by two different doctors. We believe this has been a problem for several years, but is getting much worse. We are planning, as a family, to ask her to go into treatment. We would like you to write a letter supporting treatment as necessary for her health. Would you be willing to write a letter and mail it to us?"

The book *Aging and Addiction: Helping Older Adults Overcome Alcohol or Medication Dependence,* by Debra Jay and Carol Colleran, offers advice on building a team for an older adult intervention:

> The number of people on your team should be determined by evaluating the needs of the older adult. If the older adult has a problem with dementia, use a smaller team. Too many people may confuse an older adult with cognitive problems. Late onset alcoholics (who develop the disease after the age of fifty) respond more favorably to a smaller team due to shame issues. Early onset alcoholics (who have been alcoholic since young or middle adulthood) are more resistant to accepting help, so larger teams help break through denial. These are guidelines, not steadfast rules.

Every so often, adult children resist asking friends or relatives to participate in the intervention. The reasoning usually has to do with avoiding embarrassment. We find that intervention is more effective when relatives and longtime friends are involved. Older adults find it easier to refuse their adult children, but are more inclined to agree to treatment when friends or other relatives are on the team. Friends may have been reluctant to voice concerns in the past because they didn't feel it was their place. During the training and rehearsal, however, they usually open up.

Intervening on a parent is especially difficult. Adult children can be uncomfortable with the role reversal—they are now parenting their parent. We've also seen adult children quickly revert to feeling twelve years old again. Early family-of-origin issues can unexpectedly overwhelm some of the siblings. In addition, disagreements may arise. Or a sibling may have her own drinking problem and cause disturbances among team members. In some cases, adult children fear being disinherited. Because of the many complexities, working with a professional experienced in older adult intervention is advisable.

Once the older adult is in treatment, call and inform the doctor. By obtaining a signed release of information, the treatment center can send the doctor a summary of treatment and aftercare recommendations. It is critical that doctors understand they cannot prescribe mood-altering drugs again except when absolutely necessary, such as after surgery. Do not assume doctors won't prescribe mood-altering drugs to recovering alcoholics and addicts. We worked with an elderly woman whose doctor sent her to treatment due to her twenty-five-year addiction to prescription drugs. Within two weeks after discharge from the treatment center, the same doctor gave her a prescription for sleeping pills and told her, "Now you know how to keep this under control, so we shouldn't have any future problems." The doctor didn't understand that recovery requires abstinence and that addicted people can't use drugs in the same way nonaddicted people use them.

Because of their heightened sense of shame, intervening on older adults requires sensitivity. Most grew up believing that character flaws and moral failings cause addiction. For this reason, avoid words such as *alcoholic, alcoholism, addict,* and *addiction* during the intervention. These words create pictures of skid row bums in the minds of many older adults. This can trigger defensiveness by creating feelings of shame. It's far better to say something like this:

Mom, I've seen alcohol have an increasingly negative effect on your life. You've had falls. You shake in the morning. You have frequent lapses of memory. I found you unconscious in the living room last Thursday. It isn't unusual for alcohol to become a problem as people age and their bodies change. Science has learned that alcohol is more destructive to the older person's body and brain. Alcohol problems sneak up on people in their later years without anyone realizing it is happening. The American Medical Association identifies this as a disease that responds well to professional treatment. I'm here today to ask you to get help for this serious problem that is damaging your health and your soundness of mind.

You'll notice that this example addresses alcoholism as a medical issue. It mentions the American Medical Association, describes the problem as common among people in later life, and explains that physical changes affect how aging people respond to alcohol. All these things help reduce shame, which means less defensiveness during the intervention.

We've also found it helpful in some older adult interventions to mention that President Gerald Ford and his family intervened on Betty Ford in just the same way we're intervening on the older adult. The former first lady describes her intervention in her book *Healing and Hope*: "Surrounded by the family who loved me . . . this intervention saved my life."

When selecting a treatment center, look for a program designed for older adults. They are designed to address the special needs of this age group, which are often overlooked in treatment programs designed for younger people. Older adults require a longer detox, scheduled rest periods during the day, more time to walk from place to place, and their progress in treatment is slower. They also have a hard time relating to twenty-something or thirty-something drug addicts. Oftentimes, the younger adults use language they find offensive. They resist participating in group therapy, don't respond well to direct confrontation, and need more one-on-one contact with their counselor. They also have grief issues specific to their age. Older adult treatment programs are designed to meet these special needs. If there are no older adult programs in your home area, go to the resources section in the back of the book to locate one.

According to the Substance Abuse and Mental Health Services Administration (SAMHSA), older adults have higher success rates in treatment than any other age group. Transformation is nothing less than miraculous when older adults are given enough time in treatment. Most regain health, vitality, and a sense of purpose. Cognitive impairment improves or disappears entirely. Permanent brain damage is a reality for some, but not for most. We've heard many people say, "They're old. Let them drink." Advanced age doesn't make a life dispensable; older adults play an important role in communities and families.

We worked with a seventy-two-year-old grandmother as a patient several years ago. She came into treatment malnourished, bruised from head to toe, shaky, and confused. She was mixing alcohol with prescription mood-altering drugs. A neighbor found her passed out in her driveway one morning. Her kids didn't trust her with the grandchildren anymore. She stopped going out with friends. She didn't eat, shower, or clean her house. There is nothing romantic about this picture. But once she got into recovery, her life changed. Her family came together, she enjoyed her grandchildren, and she began traveling. She sent us postcards from her snorkeling adventure in the Caribbean and her hiking trip in the mountains of Arizona. This was a woman who could barely walk when she came into treatment. In recovery, she was free to enjoy the true gifts of life and family.

We see differences in the older population according to what generation they belong to. The leading-edge baby boomers are entering treatment addicted to illicit drugs in addition to alcohol and prescription medications. Baby boomers are more demanding, questioning of authority, and want more of a say in the treatment process. They request more services and conveniences while in treatment; therefore, more treatment centers are offering yoga, acupuncture, holistic medicine, vegetarian cuisine, massage therapy, and the list goes on. When intervening on a baby boomer, there's a greater possibility that the person is divorced, remarried, and has children from the second marriage or stepchildren. The family dynamics can be very different from those of the WWII generation. Baby boomers are determined to stay young, athletic, and sexually active. It can be helpful to understand this when intervening by expressing how alcohol and other drugs are robbing them of their good looks, youthfulness, and health. Baby boomers have grown up hearing that alcoholism is a disease, so their belief system isn't as much of a barrier to treatment. They are also generally more open to the concept of spirituality and self-help groups.

A high level of family involvement throughout the treatment process will benefit everybody. Attend the family program and speak to the older adult's counselors regularly. Ask for a copy of the aftercare recommendations the older adult needs to follow when returning home. The clinical team can also help you identify ways to be supportive of early recovery.

Older adults have many struggles in treatment, but the end result is worth it. Older adults in recovery live longer and, more important, have a life worth living.

What an Intervention Looks Like

Let's take a look at what an actual intervention looks like. We've re-created a typical intervention to give you a picture of what you'll probably experience. Read how the chairperson handles objections, how team members deliver bottom lines, and how the intervention is concluded.

Most interventions unfold just as the following dramatization does. The alcoholic rarely interrupts members of the team as they read their letters, almost never walks out during an intervention, and, in most every case, will become tearful rather than angry. Most alcoholics and addicts agree to accept help the same day or shortly thereafter.

Since we can't predict with complete accuracy whether a particular intervention will end with an agreement to accept help, we must be prepared for all possible outcomes. We offer different endings to our sample intervention to prepare you for a variety of possible responses from the addicted person.

When an alcoholic refuses help and isn't swayed by bottom lines, we can suspend the rule that the chairperson alone speaks to the alcoholic. While we never dissolve into free-for-all arguments during interventions, a few well-chosen words from a team member with significant influence may help change the alcoholic's mind. This is a last resort effort and your team must play this one by ear. Stay true to the rule that no one resorts to anger, blame, or admonishment, and you should be all right. If it's clear that you are not getting anywhere, end the intervention. Ultimately, you must preserve the alcoholic's dignity and leave the door open to future opportunities.

Intervention: A Portrayal

Characters

Greg, *a thirty-five-year-old with an alcohol problem*
Audrey, *his seventy-nine-year-old grandmother*
Rose, *his mother*
Katie, *his younger sister, and the detail person*
Janet, *his wife*
Ashley, *his thirteen-year-old daughter*
Ken, *his best friend, and the chairperson*
Judy, *his workplace supervisor, unable to attend*

The intervention is taking place in the living room of Greg's grand-parents' home. Greg thinks the family is gathering for Sunday brunch. Greg is expected to arrive with his wife, Janet, and daughter, Ashley, at 10:00 a.m. The other family members will arrive thirty minutes earlier.

Greg's supervisor, Judy, could not attend but wrote a letter for the intervention. Her letter is read by Ken.

Greg is not expecting his best friend, Ken, to attend the brunch, so Ken parks his car in a discreet location.

A day earlier, during the rehearsal, the team drew up a seating plan for the intervention. Everyone has taken their place before Greg arrives. Greg's wife and daughter will immediately go to their assigned seats upon entering the grandparents' home. Ken, as chairperson, will greet Greg and escort him to his seat, which the team has preselected for him.

Greg has a devoted relationship to his mother, Rose, and his best friend, Ken. Therefore, he is seated on the sofa between the two of them. Greg is seated away from the door. To leave the intervention, he'll have to walk past his best friend, his daughter, and his grandmother. Greg has deep respect for his grandmother and great love for his daughter. The two of them are seated together to create a strong emotional force. Greg and his wife, Janet, love each other, but their relationship is filled with anger. For this reason, Janet is farther away from Greg. Putting space between Greg and his wife helps prevent angry flare-ups. Greg has always been close to his sister, Katie, so she is seated next to Janet to help neutralize the anger between Janet and Greg.

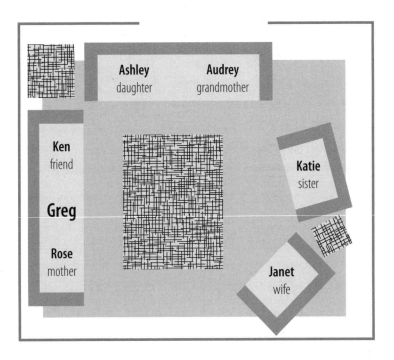

The time is 9:45 a.m. Members of the intervention team take their seats in the living room. Greg, his wife, and daughter are expected to arrive in fifteen minutes. All beverages, food, and cigarettes are put away. Telephone ringers and cell phones are turned off. The dog is moved to the basement. The team waits, listening for the sound of Greg's car pulling into the driveway. When they hear a car pull up and car doors slam, Ken, as chairperson, gets up to greet Greg at the door. The doorbell rings, and Ken opens the door.

Greg: *[surprised]* Ken, what are you doing here?

Janet and Ashley walk past Ken and go to their seats in the living room.

Ken: *[warmly, putting his hand on Greg's shoulder and looking him straight in the eye]* Greg, your family loves you very much and so do I. We've come together today because we have some important things we want to share with you. Come on in with me.

Ken's hand moves from Greg's shoulder to his back, gently guiding Greg toward the living room.

Ken: *[gesturing toward the couch where Rose is seated]* Here. Take a seat next to your mom.

Greg sits down next to his mother and Ken sits down on the other side of Greg. Greg looks around the room at everyone. The room is silent.

Greg: *[tentatively]* Hey, how's everyone doing? What's going on?

Ken: *[calmly]* Greg, we're all doing just fine. We've gotten together because each of us has taken some time to write you a letter, and we'd like to share them with you. We ask you to just listen as we read, and your sister would like to read her letter first.

Katie looks up at her brother, smiles, and after a two-second pause begins to read her letter.

Katie: Dear Greg, you're my big brother, and I've looked up to you my whole life. You were always the smartest and the funniest of anybody. You don't know how proud I was to tell people you were my big brother. I always felt like I was something just because I was related to you. I was so shy growing up, and you were always there to take me under your wing. Like when I had that huge crush on Billy Olson, and you started inviting him over to play touch football just so I could get to know him. You've always put other people before yourself. It is this generosity of your spirit that I so admire. I don't say it nearly enough but I love you more than anything.

Katie finishes her letter by talking about the alcohol problems she's witnessed firsthand and by asking Greg to accept help today. Greg stares down at his hands. Ken glances at Janet to cue her that it's her turn to read her letter.

Janet: Dearest Greg, you are my husband and my best friend.

Greg's demeanor stiffens as Janet begins to speak. His eyes flash with anger as he looks up at her.

When I first met you, I was so infatuated with you. You made me laugh all night long. You have the funniest sense of humor. But more importantly, your warm heart and compassion for others shines through everything you say and do. That's as true today as it was then. It's what I love most about you. I know we've had some hard times lately, but don't ever doubt my love for you. I'm so sorry for all of the harsh and unloving things I've said to you. I just didn't know what to do, and I let my anger take over. But you must know that it's the depth of my love for you and my devotion to our marriage that I've been fighting for—I don't want to lose you. I love you too much.

Janet finishes her letter by talking about the alcohol problems she's witnessed firsthand and by asking Greg to accept help today. Greg's jaw is set and he looks at her accusingly. Ken glances at Audrey, Greg's grandmother, to cue her that it's her turn.

Audrey: *[gazes at Greg steadily for a few seconds and then reads her letter]* Dear Gregory, I was with your mother when she went into labor with you, and I drove her to the hospital. Your dad showed up a few minutes later, and I sat with him in the waiting room, calming his nerves. When the nurse came out holding you in her arms, the first thing your dad asked was, "Is Rose all right?" When the nurse assured him that your mom was just fine, he looked down at you with so much pride. The nurse said, "It's a boy. You have a son." Your dad started crying right then and there. If your dad was still with us today—and I think he is looking down on us right now—he'd tell you that you were his whole world. *[Audrey starts to cry.]* He loved you with his heart and soul. He'd do anything for you. And so would I. After all, you were my special boy from the start. The first time I held you, you looked up at me and I knew it was an instant bond between you and me.

Audrey finishes her letter by talking about the alcohol problems she's witnessed firsthand and by asking Greg to accept help today. Greg's head is in his hands and tears are running down his cheeks. Ken nods at Rose, Greg's mother, to cue her that it is her turn.

Rose: *[crying softly as she begins to read]* Dear Greg, I'm so proud of you, son, for everything you've accomplished in your life. From the very beginning you've been a ray of sunshine in my life. When you were three, and I was pregnant with Katie, you asked me where babies came from. I told you that if God smiled down on a mommy and daddy, they got a baby. God definitely smiled the day you were born. He gave you a kind and generous heart, and the gift of laughter. I've always felt that you were a wonderful gift to me. When your father died, you were my strength. You came to see me every single day. You took care of the house, the car, and the yard. You made me laugh when I thought I would never laugh again. If it hadn't been for you, I don't think I could have gotten through that first year after your father's death. Son, I love you more than life itself.

Rose finishes her letter by talking about the alcohol problems she's witnessed firsthand and by asking Greg to accept help today. Greg nods yes to her request, tears in his eyes. Ken nods to Ashley, Greg's daughter, who begins reading her letter.

Ashley: *[looks at her dad and then down at her letter]* Dear Dad, I think you must be the best dad anybody could ever have. We always have a lot of laughs kidding around, and you always think of the most fun things to do. When I want to get permission to do something, I always ask you, because—like Mom says—you're the softie and can never say no. I love you so much, Dad. *[starts crying and takes several deep breaths to compose herself before reading again]* But lately things have been different. You and Mom fight all the time, and I've seen you drunk. It scares me. I know you don't mean it, and it's not really you. I've learned that this is a disease and it takes help to get better. I want you to get better. I want to have a happy life for all of us. Please, Dad, accept help today. I love you. Your daughter, Ashley.

Greg: *[crying]* I love you too, Pumpkin. I love you too.

Ken: *[turns toward Greg and begins to read]* Dear Greg, we've been best friends since the ninth grade. That's twenty-one years now. You were always the guy ready to try anything. You've never let anything get in your way when you wanted to accomplish something. I may not have told you this before, but you have always been an inspiration to me. I've pushed myself harder to accomplish more in my life because of the example you've set.

You were best man at my wedding, and you're my son's godfather. This makes you more than my best friend—you're a member of my family. The kids call you "Uncle Greg," and they love you very much. Lately, however, they've asked me what's wrong with you. The last several times you've been over you've gotten pretty intoxicated, and the kids have been confused. You get too loud and your play becomes too aggressive. The kids have always adored you, but the alcohol changes you. We've explained to them that you have an alcohol problem and that it's an illness. Christopher asked us why nobody was helping you. At that moment I realized that I was avoiding you more and more when I should be helping you instead. I promised Chris I would do whatever I could to help.

That is why I am here today. I've always considered myself a good friend to you, but I've known for some time that alcohol is a problem in your life and I chose to look the other way. That's not what friends do. Today I am willing to do the tough thing and ask you to accept treatment for your alcohol problem. We've made all of the arrangements for you to check into a really great treatment center today. Greg, will you accept the help we are offering you? Your friend, Ken

Silence

Ken: [*looking directly at Greg*] Greg, are you willing to go into treatment today? We have made all the arrangements at an excellent treatment center. Everything is taken care of for you.

Greg: [*composing himself*] You're probably right. I might have a bit of a problem. But I can't go anyplace today. We're in the middle of a big project at work, and it's not as if I can just disappear from my job. Maybe in a month I'll go. But, really, I think I can handle this on my own. I promise you all that I won't drink anymore. Not a drop.

Ken: [*calm and steady*] In the past, you've gone on the wagon. You've attempted to control this problem, but it hasn't worked. We've learned that recovery requires getting help from others.

Also, we have a letter from your supervisor, and she asked us to read it to you. She writes: "Dear Greg, our company has a policy that supports treatment for alcohol problems. I have made arrangements for your medical leave. The only thing you need to do is to make a phone call to me once you've been admitted into treatment. You can be assured that the reason for your leave will be kept confidential and your job will be waiting for you upon completion of treatment. On a more personal note, I have a son who is recovering from alcoholism, so I have an intimate understanding of this problem. Please know that I support you in your decision to accept help today. Sincerely, Judy."

Silence

Greg: *[deep sigh]* I guess I don't have much choice, do I? Okay, I'll go. But how long do I have to stay?

Ken: Greg, that is for your treatment team to decide, but typically it's about twenty-eight days. This problem didn't happen overnight and it doesn't get fixed overnight. We'd like you to commit to the entire program.

Greg: *[nods]* It's a long time to be away, but yeah. I will.

Ken: *[smiling]* I think I can speak for everyone in this room when I say we're really proud of you.

Everybody gets up and hugs Greg. Ken and Katie walk Greg out to the car. Greg's suitcase is already in the trunk. Greg, Ken, and Katie drive away. Rose calls the treatment center's admissions department to tell them Greg has agreed to accept help and is on his way. Everybody drives to join Greg, Ken, and Katie at the treatment center.

A Different Ending

The scenario you just read ended positively, but sometimes alcoholics and addicts refuse to accept help even after all objections are discussed and answered. When this happens, the chairperson introduces the bottom lines just as Ken does below.

Greg: *[annoyed]* I have too many things going on right now and my answer is no. I am not going to treatment. That is my final answer.

Ken: *[calmly]* Each of us in this room loves you very much, and we understand that you have the right to make this decision for yourself. We hope you can respect the decisions we've made. None of us is willing to do anything that continues supporting your alcohol problem. Also, if you do not choose treatment, we must take care of ourselves. We'd like to share our decisions with you.

Katie: *[reading]* Greg, you must know how much I love you. Watching what alcohol is doing to you is more than I can bear. I can't pretend everything is all right, because by doing so, I am letting the alcohol take you away from me. I can no longer look the other way when you drive drunk. I'd never be able to forgive myself if you killed yourself or someone else. I can't stand by and do nothing anymore. As difficult as it will be, I will call the police if I see you drive drunk. Please accept the help we're offering so it never comes to that.

Greg: *[impatiently]* Listen. I can handle this problem on my own. Besides, I don't think this is anybody's business. This is my life, and I'm not hurting anybody.

Ken: *[calmly]* You've tried to handle it on your own before without success. We've taken time to learn about this problem and know that recovery requires getting help. And it is our business. Each of us has been hurt by this problem. It affects all of us more than you can know. Now let's hear what your grandmother has to say. *[nods to Audrey]*

Audrey: *[reading]* Gregory, I love you, but I've always been straight with you. Your drinking has caused your grandfather and me a lot of concern and worry. When you show up in the morning smelling of liquor, it's really hard on your grandfather, especially since his stroke. His health can't take the stress. Until you do the right thing and get the help you need, you can't come to the house. As long as you refuse help, you're telling me that alcohol is the most important thing in your life and that hurts me. I feel I'm playing second fiddle to a bottle of booze. It's time you make a choice about what's really important in your life. Won't you accept help today?

Rose: *[reading]* Greg, I've learned that I've enabled you to continue drinking. I'm not proud of it, and I've vowed to stop doing it. I let you stay at my house when you and Janet have fights, and many times you've shown up drunk. I've cleaned you up, put you to bed, fed you in the morning, and never said much about the drinking. I've let you come home whenever you want, making it easy for you to run from the responsibilities of your family. I'm ashamed to say that I've even blamed Janet for your problems when it's really the drinking. I'm not going to bail you out anymore. If you get thrown out of the house, you'll either have to get help for your drinking or find another place to stay. I won't help you while you're drinking anymore, but I will help you if you want to get better. Will you accept help today?

Ken: *[reading]* You're my best friend and you can always call me if you change your mind and decide to get help. I'll pick you up and drive you to treatment anytime. But I'm going to ask that you don't come by the house until you get help. If you choose alcohol over treatment, you can't be around the kids. They've already been affected by your drinking problem, and their welfare is a priority. It doesn't mean we don't love you. It means we must take care of ourselves. Won't you take care of yourself and get help today?

Janet: [reading] Greg, as much as I want to save our marriage, I can't live with your drinking anymore. If you decide not to get help, I have to think about Ashley and myself. We can't keep living like this. Until you get help, you need to find another place to live. If you want to drink, you can't live in our house any longer starting today. But if you choose help, I'm willing to do my part, too. I know we can rebuild our marriage if the alcohol is no longer an issue. I want our marriage and family to work. Will you please accept our help today?

Ashley: [reading] Dad, Mom talked to me about her decision to ask you to leave the house. I don't think I've ever cried so hard. I never thought this would happen to us. I don't want our family to break up, but I understand why Mom is doing what she's doing. Our life at home has been pretty bad lately. Won't you go to treatment instead? [begins to cry] I told Mom you'd get help if we asked.

Ken: Greg, we'll all stand by you if you reach out for help. Will you accept the help we're offering you today?

Greg: [visibly shaken] I need a minute to think. Grandma, is there any coffee out in the kitchen?

Audrey: Yes. There's some in the pot.

Greg gets up and walks into the kitchen.

Ken: [quietly, to the team] Everybody remain seated and silent. Let him have a moment to think.

After a few minutes pass, Ken motions to Audrey.

Ken: [quietly] Maybe you should go check on him.

Audrey gets up and goes into the kitchen to talk to Greg.

Audrey: How're you doing?

Greg looks at his grandmother and shrugs his shoulders.

I know we're asking you to do something you don't want to do. It's not about wanting to go, Greg. It's about needing to go. One thing I've learned about life, success usually requires doing things we don't want to do. This is going to take guts. It may be the toughest thing you ever do. You're going to have to say yes when everything in you wants to say no. *[putting a hand on his shoulder and looking him in the eye]* Are you ready to do what you need to do?

Greg: *[sighs deeply]* Okay, Grams, okay. I'll do it.

Audrey: *[patting his cheek and smiling]* Let's go tell the others.

Together, they walk out of the kitchen back toward the living room.

A Variation to the Ending

When an alcoholic refuses treatment today but promises to go later, we first try to explain why going today is the better choice. With time to think, the addiction can convince any alcoholic or addict that she doesn't need help after all. You may also have purchased plane tickets that are nonrefundable. If you can't get an agreement for today, negotiate the soonest possible date for treatment. Ask the alcoholic to give the team her word that she will keep her promise to go. Have her get on the phone, along with another team member, to call the treatment center and change the admissions date. Decide who will escort her to treatment. Don't read bottom lines unless she doesn't go on the promised day.

Every so often an alcoholic or addict steadfastly adheres to his decision not to accept help even after the bottom lines are read. There are two primary reasons. First, he doesn't believe the team will follow through with their bottom lines and is testing them. Learning the hard way that everyone means business, he eventually agrees to treatment. This can take days, weeks, or months. Second, the alcoholic needs to feel in control. He first wants to try to stay sober on his own. If this is the case, negotiate with him. Ask him to give his word that if he starts drinking or taking other drugs again, he'll go into treatment immediately.

Other times, the alcoholic is so emotionally withdrawn from the family, she's no longer influenced by what they think or say. Occasionally the alcoholic has been drinking before the intervention, making it difficult to break through his denial. If the alcoholic or addict has a love interest on the side—especially one that drinks or takes drugs with him—it can be more difficult.

Invite the alcoholic who is refusing treatment to tell the group why he won't accept help. Listen to him closely. He may provide the information you need to help him change his mind. If not, the chairperson closes the intervention as Ken does below:

> **Ken:** We respect the fact that getting help is ultimately your deci-
> sion. We've told you our decisions and ask that you respect them
> as well. *[pause]* The last thing I have to say is that we came to-
> gether today out of love for you. We want only the best for you.
> If you change your mind, please come to us.

The chairperson stands after closing the intervention, cue-ing everyone else to do the same. The alcoholic or addict will usually leave at this point. It's a good idea for the treatment team to reassemble and discuss their feelings with each other. Pay special attention to children who've participated in the intervention. They need to hear that they did a good job and that the alcoholic's refusal to accept help doesn't mean she doesn't love them. It's a good idea for someone to spend the night with the spouse and children of the alcoholic. In the last scenario where Greg refuses help, Janet and Ashley plan to spend the night with Katie and Rose in case Greg returns drunk or angry.

If an alcoholic threatens to hurt himself—something that almost never occurs—call 911. Never leave a suicidal person alone. If the person you are intervening on has had past suicidal thoughts or attempts, work with a professional. Intervention doesn't cause suicide, but addicted people have a higher risk for suicide than the general public.

When an alcoholic refuses help, it doesn't mean she won't ever choose recovery. It just means the process is going to take longer. This is when faith counts. You can't see what's ahead but you've initiated change. Stick with your plan. Keep a loving mind-set, follow through with bottom lines, and make decisions as a team. If you do, there's a very good chance the alcoholic will eventually go into treatment or join Alcoholics Anonymous.

Helping without a Family Intervention

If you aren't ready for a full family intervention right now but want to do something to help the alcoholic, there are a couple of other options. Statistically, the following techniques don't have the high success rate of family intervention, but they are worthwhile alternatives.

The method recommended by Al-Anon is to detach from the problem, begin your own program of recovery, and stop enabling the alcoholic. Some people call this *soft intervention*. When you stop helping the alcoholic avoid the consequences of his addiction, and troubles begin stacking up, he may eventually decide to go to an Alcoholics Anonymous meeting or into treatment. No one can predict when or if this will happen. Every situation is different. But some people estimate that the success rate of soft intervention is about 50 percent. If the alcoholic never chooses recovery, you will at least take care of yourself by practicing the principles of Al-Anon.

Another way to approach the alcoholic is to calmly tell her you are concerned about her drinking and to ask if she wants help. As we discussed earlier, talking to the alcoholic one-on-one is not highly effective but there are ways you can increase your chances of success. Talk to the alcoholic when he's sober and in a receptive mood. Approach him with love and concern. Don't resort to anger or engage in debate. Follow the same guidelines used for intervention, but don't write a letter or go into a long discussion about the addiction. Instead say something like: "Meg, you're my best friend. I value your friendship beyond all others. For this reason, I feel I need to talk with you about the toll alcohol is taking on your health. I believe it is causing significant problems in your life. I'm afraid for you and don't want to lose you. Would you be willing to talk to a counselor about it? I'll go with you if you like."

If the alcoholic says no, drop it. Don't try to cajole or plead. Simply say, "Okay, I just want you to know I love you. If you ever want to talk about this, you know you can come to me." You'll have a more profound effect on the alcoholic by respecting his response to your offer for help. This will keep the door open for future opportunities.

If the alcoholic agrees to get help, be prepared to respond immediately. Have the name and telephone number of an addictions counselor in your pocket. Pull it out and say, "I took the time to find a good counselor. Her name is Carolyn Johnson, and I have her number right here. I'll give her a call. She said she has an opening this afternoon." The sooner you get the alcoholic into the counselor's office, the less likely he'll change his mind about going.

A third approach is to wait until a crisis intervenes on the alcoholic or addict and then take action. The intervention might be a drunken driving arrest, job loss, divorce, hospitalization, financial problems, or any number of things. Negative consequences can open the door of opportunity for you. The alcoholic will be more receptive to treatment when she's in trouble. The bigger the trouble, the more receptive she'll be. Approach the alcoholic at the peak of the crisis rather than waiting until problems subside. Once pain diminishes, denial can snap back into place. When crisis is the intervention, timing is everything.

Executive-Style Intervention

There are times when a full-scale family intervention isn't our best first step. If an alcoholic has major anxiety disorder, for instance, a large group of people might trigger a panic attack. High-profile careers may require greater discretion. Sometimes we don't have family members or friends in sufficient numbers to create a team. Or the addict has already been through a family intervention and relapsed. In these circumstances, we can choose a different route: executive-style intervention.

Executive-style intervention brings together one to three people who will speak privately with the alcoholic. We call these people *emissaries*. They can be friends, relatives, co-workers, employers, clergy, teachers, or professional interventionists. Since we aren't using a full intervention team, emissaries should have substantial leverage or considerable influence. In most cases, they should also work with a professional interventionist.

If a CEO of a corporation is in need of alcoholism treatment, it won't be in the company's best interest for this information to leak to the press. An executive-style intervention would restrict knowledge of the problem to a very small number of people. The chairperson of the board and a professional interventionist may be the only ones who approach the CEO.

The chairperson has the power to decide the CEO's future with the company. As head of the board of directors, he is capable of delivering immediate consequences—the loss of a very prestigious and well-paying job. The interventionist is present to guide the discussion, offer treatment options, answer questions, field objections, take care of details, and escort the CEO to treatment. Together, they create an atmosphere of teamwork—coming together to make the best decisions for the well-being of the CEO and the company. In this case, the CEO knows where the power lies and is unlikely to refuse treatment.

When an addict suffers from a debilitating anxiety disorder, a ten-member intervention team may be more than she can handle. If she has a panic attack, she won't be able to listen to the intervention letters or respond to the love and concern of her family and friends. She may even flee the room. In such situations, consider an executive-style intervention, and contract the services of a professional interventionist. Select one or two people the addict respects and trusts. They will work with the interventionist as emissaries. This small team can say, "All our family members and friends are deeply concerned and so they thought they should do a big family intervention, but we thought it might be better if we talked with you first. We thought you'd rather make the decision to get help without talking to everyone. So we brought along an expert on treatment and recovery. He's been through this himself. He can answer questions and help us come up with the best solutions."

Some people complete treatment and then relapse. Once they've started drinking or using drugs again, the family often doesn't know what to do. Another structured family intervention is often unnecessary. Instead, a carefully planned meeting with a few emissaries from the original intervention team may be sufficient. If your loved one had been attending Alcoholics Anonymous and has an AA sponsor, the sponsor will serve as a good emissary. Select two or three of the most influential people from the original intervention team. If you have a relapse agreement (see "Preparing for the Possibility of Relapse" in section 5, page 238), bring a copy to the meeting. If not, you'll need to decide the next step for the alcoholic. If the alcoholic had a short slip, perhaps it's enough to begin attending more AA meetings with his sponsor. If his relapse is more substantial, he may need medical detox. If he hasn't been working a program of recovery in AA (to learn what this entails, read "A Few Words about Alcoholics Anonymous" on pages 235–237), he probably needs a treatment center with a relapse prevention track. Other questions you may need to get answers to: Will outpatient be sufficient or does he need inpatient treatment? Are there low-cost options? Should he consider going to a halfway house? Is there something else blocking his recovery? If you don't know the answers to these questions, consult with an addiction professional.

Some addicts are estranged from their families, or their closest relations are also chemically dependent. There is no team, so a structured family intervention isn't a possibility. Maybe it's a friend who wants to help. Executive interventions can work in such cases, but should be done with guidance from a professional interventionist. Often, there is little or no leverage, so we must rely on the influence of the friendship and the expertise of the professional. If the addict is experiencing a crisis—fired from a job, evicted from her apartment, losing custody of children, or suffering from depression—we can present ourselves as the gateway to putting her life back together. Giving the addict a sense of importance and a vision of a brighter future may be the greatest motivating force.

When significant shame is associated with the addiction, executive-style intervention is a good choice. For example, sex addiction and the resulting behaviors are usually too humiliating to share with a large group. It's better to work with an interventionist and a few close friends or relatives. For instance, a husband addicted to pornography and prostitution will do better with his father, brother, and best friend as emissaries rather than facing a full family intervention that includes his wife, mother, and sisters.

When doing an executive-style intervention, we position ourselves as allies of the alcoholic. We're the ones coming in at the eleventh hour to save him from imminent consequences. We work with him, offering solutions, and hopefully we come to a satisfactory agreement about treatment and recovery.

Executive-style intervention is less structured and more difficult to navigate, so using a professional is highly recommended. If the alcoholic refuses to accept help, be prepared, whenever possible, to execute a structured family intervention in the next day or two using a full team.

Here are a few tips for planning an executive-style intervention:

+ Determine if you need to work with a professional interventionist. Refer to the chapter "Do You Need a Professional Interventionist?" (page 118).
+ Begin the planning process as you would for a standard family intervention: assemble your team, gather information, write letters, prepare bottom lines, choose a treatment center. Then put the family intervention on hold.
+ Choose one to three emissaries from your team who will meet with the addict. Select people the addict trusts and respects.
+ Determine your leverage and influence. Is there a job or a marriage on the line? Are there pending legal consequences?

Financial problems? Do emissaries have significant emotional influence?

+ Approach the alcoholic early in the day. Choose a day when she has the fewest commitments and is most likely to be sober.

+ Begin by explaining your concerns. Be respectful and use loving honesty. Speak of addiction as a disease.

+ Explain that you chose a quieter approach rather than bringing together a large group to do a family intervention.

+ Suggest that the alcoholic take control of the process by moving quickly and getting into treatment before further consequences materialize.

+ At some point, the alcoholic might ask to speak privately with one of the emissaries. Sometimes a heart-to-heart with a trusted friend or favorite uncle can result in agreeing to treatment, but only if the alcoholic isn't allowed to become manipulative. A professional interventionist can also play the role of confidant.

+ If the alcoholic doesn't agree to treatment, use your leverage. Remain nonconfrontational. The alcoholic will likely understand without being lectured or threatened. You'll be more successful if you adopt a "we're all in this together" attitude.

+ Maintain a calm and conciliatory approach throughout the process. By doing so, you preserve the alcoholic's dignity and help him understand it's in his best interest to make the right decision, no matter how difficult.

+ If the alcoholic still refuses, don't get into a battle of wills or an argument. Leave on good terms and proceed with your plans for a full family intervention.

+ If a structured family intervention isn't feasible, wait until the addict experiences a crisis and repeat this process. Most addicts are more willing to accept help when suffering from emotional or physical distress.

Section 5

After the Intervention

Talking to People Who Did Not Take Part in the Intervention

Are there significant people in the alcoholic's or addict's life whom you did not include on the intervention team? Did you decide not to include them because you felt they were not appropriate for an intervention? Will any of these people do things to help the alcoholic get out of treatment? If so, you may need to contact them after the intervention.

Some people think the best way to help the alcoholic is to spring him from treatment, give him a free place to stay, lend him money, or even provide him with drinks or other drugs. These are people the alcoholic may turn to if he decides to leave treatment early. It is often prudent to call people who may try to "rescue" the alcoholic before the alcoholic calls them. Tell potential enablers that the alcoholic checked into treatment after the family asked him to get help. Explain that he may have a tough time and could decide to leave before completing the program. Make sure they understand the seriousness of this possibility. Let them know that you believe the alcoholic may turn to them for help. Take the time to explain how this could seriously hurt the alcoholic. Tactfully suggest a way they can respond to the alcoholic's request for help and still be a friend. We suggest something like: "I'd love to help you out, you know that. But your family called and asked me not to get involved in this problem. They are really worried about you. If you want to leave treatment, I think you have to work that out with them." By implicating the family as the reason he can't help, the friend is off the hook.

We worked with a family who decided not to include one of the alcoholic's close friends on the intervention team because he had his own drinking problem. The family thought he might warn the alcoholic about the upcoming intervention. After the alcoholic was admitted into treatment, his mother called her son's friend. She purposely did not use the word *intervention* during the conversation because she thought he might have false ideas about what that meant. Instead she said: "The family got together today and talked to Leon about his drinking. We asked him to get help. We waited until now to tell you because the two of you are so close. We didn't want to put you in the middle." The friend surprised everyone by responding, "It's about time someone talked to him. His drinking has been out of control lately." When the mother asked the friend not to help the alcoholic leave treatment early, he readily agreed.

Some people may not want the alcoholic to get sober. An addicted spouse, girlfriend, or boyfriend will view treatment as a threat. Alcohol or other drug use is the essence of their relationship, and when one person gets sober, the relationship doesn't work anymore. In this situation, some families intervene on both addicted people. This requires two interventions that take place one right after the other. We recently intervened on a husband and wife. The members of the first intervention team were from the husband's family. The husband's employer was on the team, too, so the intervention took place in his office. When the husband agreed to treatment, his family drove him to a local facility. The members of the second intervention team were from the wife's family. They went to the wife's house and intervened on her. When they told her that her husband was on his way to treatment, she agreed to accept help. The family drove her to a different treatment center in a nearby city.

If a double intervention isn't possible, notify the treatment team about the addicted partner. Also tell them about drinking buddies who might cause problems or other people who may enable the alcoholic. If counselors have this information, they can help the alcoholic examine destructive relationships and understand why they're incompatible with sobriety. You can't control what the alcoholic does, but you can open the doors of communication so that problems don't remain secrets. Resolving problems requires bringing them out into the open.

Sending Your Intervention Letters to the Counselor

Intervention letters are powerful therapeutic tools during the early treatment experience. After the intervention, the detail person should collect all the letters, put them in a large envelope, and give them to the counselor. Collect the bottom-line statements, put them in a separate envelope, and hold on to them for now. Bottom lines play a separate role that we'll discuss in a later chapter.

Before mailing or delivering letters to the treatment center, call and ask for the name of the alcoholic's or addict's counselor. The treatment staff can give you this information only if the alcoholic has signed a release of information form. Without this release, they are not allowed to share any information. In this case ask for the name of the clinical director. Send the letters to the director with a request that they be forwarded to the counselor.

If the alcoholic has refused to sign a release form that gives the counselor permission to talk with family members, don't let that stop you. You can provide counselors with information even if they can't talk to you. Call the treatment center and say, "I know the laws on confidentiality do not permit you to say whether Jane Smith is or is not a patient at your facility.

However, that does not prevent me from talking to you. May I please talk to a counselor available at this time?" Counselors have very little free time. You may have ten minutes or less before the counselor has to leave for an appointment, so prepare yourself. Write down the most important points on paper before you call.

Intervention letters can help the alcoholic work through anger. Carol Colleran, executive vice president of the Hanley Center in West Palm Beach, Florida, told us that their patients read intervention letters during a counseling session in the counselor's office. They then read one or two letters during a group therapy session and ask for group feedback. She reports that group members often express thoughts such as, "Your family must love you very much to do what they have done. I wish my family had done the same for me." Feedback from the group can help move alcoholics out of anger and into acceptance. Acceptance is the first step toward gratitude.

Intervention letters help break through denial. Most alcoholics and addicts minimize, rationalize, and deny their drug problems. Even if the consequences of addiction are severe, the addict may have difficulty seeing the problem clearly. Counselors and other patients can point out the discrepancies between the alcoholic's account of his drug problem and his family's account as reported in the intervention letters.

When an entire group of people can recognize the addiction, the implication is too great for most alcoholics to ignore. For example, if one person comes up to you and says your nose has turned green, you'll laugh it off as a joke. But if several people comment on your green nose, you'll head for the nearest mirror to take a look. Intervention letters can do the same for the alcoholic. With so many people acknowledging the problem, the alcoholic takes a second look at what is happening in her life.

Include a note to the counselor with the letters. Some counselors may not have experience using intervention letters as therapeutic tools. Here's an example letter:

Dear Ms. Counselor:
I am writing regarding my wife, Jane Smith. As a family, we used intervention to motivate Jane to accept treatment for her cocaine problem. During the intervention, each of us read a letter to Jane expressing our love and our hope that she would accept help. I am sending you copies of those letters.

I realize that Jane may be experiencing anger and denial at this early stage of her treatment. Our intervention team was informed that these letters are a valuable therapeutic tool for the treatment staff. It is our understanding that you may want Jane to read and discuss these letters during a one-on-one counseling session or read a couple during group therapy and ask for peer feedback. I hope the love and eyewitness accounts presented in our letters will help Jane work through her anger and overcome denial.

Please feel free to call me at 555-1294. I am very supportive of Jane's recovery and will do my part by attending the family program and Al-Anon.

Sincerely yours,
John Smith

Most counselors understand the special needs of patients entering treatment after an intervention. Anger is common among all people entering treatment, but it is often more intense after an intervention. For this reason, working through anger is usually the first priority of the treatment team. Your letters will help. Have them delivered to the counselor as soon as possible.

Understanding What Goes On during Treatment

Most people know about treatment, but few can describe what it is. When an alcoholic or addict goes into an inpatient treatment center, families and friends often have no idea what to expect. An alcoholic's account of treatment can vary depending on her attitude. Some alcoholics refuse to give the treatment staff permission to talk with family members, denying the family information from the counselor. So let's take a look at what happens in many inpatient treatment centers. Keep in mind that programs vary and not all programs will exactly match our example.

When the addict enters treatment, a doctor performs a physical exam, including blood and urine screenings. The medical team closely monitors the addict until he is fully detoxed and medically stable. When necessary, alcoholics and addicts are given medications to ease withdrawal symptoms. Nurses check vital signs to monitor withdrawal symptoms. Withdrawal from some drugs, such as alcohol or Valium, can cause seizures and can be fatal. To detox the addict safely, medications are necessary. Other drugs—such as heroin and pain medications—cause severe withdrawal symptoms, but they aren't life-threatening. In these cases, medications may be used to reduce discomfort.

Otherwise, addicts may not be able to bear the pain and, as a result, leave treatment. Don't be alarmed if the addict tells you the doctor is prescribing mood-altering drugs. This is sometimes a necessary aspect of detoxification and is terminated once the alcoholic is physically stable.

Treatment centers rarely provide private rooms because alcoholics and addicts tend to isolate themselves from other people, and isolation blocks recovery. For this reason, almost everyone in treatment has a roommate. If the alcoholic calls complaining about sharing a room, remember that this is an important part of the treatment process.

Each patient is assigned a counselor who will work with her throughout treatment. Counselors don't work alone. They are part of a clinical team including some or all of the following: a psychologist, a psychiatrist, a medical doctor, nurses, addictions counselors, clergy, relapse specialist, aftercare specialist, and activities director. The clinical team meets to discuss each patient's needs and progress. Even though the addict's primary counselor manages her case, the entire team treats the addict.

During the first few days of treatment, patients go through an assessment process. The medical team assesses a patient's physical health and makes recommendations for health care needs. For instance, if the patient has a bladder infection, the doctor will prescribe antibiotics. Problems that don't require immediate attention will be referenced in the patient's aftercare plan. This aftercare plan lists everything the patient needs to do after discharge from treatment. The doctor also will alert counselors to problems that might hinder progress in treatment such as hearing loss or limited mobility. These problems require immediate solutions, so the patient gets the most from his treatment experience.

In some centers a psychologist or other mental health professional does a psychological assessment, using testing and personal interviews. If problems beyond chemical dependency exist, the psychologist will inform the team of what is called *co-occurring disorders*. This means two or more problems exist together but each is a separate diagnosis. For example, a patient may have an anxiety disorder as well as alcoholism. One doesn't cause the other, although they may make each other worse. The psychologist or psychiatrist determines what additional clinical services are needed for patients with co-occurring disorders. Ideally, these services will be integrated with the addiction treatment plan.

An addictions counselor usually does an assessment of the patient's history of alcohol and drug use. The patient and the counselor also discuss legal, financial, marital, family, employment, and social problems. If these problems are not addressed, the addict may cope poorly in early recovery and resort to using alcohol or other drugs again. The counselor also needs to gather information from the family, but must obtain a release from the patient to do so.

When assessments are complete, the clinical team reviews the information and makes treatment recommendations. Based on these recommendations and input from the patient, the counselor writes a treatment plan. The treatment plan lists the problem areas identified by the clinical team, and then each problem is matched with a goal for treatment. To help the patient reach treatment goals, the clinical team adds assignments to the treatment plan. The counselor monitors the patient's progress as she works on these assignments. If her work is unsatisfactory, the counselor meets with the patient to identify problems blocking her progress.

Alcoholics and addicts often come to treatment expecting to spend most of their time talking one-on-one with a counselor. In actuality, group therapy is the focal point of treatment. Patients go to several groups each day, and meet individually with their counselor only two or three times a week. The counselor is a patient's guide throughout treatment, but recovery happens primarily through group therapy. So if the alcoholic calls complaining that he doesn't meet with his counselor often enough, ask him how many group sessions he has every day.

Recreation is an important activity in treatment. We've heard people scoff at treatment centers with swimming pools or yoga classes: "This is nothing but a country club." This statement ignores the long hours and difficult personal introspection required of people in treatment and underestimates the importance of setting aside time for fun. Alcoholics and addicts don't know how to have fun sober, and they need to learn. If an addict is miserable and bored in sobriety, she is at greater risk for relapse. Many treatment centers offer pools, gymnasiums, game rooms, or workout centers; they employ activities directors and schedule recreation as a part of daily schedules. So if the alcoholic tells you about the great swimming pool or the terrific volleyball games, don't resent the good time she's having in treatment. She needs to practice having fun without alcohol or other drugs.

Although daily schedules vary from treatment center to treatment center, they're more alike than different. We put together the following schedule based on our experiences working in treatment. It gives you a general idea of what an alcoholic or addict does during a typical day in an inpatient treatment setting:

7:00	Morning Meditation Reading/Discussion
7:30–8:15	Breakfast
8:15–8:45	Personal Time/Work on Assignments
8:45–9:30	Lecture and Discussion
9:30–10:00	Personal Time/Work on Assignments
10:00–11:30	Group Therapy
11:40–12:15	Relapse Prevention Group
12:20–12:50	Lunch
12:50–1:15	Personal Time/Work on Assignments
1:15–2:00	Lecture and Discussion
2:10–3:00	Alcoholics Anonymous Orientation/Big Book Study
3:00–4:15	Pool or Gym
4:30–5:15	Sober Living Planning Group
5:15–5:45	Relaxation Therapy
5:45–6:30	Dinner
6:30–7:45	Lecture and Discussion
8:00–9:00	Alcoholics Anonymous Meeting
9:00–10:30	Personal Time
10:30	Lights Out

Individual sessions with an addictions counselor are scheduled during a patient's personal time. Other groups offered by many treatment programs include grief group, Twelve Step study, aftercare planning, nutrition guidance, HIV/AIDS education, and family program. Some treatment centers set aside Sunday afternoons for relaxation and family visitation.

Before a patient is discharged from treatment, the clinical team develops his aftercare plan. This plan outlines what the patient needs to do to maintain sobriety and to successfully work through other problems in his life. Following are two examples of aftercare plans.

1. For ongoing sobriety, attend four or more Alcoholics Anonymous meetings per week; ask five Alcoholics Anonymous

members for their telephone numbers and talk to at least one of them daily; obtain an Alcoholics Anonymous sponsor within two weeks of discharge from treatment; work the Twelve Steps with your sponsor. Attend the Aftercare Support Group every Wednesday at 6:30 p.m. for six months. Set up a credit counseling session at a nonprofit, no-cost organization by calling 555-1625. Begin marriage counseling within six months after discharge from treatment or as determined appropriate by your aftercare counselor. See your medical doctor, as necessary, for ongoing medical problems. Make an appointment at a pain management clinic to discuss biofeedback techniques for managing back pain.

2. Upon discharge, transfer to a halfway house program for four months. Attend Narcotics Anonymous meetings as determined appropriate by halfway house staff and obtain a Narcotics Anonymous sponsor to help you work the Twelve Steps. Follow all halfway house expectations. Seek individual counseling to deal with problems related to but beyond chemical dependency. After completion of the halfway house program, follow the aftercare recommendations provided by the halfway house staff.

Sometimes patients refuse to comply with aftercare plans. When this happens, the clinical team holds a conflict resolution meeting with the patient. The team members listen to the reasons the patient doesn't want to comply and then explains why they feel the recommendations are necessary and appropriate. They may ask the patient to discuss her reluctance with her peer group and ask them for feedback. Family bottom lines can be used as leverage. Many patients finally agree to comply. Those who don't are at high risk of eventually returning to alcohol or other drug use.

If a patient stubbornly refuses to follow his aftercare plan, the treatment team will write a secondary aftercare plan. For instance, if a halfway house program is refused, the team may recommend an intensive outpatient program. In this case, the secondary aftercare plan does not provide as much support as the clinical team believes the alcoholic needs in early recovery, but is the next best option. When a patient refuses to attend Alcoholics Anonymous, most clinical teams will not eliminate Alcoholics Anonymous from the aftercare plan. Attending a Twelve Step program is not an optional part of recovery.

Family members should be familiar with aftercare plan recommendations before the alcoholic is discharged from the treatment facility. If the alcoholic refuses to let the counselor share aftercare planning with the family, she's probably not serious about long-term recovery.

Family involvement during treatment is very important. Counselors need family input since alcoholics often deny and minimize their problems. Without talking to families, counselors can't be certain that the information they get from patients is accurate. An alcoholic's account of his problem and his family's account are often vastly different. If the counselor doesn't contact you in the first two days of treatment, initiate the call yourself.

Preparing for Objections during Treatment

Once the alcoholic or addict is in treatment, denial often resurfaces. This happens to people whether or not they've gone through an intervention. Denial is like a punching bag. When you knock the bag down, it pops right back into place. Denial has to be knocked down over and over.

When denial pops back up, the alcoholic may start looking for escape routes out of treatment. You'll know when she's found one, because she'll tell you about it in the form of an objection. The alcoholic will probably call a family member she thinks she can easily influence and present her objections to treatment. Here are some of the most common objections:

+ I understand everything they're telling me. I really don't need to stay here any longer. I know what to do. There is nothing more they can teach me.
+ The people here are all worse off than I am. There's a guy who used heroin and another one was a crack addict. Get me out of this place.
+ I've got important business to deal with right now. It can't wait. I've got to leave.
+ It's not right to be away from my kids this long. They need me. I've got to come home and take care of them.

+ I can't afford treatment, and I refuse to let anyone else pay for it.
+ I see the error of my ways. I'll never drink or drug again. I've really learned my lesson this time.
+ The food here is terrible, and I can't sleep in a strange bed. I'm miserable, and I don't have to subject myself to this.
+ They're making me share a room with two other people. I have no privacy, and I don't trust these people. I'm not going to stay in this place.
+ The staff here doesn't know what they're doing. I'm not being seen enough, and my counselor is incompetent.
+ This program is the pits. I'm not getting a thing out of it.

Prepare yourself for treatment objections in the same way you prepared for the intervention. Brainstorm with team members. Write down possible objections and how you'll answer them. Every team member should be prepared for the alcoholic to call with reasons why he needs to leave treatment early. If the alcoholic presents an objection, try one of the following answers: "I suggest you discuss that problem with your counselor," or "I don't know what to tell you. I'd recommend that you take that to your group," or "I understand that you have a problem with the food (roommate, bed, being away from the children) but your most important problem is your chemical dependency. Recovery takes precedence over all other concerns." If the alcoholic continues to object, use the broken record technique by repeating the same answer over and over again. If the alcoholic becomes angry, calmly tell him that you must end the conversation. Don't start reacting to the alcoholic's anger. If you are tempted to engage in debates or arguments, tell yourself to stop. End the conversation and call a member of the intervention team for support.

If you find yourself believing the alcoholic's objections, warning bells should go off in your head. When the alcoholic's objections begin making sense, the addiction is running the show. If this happens, slow everything down. Stop and think. You don't have to make an immediate decision. Respond by saying, "I'll have to think about that." The alcoholic will probably pressure you for an immediate answer, but don't rush into anything. Call your team members and the counselor to ask for advice. By using the group to make your decisions, the alcoholic is less likely to manipulate you into doing the wrong thing. If the alcoholic won't allow you to speak with her counselor, that's a sign that she's trying to control you.

Of course an alcoholic doesn't need the family's permission to leave treatment. He can leave anytime. But if the family is using influence and leverage, the alcoholic knows he will experience consequences. He'd rather convince the family that the treatment center isn't working for him or that he doesn't belong there. Then he can leave treatment with the family's blessings and avoid negative consequences. A family prepared for treatment objections is less susceptible to this kind of manipulation.

If your alcoholic tells you she is leaving treatment early, put your bottom lines to work. Ask the counselor if the family can come to the treatment center and do a conflict resolution with the staff. Family members can read their bottom lines to the alcoholic with the clinical team present. Of course, this is only possible if the alcoholic has signed release forms for the family members. If you can't meet with the alcoholic in treatment, deliver bottom lines to the counselor.

Once the alcoholic is in treatment, some families start blaming the treatment staff for the alcoholic's problems. Like the alcoholic, the family begins resisting the recovery process. This is often a sign that the family feels they've lost control over the situation. They don't know what to expect anymore. The alcoholic doesn't seem to be getting better. Everything is changing. Recovery is puzzling and new. As a reaction to these uncertainties, the family turns against the treatment team. When this happens, they provide the alcoholic with an excuse to leave treatment.

If you start viewing the treatment team as the problem, discuss your concerns with the alcoholic's counselor and ask for feedback. Begin looking for solutions that support recovery. Check your expectations for early recovery. Are they realistic? Are you expecting too much too fast? How are you feeling about yourself? Do you sometimes think it would be easier to go back to the way things used to be? Are you afraid the alcoholic won't need you once he gets well? If you're blaming others rather than focusing on the recovery process, something is probably making you uncomfortable. Blame becomes your refuge and blocks recovery. Make a choice to deal with uncomfortable feelings in a different way: talk to the addictions counselor, go to Al-Anon, sign up for the family program, start seeing a counselor who works with families of alcoholics and addicts. Do something that will help you make positive change in your life.

Supporting the Alcoholic or Addict during Treatment

Support your alcoholic with actions. They speak louder than words. It's one thing to tell the alcoholic or addict that you support what she's doing; it's quite another to get busy yourself. Once the alcoholic is in treatment, it's time for you to participate in the recovery process. Remember, recovery is not a spectator sport. Everybody in the family is part of the team.

The first thing to do is to sign up for the family program offered by the treatment center. Once you know the dates and times of the program, make child care arrangements and talk to your boss about taking a few days off work. Let nothing interfere with your attendance. We suggest that everyone who participated in the intervention participate in the family program. If this isn't possible, the people closest to the addict should attend.

Some people mistakenly believe that the family program will be a grueling, unpleasant experience. Nothing could be further from the truth. Families routinely count it among the best experiences of their lives. A family member of ours, who was very reluctant to go, called us after completing a four-day family program and couldn't stop talking about his amazing experience. He had so much to say that he kept us on the phone for nearly an hour.

As good as your intentions may be, without the family program, you will not be well prepared to deal with early recovery. You'll likely experience confusion and frustration, and your newly recovering alcoholic will probably feel alienated and misunderstood. At first, relationship problems may grow rather than lessen. In early recovery, added pressures are placed upon the family. Properly coping with these pressures demands that you learn new ways to handle the challenge. So don't think of the family program as an elective. It's a required course for family recovery.

Counselors usually suggest the best time to attend the family program. Typically families come the third week of treatment. By this time, most alcoholics have had major breakthroughs and are doing well. The family's arrival doesn't cause turmoil or the desire to leave treatment early, as it might at an earlier date. You could also attend the week the alcoholic is being discharged, and everyone can go home together.

If the treatment center does not offer a family program, call other local treatment centers. Many will welcome people who do not have a family member in their rehab program. If you don't find any locally, investigate nearby cities or some of the centers listed in the resources section.

Next, choose a Twelve Step program that's right for you. Al-Anon is for families of alcoholics, Nar-Anon is for families of people addicted to other drugs, and Families Anonymous is for both. Many members of Families Anonymous are parents of adult children with alcohol or other drug problems. Find a meeting close to your home or workplace and begin attending. Use your phone book or call local information for a listing. The resources section lists Web sites and telephone numbers of Twelve Step programs.

Most treatment centers set aside time for visitation once a week, usually Sunday afternoons. If your loved one has just arrived and is emotionally volatile, you might want to wait a week or two before visiting. Talk to the counselor for guidance. Seeing family isn't always recommended initially. It can be more helpful not to visit the alcoholic for the first week or more.

When your loved one is in treatment, you'll be supportive by keeping phone calls to a minimum. Most treatment centers ask patients to spend no more than ten minutes on a call, so keep calls short and infrequent. Don't call daily. Once or twice a week should be sufficient. Some treatment centers don't allow phone calls. Patients who get a lot of calls aren't keeping their focus on treatment. They are more concerned with what's going on at home or work and aren't getting the full benefit of the program. If you feel the need to talk to the alcoholic frequently, find another family member to talk to instead.

Rather than calling, send cards, upbeat letters, and photos. Have the kids draw pictures and make their own cards. If you send gifts, keep them small and inexpensive. Expressing your love shouldn't stop when the intervention ends. When the mail arrives, patients line up hoping for letters. Be sure your loved one isn't disappointed.

Your First Al-Anon Meeting

Making the decision to go to an Al-Anon meeting can be difficult for many people. Some people feel intimidated because they don't know what to expect. Others think they don't belong or believe they can handle things on their own. Still others insist they don't have time or that it's the alcoholic's problem. And some are afraid they might run into people they know. This is exactly how the alcoholic or addict is feeling about going to his first Alcoholics Anonymous meeting.

Just about everyone resists going to their first meeting. Knowing what to expect can help you feel more comfortable. When you walk into an Al-Anon meeting, the first thing you'll notice is that the members look like people you see at the grocery store, your church, around your neighborhood, in school, and at work. You'll find homemakers, schoolteachers, shopkeepers, college students, nurses, business owners, electricians, doctors, computer programmers, artists, salespeople, lawyers, clerks, and so on. You'll find retired people, young people, middle-aged people, the rich, poor, and middle class. You'll find people who've been going to Al-Anon for years and those coming for the first time. Despite individual backgrounds, everyone at Al-Anon comes because they have been affected by someone else's drinking. Everyone at the meeting has a common problem.

Most Al-Anon meetings are held in churches, but they are also found in hospitals, office buildings, schools, and government facilities. Al-Anon is available most days of the week and holidays, depending on your location. There are morning, lunch, evening, and weekend meetings. There are men's meetings, women's meetings, and mixed meetings. There are beginners' groups. Some Al-Anon meetings are at the same time as Alcoholics Anonymous meetings, but in separate rooms. Most meetings are nonsmoking. Some meetings offer child care. All meetings are anonymous and confidential.

When you walk into an Al-Anon meeting, look for a display of Al-Anon literature. Ask for the free packet of information for beginners. Some people prefer to listen without speaking during their first meeting; if you're invited to talk and you prefer not to, say "I'll pass." If you choose to speak, let people know it's your first meeting.

Before the meeting begins, someone will read the preamble to the Twelve Steps. This gives you an overview of Al-Anon. Next, the group recites the Twelve Steps, which provide ideas and guidance for personal growth and improved relationships. Then one of the Twelve Traditions is read. The Traditions guide the group so it can function smoothly. Since Al-Anon is not a structured organization and individual members are not expected to follow rules, the Traditions help ensure that individual decisions don't interfere with the welfare of the group.

Once the Steps and Traditions are read, members recite the Serenity Prayer and begin the meeting. Some meetings are called speaker meetings. At a speaker meeting, an Al-Anon member will share her story. Stories tell how it was in the person's past, what happened to initiate change, and how it is today. Other meetings are discussion meetings. At some discussion meetings, the group selects a discussion topic such as "controlling behavior" or "perfectionism." At others, the group discusses one of the Twelve Steps or an Al-Anon slogan. Examples of Al-Anon slogans include *First Things First; Easy Does It; Live and Let Live; Keep It Simple; How Important Is It?*

Members don't give counsel to one another during meetings. There shouldn't be any cross talk during discussions. In other words, only talk about yourself and don't comment on or advise other members. Members learn how to solve their common problems by listening to what has worked for others. This doesn't mean you'll necessarily agree with everything you hear. Al-Anon suggests you take what you like from a meeting and leave the rest behind.

Al-Anon is about you, not the alcoholic. By attending meetings you will find support for yourself and learn to detach from the alcoholic's problems. You'll begin to identify the ways you've changed as a result of your relationship with an addicted person. Since many of these changes are incompatible with a happy, contented life, Al-Anon helps you transform defects into assets and broken relationships into healthy ones.

There are no leaders in Al-Anon. A chairperson is a volunteer who opens and closes the meeting. Nobody acts as group facilitator or counselor. Al-Anon is nonprofessional, nonreligious, and has no political affiliations. Al-Anon discourages discussions of therapy techniques, psychology, religious affiliation, non-Al-Anon literature, intervention, and treatment programs during meetings. Discussions focus on the principles of Al-Anon. This preserves the purity of the program. There are no dues for membership, but during each meeting a basket is passed around to collect donations for group expenses. Most members put a dollar or two in the basket but contributions are strictly voluntary.

Before deciding if Al-Anon is right for you, attend at least six meetings. If you don't like a particular meeting, try another one. If you attend a meeting and members are giving each other advice, cross talking, or discussing the latest pop psychologist, find another meeting. Those conversations can happen before or after meetings, but not during. Look for meetings that uphold the Twelve Traditions and stay focused on Al-Anon literature. Then make a commitment to attend at least once a week. As they say in Al-Anon, "Keep coming back. It works if you work it."

Nar-Anon and Families Anonymous are based on the principles of Al-Anon. Most Twelve Step programs follow the same protocol as Al-Anon, so our description will prepare you for just about any Twelve Steps meeting you attend.

A Few Words about
Alcoholics Anonymous

Alcoholics Anonymous (AA) was not developed by physicians, psychologists, or researchers. It came about as a result of the successful experiences of alcoholics who stayed sober by helping others. Before Alcoholics Anonymous, the likelihood of an alcoholic staying sober was considered nothing short of a miracle. Today, Alcoholics Anonymous helps millions of alcoholics achieve long-term, contented sobriety. Using the principles of Alcoholics Anonymous, Narcotics Anonymous does the same for people addicted to other drugs.

Alcoholics Anonymous describes itself in the following way: "Alcoholics Anonymous is a fellowship of men and women who share their experience, strength, and hope with each other that they may solve their common problem and help others to recover from alcoholism. The only requirement for membership is a desire to stop drinking. There are no dues or fees for Alcoholics Anonymous membership; we are self-supporting through our own contributions. Alcoholics Anonymous is not allied with any sect, denomination, politics, organization, or institution; does not wish to engage in any controversy; neither endorses nor opposes any causes. Our primary purpose is to stay sober and help other alcoholics to achieve sobriety."

This preamble underscores some of the central facts about Alcoholics Anonymous: (1) members rely on sharing "experience, strength, and hope" to stay sober; (2) Alcoholics Anonymous members are dedicated to helping others; and (3) there are no religious, political, or financial aspects to the organization.

Some people erroneously believe Alcoholics Anonymous is a religious organization. This is not the case. Alcoholics Anonymous has a spiritual dimension, but it is not religious. Spirituality in Alcoholics Anonymous is defined as the ability to reach out for help and, as a result, achieve a changed personality. Alcoholics Anonymous members turn to other alcoholics and a Higher Power for help, but Alcoholics Anonymous does not define Higher Power for its members. Alcoholics Anonymous explains spirituality in the pamphlet *A Newcomer Asks* this way: "The majority of AA members believe that we have found the solution to our drinking problem not through individual willpower, but through a power greater than ourselves. However, everyone defines this power as he or she wishes. Many people call it God, others think it is the AA group, still others don't believe in it at all. There is room in AA for people of all shades of belief and nonbelief."

Alcoholics Anonymous is the most important part of any recovery program. The majority of alcohol and drug rehabilitation centers base their treatment programs on the Twelve Steps of Alcoholics Anonymous. Studies show that Alcoholics Anonymous attendance is the best predictor of long-term sobriety. For the newly recovering alcoholic, working a program of recovery in Alcoholics Anonymous requires following a few guidelines:

1. *Attend meetings.* A newly recovering alcoholic should attend a minimum of four Alcoholics Anonymous meetings every week.

Some Alcoholics Anonymous members recommend ninety meetings in ninety days.

2. *Choose an Alcoholics Anonymous home group.* A home group is a meeting where the alcoholic finds his Alcoholics Anonymous sponsor, volunteers for service work, and makes lifelong friends. He rarely misses this meeting.

3. *Get an Alcoholics Anonymous sponsor.* An Alcoholics Anonymous sponsor is a person who guides the alcoholic through the Twelve Steps. She helps the alcoholic over the rough spots of early recovery and, if the alcoholic relapses, encourages him to return to the meetings. A sponsor is not a therapist or personal financier. She doesn't solve problems for the alcoholic or lend her money. A sponsor is a recovering alcoholic who shares her experience, strength, and hope and, by doing so, points the way to a new life of contented sobriety.

4. *Follow the directions* by adhering to the principles of Alcoholics Anonymous and just about anybody can achieve sobriety. Alcoholics who don't follow the directions usually drink again. As it says in the Big Book of Alcoholics Anonymous, "Rarely have we seen a person fail who has thoroughly followed our path. Those who do not recover are people who cannot or will not completely give themselves to this simple program, usually men and women who are constitutionally incapable of being honest with themselves."

There are now millions of people around the world who have found help and recovery through Twelve Step programs. The Twelve Steps translate across geographical and cultural boundaries. As Bill Wilson, the co-founder of Alcoholics Anonymous, so aptly put it: "The unique ability of each Alcoholics Anonymous to identify himself with, and bring recovery to, the newcomer in no way depends upon his learning, his eloquence, or any special individual skills. The only thing that matters is that he is an alcoholic who has found a key to sobriety."

Preparing for the Possibility of Relapse

Many families begin worrying about relapse before the alcoholic or addict even gets into treatment. These fears are not unfounded, because staying sober can be very difficult for alcoholics in early recovery. However, families who have done an intervention are better prepared to handle relapse than most families. As a team, the family can use its influence and leverage to motivate the addict to get back into recovery if a relapse occurs.

Relapse begins before the recovering alcoholic ever takes the first drink or drug. Relapse is a way of thinking and acting that leads the alcoholic back to drinking. For this reason, a return to alcohol or other drugs is always preceded by relapse warning signs. Common warnings include the following:

+ lack of a recovery program
+ risky lifestyle choices such as going to bars
+ unresolved stress
+ relationship problems
+ peer pressure to drink
+ cravings for alcohol or other drugs
+ too much unstructured time

+ isolation
+ lingering resentments
+ compulsive behaviors such as overworking
+ overconfidence
+ feelings of hopelessness or defensiveness
+ dropping out of treatment or Alcoholics Anonymous

Terence Gorski answers the question "What are some things an alcoholic or addict might do that would cause a relapse?" in his book *Passages through Recovery:* "You don't have to do anything. Stop using alcohol and other drugs, but continue to live your life the way you always have. Your disease will do the rest. It will trigger a series of automatic and habitual reactions to life's problems that will create so much pain and discomfort that a return to chemical use will seem like a positive option." Avoiding the pain and discomfort that lead to relapse requires a program of recovery. Recovery requires a willingness to do things differently.

Not all recovering people experience relapse, but relapse experts estimate that approximately 50 percent are likely to relapse during the first three months after treatment. Relapse is a sign that something is missing from the recovery program, causing the alcoholic to become increasingly uncomfortable in sobriety. Many things can create gaps in recovery programs, including trying to recover without help; not following directions or following them only part of the time; attending Alcoholics Anonymous but never getting involved; hanging out with drinking or drugging buddies; not getting enough sleep; eating poorly; participating in the program intellectually but never emotionally; and isolating from people. Addicts who decide they don't need a program of recovery underestimate the power of addiction and are at high risk for relapse.

Many newly recovering alcoholics work solid recovery programs in Alcoholics Anonymous. They go to several meetings each week. They find sponsors who help them work the Twelve Steps. They do service work at meetings, such as greeting newcomers or making coffee. They develop friendships with other recovering people, and they read the literature published by Alcoholics Anonymous. Alcoholics who consistently do all of these things rarely relapse. If they do, they have so much support from the people in Alcoholics Anonymous that they get right back into recovery. The same holds true for addicts attending Narcotics Anonymous.

In some cases, a recovering alcoholic or addict may suffer from another problem that blocks recovery until it is properly treated. This may be an eating disorder, gambling addiction, or other psychological problem. These problems exist separately from the chemical dependency but must be addressed before successful recovery can be maintained. Jerry Boriskin, Ph.D., psychological services director for Advanced Recovery Center in Delray Beach, Florida, explains:

> Potent triggers that lead to repeated relapse often result from undiagnosed or untreated psychological issues. Over 80 percent of those with post traumatic stress syndrome, for instance, also suffer from addiction. Individuals who have experienced trauma or who suffer from conditions such as bipolar disorder need to focus on those issues in addition to Twelve Step work if a lasting recovery is to be achieved.

If your loved one is working a strong recovery program in Alcoholics Anonymous or Narcotics Anonymous but continues to repeatedly relapse, it would be wise to get further evaluation by a professional experienced in addictions and co-occurring disorders. Ask a treatment center for a referral.

Families need to prepare for relapse before it happens. We highly recommend meeting with the alcoholic and her counselor to write a relapse agreement. Set this meeting up toward the end of treatment. Ask the alcoholic what she wants the family to do if she relapses. By asking her rather than deciding for her, you preserve her dignity and give her the opportunity to participate in this important decision. If she relapses, she's more likely to respond positively to a relapse agreement she created. The counselor will guide the alcoholic so her plan is befitting a good relapse agreement. Once the counselor and alcoholic are satisfied, ask the alcoholic to write the agreement down on paper. Then you, the counselor, and the alcoholic sign it. Each member of the intervention team should get a copy. It will help everyone understand what to do if the alcoholic relapses. It also provides the alcoholic with a sense of accountability because she knows that the family is prepared to act if she returns to drinking or drugs. And you've accomplished this by working with the alcoholic, not against her.

Families who attend the family program and go to Al-Anon create an environment that supports recovery. It's more difficult for alcoholics and addicts to return to addiction when the whole family is participating in the recovery process. If the alcoholic does relapse, families attending Al-Anon are better prepared to cope with relapse in a more productive way than families that don't attend.

Having already done an intervention on your loved one, you are capable of quickly putting together an executive-style intervention if a relapse occurs. You can refer to your relapse agreement if you have one. You can also call the alcoholic's former counselor at the treatment center for advice. If the alcoholic isn't involved in Alcoholics Anonymous, the counselor will likely want him to return to treatment. If he has been working a solid recovery program and has a sponsor in Alcoholics Anonymous, he may just need to talk with his sponsor and go to more meetings. If you suspect another problem in addition to addiction, get a professional evaluation. Approach the alcoholic with love. Diffuse the shame of relapse by saying you understand that relapse is a symptom of addiction and a sign that he needs more support in his recovery program. Ask the alcoholic to follow the counselor's recommendations. If the alcoholic refuses, go back to your bottom lines. Explain that you won't support the disease of addiction and you must take care of yourselves.

Relapse doesn't mean the alcoholic or addict won't recover. Sometimes relapse is what helps an alcoholic finally accept that she's powerless over alcohol and other drugs. As they say in Alcoholics Anonymous, "I guess he had to do a little more research."

Using Family Intervention for Other Problems

Family intervention was developed to help motivate alcoholics and addicts to accept help, but intervention techniques work well to help people with other issues, too. Many of the symptoms of chemical dependency—denial, minimizing, and rationalizing—are common among people dealing with a range of problems. Families can use intervention to break through denial, whether it is associated with compulsive disorders and process addictions, such as gambling, or with alcoholism and drug addiction. It's also an effective tool when an older relative needs assisted living but is resistant to leaving the family home, or is no longer able to drive a car safely but refuses to surrender his driver's license.

If your loved one is suffering from a compulsive behavioral disorder such as sex addiction, compulsive gambling, eating disorders, computer addiction, or shopping addiction, consult with a professional specializing in that disorder to help you prepare for the intervention. Each of these disorders has specific characteristics and nuances that may require special handling. For example, chronic pain and opiate use can lead to dependence or addiction, requiring family intervention.

The following provides you with general information about some of the disorders that can be approached through intervention.

Compulsive Gambling

Compulsive gambling adversely affects family relationships, friendships, employment, finances, school performance, and physical and mental health. Signs of a gambling problem include the following:

+ spending longer and longer periods of time gambling
+ unexplained disappearances from home or work
+ waging higher stakes to win back losses
+ gambling until there is no more money left
+ lying about gambling debt
+ stealing or other criminal activity to finance gambling or pay debts
+ being mentally preoccupied with gambling, negligent of family responsibilities, declining in personal care such as sleep and nutrition, and threats of suicide related to gambling problems

When intervening on a gambling addict, use a professional interventionist experienced in this area. Patrick Witri, a limited licensed psychologist with a specialty in gambling addiction, explains: "Substantial information about a gambling addiction is harder to corroborate. It's more ethereal and more subject to manipulation than substance use disorders and other process addictions. Ultimately, intervention will almost always require professional assistance in order for the team to come to trust what they know, even if they can't prove it. With gambling, intervention team members struggle with their own minimization and denial throughout the process."

Gambling addiction hijacks the brain's reward system, as do other addictions. The craving to be "in action" is as intense as it is for meth or crack, and some would say even worse. Patrick Witri adds: "My experience with gamblers is that the incidence of co-occurring mental illness, usually depression, is higher than with other addictions. Additionally, gamblers can have very real reasons to fear the collapse of their financial schemes, including foreclosure by legitimate lenders and violence from street lenders." The many issues facing gamblers make the prospect of intervention difficult if not overwhelming for families, so don't attempt to intervene without professional help. Treatment resources are scarce and insurance rarely pays to treat this disorder. See the resources section for treatment providers.

Sex Addiction

Sex addiction can involve a wide variety of behaviors, and the addict may have one unwanted behavior or many. Sex addiction harms relationships, careers, finances, and mental and physical health. Signs of sex addiction include the following:

+ secrecy about sexual activities
+ leading a double life
+ involvement in sexual activities that violate deeply held spiritual or religious beliefs
+ sexual involvement with people not considered acceptable as partners
+ greater frequency and variety of sexual exploits needed to reach the same level of stimulation
+ compulsive masturbation
+ disregard for dangers of sexually transmitted disease, pregnancy, violence, or arrest

The addict often becomes preoccupied with pornography or Internet cybersex. Consequences include loss of relationship with primary partner or spouse and threats of self-destruction or suicide.

As discussed earlier in the book, an executive-style intervention is the preferred method for sex addiction. Choose a small group of people the sex addict respects, often of the same gender. Many of the behaviors are secretive and well hidden from others, so the team won't have all the facts. Leverage is important. The spouse should be willing to initiate a separation if treatment is refused. Working with a professional is recommended.

Eating Disorders

The stomach, ovaries, kidneys, teeth, salivary glands, blood pressure, hormones, and electrolytes all may be adversely affected by eating disorders. Extreme loss of body weight can lead to death, as can purging.

Anorexia

Anorexia involves an intense fear of gaining weight, causing continual dieting and self-starvation. It usually occurs in young women in their teens, but men and older women are also susceptible. While people who are anorexic habitually restrict food intake, they sometimes resort to binge eating and purging by vomiting or using laxatives. Signs of anorexia include the following:

+ severe weight loss
+ avoiding meals with the family
+ obsession with diets

+ feeding others but depriving self of food
+ cessation of menstrual cycle
+ mood swings
+ constant complaints about being overweight
+ wearing baggy clothes to hide weight loss from others
+ distorted body image

Some anorexics are compulsive exercisers, or use speed or cocaine for weight loss purposes.

Bulimia

Bulimia is a problem marked by binge eating and vomiting or overexercising. Laxatives, diuretics, and other medications are also used for weight loss. Symptoms include the following:

+ a chaotic lifestyle
+ emotional and physical suffering
+ disappearing to the bathroom after meals
+ evidence of vomiting or use of medications and laxatives
+ concealing symptoms
+ fasting
+ loss of dental enamel
+ rise in dental cavities
+ scarred or callused hands or knuckles
+ irregular menstrual cycles
+ constipation

Bulimics often have normal body weight or are slightly overweight.

Compulsive overeaters

People who are compulsive overeaters lose control over the amount of food they eat and often suffer from obesity. They experience uncontrollable eating binges, consuming large quantities of mostly junk food. They usually binge in private, do not attempt to control their weight, and are typically suffering from severe obesity. Overeating is often related to complicated emotional problems, fears, emotional pain, and stress.

When intervening on an eating disorder, use a professional interventionist who is experienced in this area. This is a complex issue requiring expert guidance. The first thing to remember is that eating disorders are never about food. Emotional issues drive the disorder. Eating disorders hijack the brain, perhaps to a greater degree than addiction to alcohol and other drugs. And treating this disorder is even more difficult. The goal of intervention is not to get the person to begin eating, stop purging, or to go on a diet, but to get treatment for complex emotional issues, to address medical needs, and to develop coping skills that replace the eating disorder behavior.

Self-starvation can lead to serious medical issues, which are not always apparent to family and friends. Mortality rate is higher than for other psychiatric illnesses. Gaining weight, if not done properly, can lead to a life-threatening health issue called *refeeding syndrome*. For these reasons, inpatient treatment is often the preferred recommendation. Anorexia and bulimia may lead to malnourished brains, resulting in difficulty processing information and impaired decision-making. The brain must receive nutrition on a regular basis before the person can begin to think logically and rationally and, at that point only, will the person begin to benefit from treatment.

Often, compulsive overeaters use food to hide from their emotions. They know their eating issues are abnormal. They are at risk for heart attack, diabetes, stroke, high blood pressure, high cholesterol, kidney disease, arthritis, and bone loss.

They suffer from shame, guilt, and low self-esteem. Telling them to go on a diet is not a productive way of approaching this problem and contributes to emotional distress. This should never be the goal of the intervention. Instead, find a program that specializes in compulsive overeating. See the resources section.

Dr. Barbara Cole, author and director of the Victorian of Newport Beach, a treatment center for eating disorders, advises not to use an invitational-style intervention (where a person is invited to the intervention), but to use a surprise approach. Defense mechanisms interfere with the success of the intervention if the person with the eating disorder has advance knowledge of the intervention.

Compulsive Shopping

Compulsive shopping and uncontrollable spending lead to unmanageable debt. Signs of compulsive shopping include the following:

+ feeling "high" when shopping
+ buying unneeded items
+ not remembering what was purchased
+ using shopping to overcome negative emotions
+ buying unaffordable items and rationalizing that "I deserve it"
+ using credit cards to stretch budgets
+ delaying the ramifications of overspending

In addition, compulsive shoppers ignore household budgets, experience shopping hangovers of guilt and remorse, usually shop alone, hide purchases from others, lie about the amount of money spent, spend money needed for bills or necessities, and accumulate large credit card debt.

The compulsive shopper is skilled at hiding the problem. Even a spouse may be unaware of it. Intervention usually takes place when a crisis finally reveals the problem to others. For instance, a husband discovers multiple credit cards with high balances or hoards of hidden purchases, often with tags that haven't been removed. Individual therapy, credit counseling (find free services), attending Debtors Anonymous meetings, and reading self-help books are recommended treatments. In severe cases, appoint a financial conservator to handle the compulsive shopper's finances until he shows progress in recovery.

Compulsive Indebtedness

Compulsive indebtedness is an addiction to irresponsible debting. Symptoms may include the following:

+ obsession with managing debt
+ unrealistic solutions to debt
+ chronic mishandling of finances
+ fantasies of far-fetched business opportunities to solve financial troubles
+ paying off one debt with another debt
+ ignoring the consequences of uncontrolled debt
+ feelings of euphoria when getting new credit cards or loans
+ frequently borrowing money from friends and family
+ having illusions of being rescued from debt
+ ruined family lives
+ feelings of suicide

Intervention and treatment recommendations are the same as for compulsive shopping.

Computer or Internet Addictive Disorder

Referred to as an impulse control disorder, Internet Addictive Disorder affects family relationships, friendships, employment, finances, and emotional health. Symptoms include the following:

+ getting a "high" when on the computer
+ being overly attached to the computer emotionally
+ inability to turn off the computer
+ neglecting sleep to stay up all night on the Internet
+ experiencing cravings for the Internet
+ hiding computer activities at work
+ lying to spouse about time spent on the computer

Additionally this disorder may lead to ignoring responsibilities at home, work, or school in favor of being on the computer, neglecting personal hygiene, and not eating or eating at the computer rather than with the family. Internet chat rooms or online virtual worlds replace real-life relationships. The addicted person is unable to control the amount of time spent at the computer once online, and physical problems surface such as carpal tunnel, migraines, or backaches.

Internet addictions can culminate in shopping addiction through online auction houses, gambling addiction through online gambling venues, and sex addiction through online chat rooms, cybersex, and cyberporn. Cyber-relational disorders describe those who become overinvolved in online relationships or virtual adultery. Compulsive online video gaming, or what is commonly called *gaming addiction*, is a growing problem. Intervention can be difficult, so working with a professional is advisable. Structured family intervention is a good method.

Include people who have firsthand information when possible. A list of warning signs and a self-quiz are available at www.netaddiction.com.

Treatment typically includes individual therapy with an expert in this area. The focus is on behavior modification: planning a daily schedule, journaling mood changes that occur when using the Internet, limiting time on the computer, and expanding an *in the flesh* social life. Internet addicts work with a therapist to overcome anger and shyness and to develop assertiveness and social skills. The therapist can determine whether there are co-occurring disorders such as alcoholism, anxiety, or depression. The addict attends a support group and commits to regular exercise.

Chronic Pain Patient Psychologically Dependent on Opiates

These pain patients realize they are psychologically dependent on their medications, but they do not exhibit addict behavior where psychological dependency is also a factor. However, they believe they must stay on opiates to control pain. Typically, these patients are only taking what the doctor prescribes.

According to Scott Dehorty, a social worker specializing in pain management and addiction at Johns Hopkins, "The problem stems from the fact that when opiates are used for pain, they are supposed to be used for *acute pain*, not *chronic pain*. Our bodies build a tolerance to the medications and, over time, need more and more since the sensation of pain occurs in the brain, not the body. If you hit your finger with a hammer, your finger sends a message to your brain saying something is wrong and needs attention." He explains that when a person is dependent upon opiates, the injured part of the body sends signals to the brain with greater frequency and intensity. Once the injury is healed, the brain continues to send pain signals, because it hasn't received the all-clear signal from the body. Additionally, the body becomes hypersensitive to all pain sensation. Time and again, when people are simply tapered off the opiates, the body is finally able to give the all-clear signal to the brain, and the brain finally stops sending pain signals. Patients find themselves pain free. Without drugs, the body works the way it should.

Scott Dehorty emphasizes other consequences of long-term opiate use: "The other trade-off is that you sacrifice cognitive and physical abilities in order to get relief. Patients sleep and stay in bed for prolonged periods of time, becoming physically de-conditioned, which increases potential for injury and sensitivity to pain."

When intervening on the psychologically *dependent* person, do not use the words *addict* or *addicted*. Speak in terms of psychological *dependence*. Talk about changes in physiology caused by prolonged opiate use and how it impedes recuperation. Explain that withdrawing from opiates can make pain more manageable or eliminate it altogether. Ask them to commit to drug-free methods of managing pain.

The intervention team should help reduce shame by emphasizing that the patient has been following the doctor's recommendations—which have not worked—and now it's time to try something else. Focus on how opiates have reduced the patient's ability to function. With help, they can become the person they once were. Use an inpatient facility that can make them as comfortable as possible while tapering off medications and that offers non-opiate alternatives to pain management.

Chronic Pain Addicted to Opiates

When a patient is *addicted* to opiates, both physiologically and psychologically dependent, he does not follow the doctor's orders. He uses more pills than prescribed, has multiple doctors writing prescriptions, buys drugs off the street or the Internet, mixes drugs with alcohol, and/or steal drugs from medicine cabinets of relatives and friends. He has personality changes, mood-swings, and becomes increasingly dishonest. Without treatment, the problem progresses and consequences mount.

Intervening on addicts with chronic pain is similar to a typical intervention. The difference is in how you respond to objections. The addict may say she can't go to treatment because she cannot give up the medications due to unbearable pain. The team needs to educate the addict about opiates and pain, as we discussed above. Present the facts: Opiates are not the best treatment for chronic pain and other methods work much better without side effects. It's important not to argue about the validity of the addict's pain. It's a losing battle even if the family has reason to be skeptical. Scott Dehorty suggests that you say: "I realize you have pain. You have been very strong in dealing with it and deserve credit for that. However, it has reached a point that it is taking over your life. The medications are robbing you of your abilities."

It is important to note that most patients with long-standing opiate use are not getting much relief from their pain. In fact, their pain is about the same with or without the drugs. They may have periodic relief or slight decreases in pain, but most will tell you that their pain continues to be unmanageable despite the drugs.

Select a facility that treats alcohol and drug addiction with a specialty in pain management. The addict with chronic pain, like all other addicts, will need an ongoing Twelve Step recovery program. If someone is suffering from multiple addictions or disorders, talk to a professional about the correct sequence in which to address the problems. For instance, alcoholism and other drug addictions almost always need to be treated first or simultaneously with other disorders. If the alcoholism is left untreated, it will block the treatment of other problems. A professional can also help determine if the family has misdiagnosed the primary problem. The family may decide a loved one's gambling addiction is the most serious problem and ignore or minimize his cocaine addiction. But if the gambling addiction is treated first and the cocaine problem is left untreated, the addiction to cocaine will block the treatment for compulsive gambling. Educate yourself about the specific disorder you plan to intervene on so you approach your loved with facts rather than myths and misinformation. Talk to counselors and read books.

Elder Care Issues

Intervention is also an excellent tool for addressing elder care issues. If an older relative is no longer capable of self-care, is unwilling to consider assisted living, and is a danger to his safety and well-being, intervention can help motivate the older person to make healthier and more realistic choices. Talk to a counselor specializing in geriatric issues as part of your preparation for intervention. The counselor will teach you to listen for and discuss the fears your loved one is experiencing about aging, loss of independence, and giving up his home.

If you are planning to intervene on an older person who is unable to drive safely, focus on the following: decreased vision;

dementia; limited range of motion in the head, neck, hips, and ankles; poor coordination; foot problems; alcohol use; medications that affect alertness; and prior accidents or citations. Giving up a driver's license can signify loss of freedom.

When intervening on age-related issues, involve the older adult in the decision-making process with the goal of maintaining the highest level of independence possible. Rely on a professional for a comprehensive assessment.

Intervention is an effective tool to help loved ones who are unable to help themselves. The techniques in this book are transferable and can be used to help people with addictions and problems other than chemical dependency. However, get information and professional advice about the problem you are facing before you do an intervention. Take note of special considerations before you take action. Work with a professional interventionist with experience in the problem area you are concerned about. If that proves difficult, hire a chemical dependency interventionist who will work with a therapist who specializes in treating the specific disorder.

An Instrument of Love

Intervention organizes love and honesty and uses them to break through the barrier of addiction. We bring a moment of clarity to one who cannot see; promise to one with no hope. Rarely are we presented with such an opportunity. Intervention is a chance to be an instrument of love in the world. It opens doors to miracles and grace.

People say it is grace, in the end, that saves the alcoholic. Recovering people must agree, for all over the world they claim the hymn "Amazing Grace" as their own:

Amazing grace! How sweet the sound
That saved a wretch like me!
I once was lost, but now am found;
Was blind, but now I see.

'Twas grace that taught my heart to fear,
And grace my fears relieved;
How precious did that grace appear
The hour I first believed.

Through many dangers, toils, and snares,
I have already come;

'Tis grace hath brought me safe thus far,
And grace will lead me home.

When we've been there ten thousand years,
Bright shining as the sun,
We've no less days to sing God's praise
Than when we'd first begun.

Section 6

Tools and Resources

Tools

The following section is designed to help you gather, organize, and easily retrieve information as you prepare for an intervention. In addition, you'll find a variety of self-quizzes and other information that will guide you when preparing for an intervention.

Building a Team

Use this worksheet to list all of the significant people in the alcoholic's life. Write down everyone who comes to mind. You'll draw from this list when you finalize your team. Not everyone you list will necessarily participate in the intervention.

Name _____ Phone _____

Name _____ Phone _____

Name _____ Phone _____

Name _____ Phone _____

Name _____ Phone _____

Name _____ Phone _____

Name _____ Phone _____

Name _____ Phone _____

Name _____ Phone _____

Name _____ Phone _____

Name _____ Phone _____

Name _____ Phone _____

Name _____ Phone _____

Name _____ Phone _____

Name _____ Phone _____

The Planner

Compiling and Organizing the Details

This tool is critical for the detail person and for keeping the entire group up-to-date.

The team members

Name _____ Phone _____
Email _____
Name _____ Phone _____
Email _____
Name _____ Phone _____
Email _____
Name _____ Phone _____
Email _____
Name _____ Phone _____
Email _____
Name _____ Phone _____
Email _____

Name _____　Phone _____

Email _____

Name _____　Phone _____

Email _____

Name _____　Phone _____

Email _____

Name _____　Phone _____

Email _____

The detail person _____

The chairperson _____

Who has influence? _____

_____

Who has leverage? _____

_____

Dates, times, and location(s)

Rehearsal location _____

Date: _____　Time: _____

Intervention location _____

Date: _____　Time: _____

The financial details

Insurance card number _____

Insurance group number _____

Customer service number _____

Medicare, Medicaid _____

Other financial resources

_____

_____

_____

Treatment center choices

Treatment center #1

Name _____

Web site _____

Address _____

_____

_____

Admissions contact _____

Phone _____

Email _____

Financial contact _____

Phone _____

Email _____

Financial requirements _____

_____

_____

Copay _____ Deductible _____

Admission date and time _____

What to pack _____

_____

_____

_____

Family program schedule _____

_____

Family program contact _____

Phone _____

Email _____

Treatment center #2

Name _____

Web site _____

Address _____

_____

_____

Admissions contact _____

Phone _____

Email _____

Financial contact _____

Phone _____

Email _____

Financial requirements _____

_____

_____

Copay _____ Deductible _____

Admission date and time _____

What to pack _____

_____

_____

_____

Family program schedule _____

_____

Family program contact _____

Phone _____

Email _____

Professional interventionist

Name _____

Web site _____

Address _____

_____

_____

Phone _____

Email _____

Fee _____

Appointment place, date, and time _____

_____

Notes: _____

_____

_____

_____

Schedule the family program

Dates _____

Times _____

Lodging _____

Notes: _____

_____

_____

_____

Al-Anon, Nar-Anon, and Families Anonymous meetings

Location _____

Day and time _____

Location _____

Day and time _____

Location _____

Day and time _____

Compile facts essential to the alcoholic's or addict's treatment

Each person in the family knows different things about the alcoholic's history. Working as a group, you can create a more complete picture of the addiction. The treatment center staff will ask for this information prior to setting up the admission.

Alcoholic's address _____

_____

_____

Phone _____ Date of birth _____

Email _____

Marital status _____

Children _____

Employment _____

Legal problems _____

Dates _____

Previous counseling _____

Dates _____

Previous treatment or detox _____

Dates _____

Alcoholics Anonymous attendance _____

Dates _____

Periods of abstinence _____

Dates _____

Medical problems _____

Dates _____

Physician _____ Phone _____

Medications _____

Previously diagnosed psychiatric problems _____

_____

Dates _____

Psychiatrist _____ Phone _____

Suicide attempts or threats _____

Dates _____

History of violence toward others _____

Circumstances _____

Dates _____

Chemical use history

Alcohol:

Types _____

Age of first use _____ Last use _____

How often _____ How much _____

Notes: _____

Street drugs:

Types _____

_____

_____

_____

Age of first use _____   Last use _____

How often _____   How much _____

Notes: _____

Mood-altering prescription drugs:

Types _____

_____

_____

_____

Age of first use _____   Last use _____

How often _____   How much _____

Notes: _____

Inhalants:

Types _____

_____

_____

_____

Age of first use _____   Last use _____

How often _____   How much _____

Notes: _____

Consequences related to alcohol or other drug use:

+ Job _____
+ Relationships/friendships _____
+ Divorce/separation _____
+ Family _____
+ Finances _____
+ Legal _____
+ Physical health _____
+ Accidents _____
+ Injuries _____
+ Isolation—emotional _____
+ Isolation—social _____
+ Violence _____
+ Dishonesty _____
+ Concealing use _____
+ Blackouts _____
+ Drunk driving _____
+ Mood swings _____
+ Depression _____
+ Trauma _____
+ Paranoia _____
+ Behavior violates moral values _____

Other significant information:

_____

_____

_____

_____

The Checklist

Preparation Is the Key to a Successful Intervention

This checklist is designed to be used as an accompaniment to the book. Don't plan an intervention using the checklist alone.

[   ] Bring together three to ten people who are important to the alcoholic and are willing to learn how to help.

[   ] Read this book in its entirety for a thorough education on how to motivate an addicted loved one to accept help.

[   ] Set up a planning meeting to discuss moving forward with the intervention.

[   ] Decide if you need to work with a professional interventionist.

[   ] Identify financial resources for covering treatment costs.

[   ] Evaluate treatment centers.

[   ] Choose a detail person.

[   ] Choose a team chairperson.

[   ] Compile a master email list of team members. Email the list to all participants.

[   ] Use the planner to record and organize information.

[   ] Discuss the importance of not alerting the alcoholic to your plans for doing a structured family intervention.

[   ] Determine if an executive-style or invitational-style intervention is the method required for your circumstances.

[   ] List ways you've tried to help the alcoholic that may have actually enabled the addiction.

[   ] Put in writing all the negative consequences caused by the addiction problem.

[   ] Write a one- to two-page letter to the alcoholic following the seven-point format.

[   ] Read your letters to each other, editing out anger, blame, and judgment.

[   ] Determine bottom lines, and write them down on a separate page.

[   ] Test each other's willingness to follow through with the bottom lines.

[   ] Set a date, time, and place for the rehearsal and the intervention.

[   ] Choose a treatment center, answer its pre-intake questions, and make an appointment for admission.

[   ] Make airline reservations if the treatment center is out of state.

[   ] Create a plan likely to guarantee the alcoholic's presence at the intervention.

[   ] Identify objections the alcoholic may use to avoid or postpone treatment; then formulate answers.

[   ] Pack a suitcase for the addict using the guidelines provided by the treatment staff.

[   ] Determine who should accompany the alcoholic from the intervention to the treatment center.

[   ] Compile all information requested in the planner.

[   ] Rehearse the intervention

    [   ] Decide where each person will sit, including the alcoholic.

    [   ] Discuss the order in which you'll read your letters.

    [   ] Find a discreet place to park your cars.

    [   ] Script the chairperson's introduction and closing statements.

[   ] Review objections and answers.

[   ] Call and confirm the admissions appointment at the treatment center.

[   ] Rehearse the intervention exactly as you'll do the real thing.

[   ] Review and sign the "Family and Friends Commitment Statement" (see page 287).

[   ] Plan to arrive at the intervention location thirty minutes before the alcoholic is expected to be there.

[   ] If the intervention is taking place at the alcoholic's home, arrive as a complete group.

[   ] Hold the intervention.

[   ] After the intervention, call the admissions staff and let them know whether the alcoholic has agreed to treatment.

[   ] Collect all letters and send them to the alcoholic's treatment counselor.

[   ] Collect all bottom lines and place in a separate envelope. Deliver to the counselor using guidelines in the book.

[   ] Sign up for the family program.

[   ] Locate an Al-Anon, Nar-Anon, or Family Anonymous meeting near your home or office.

[   ] Review the resources section for Web sites, treatment facilities, books, and other helpful information.

[   ] After the intervention, team members meet to process how the intervention went and reconfirm commitment to bottom lines.

Enabling Behaviors

Out of love and fear, we do many things to protect our alcoholics. Most of the things we do, however, actually help the addiction instead. As a result, the addiction flourishes, and our loved ones get sicker. This is called enabling. The following list provides examples of behavior that enables the addiction. Check all the behaviors you recognize in yourself:

[ ] Give or lend money
[ ] Provide a place to live
[ ] Rescue or fix problems
[ ] Supply a car or transportation
[ ] Buy or provide alcohol or other drugs
[ ] Bail out of jail
[ ] Hire attorneys
[ ] Lie to cover up problems
[ ] Deny the addiction to others
[ ] Defend behaviors to others
[ ] Ignore or laugh at the problem
[ ] Argue, plead, beg, threaten, placate, or bargain
[ ] Insist nothing can be done
[ ] Keep secrets for the alcoholic
[ ] Put yourself in jeopardy

[ ] Leave minor children alone with the alcoholic
[ ] Allow drunk driving (drunk drivers should be reported to
the police)
[ ] Take over responsibilities
[ ] Protect from negative consequences
[ ] Blame other people or circumstances
[ ] Avoid social functions
[ ] Provide employment
[ ] Finance school-related expenses
[ ] Pay bills

List other ways you've unwittingly enabled the addiction:

_____

_____

_____

_____

_____

_____

_____

_____

_____

Evaluating Treatment Centers

Questions to Ask

In the planner you listed possible treatment center choices. Before deciding which you will use, learn about its program. Ask a qualified staff member the following questions:

+ Is the treatment program based—or does it include work—on the Twelve Steps of Alcoholics Anonymous? *The Twelve Steps are the most effective way to achieve long-term, contented sobriety.*
+ Is the addiction to alcohol or other drugs treated as a primary disease? *Watch out for treatment centers approaching addiction as a secondary issue. In other words, they see addiction as a symptom of another problem and believe that fixing that problem makes the addiction go away. The opposite is true. We must treat the addiction first, before we can solve other problems.*
+ Is complete abstinence of all mood-altering substances, including alcohol, the treatment goal?
+ Is inpatient, residential care available? *After an intervention, we prefer the support and concentration of residential care, at least initially. However, you may find that your insurance or other funding sources will only pay for outpatient care.*
+ Does the counseling staff consult with the family throughout the treatment process? *Counselors and family members share*

important information about the alcoholic's history, progress in treatment, and aftercare plans. If the alcoholic refuses to sign a release of information, confidentiality laws prevent counselors from speaking to family members. Families, however, are free to provide information to the counseling staff.

+ Does the center provide Alcoholics Anonymous meetings during the treatment stay? *Ongoing Alcoholics Anonymous attendance is key to long-term sobriety. When patients are introduced to Alcoholics Anonymous in treatment, they are more likely to continue to attend once discharged.*

+ Is a family program available? Is there an additional charge for this service? *Attending a family program is an essential part of the family's recovery and supports the addicted person's recovery.*

+ Can the program provide services for special needs? If the alcoholic has problems, such as illiteracy, hearing loss, limited mobility, or a co-occurring disorder, can the facility offer appropriate services so these problems do not block treatment? If the patient is an older adult, is the program designed to meet his special needs?

+ If the alcoholic wants to leave treatment early, does the staff use conflict resolution to challenge the patient to stay?

+ Is an aftercare group available? *Aftercare groups usually meet one night a week and provide support during the transition between treatment and Alcoholics Anonymous or Narcotics Anonymous.*

+ What percentage of the counseling staff is recovering in a Twelve Step program? *Counselors working their own Twelve Step programs—Al-Anon, Alcoholics Anonymous, Narcotics Anonymous, or any of the other programs—are often most effective in helping alcoholics and addicts.*

+ What percentage of the counseling staff is certified in addiction counseling? *Treating addiction requires very specific knowledge and skills. Look for a high percentage of certified addiction counselors.*

+ Is there a medical doctor on staff and a detox unit? *If not, ask whom they recommend for medical detox.*

+ Is there a psychiatrist or psychologist on staff? *This is important when alcoholics have co-occurring disorders.*

Notes:

_____

_____

_____

_____

_____

_____

_____

_____

_____

Objections and Answers

Working as a group, the intervention team needs to prepare for all possible objections the alcoholic might use to avoid accepting help. When writing your responses, keep them short and to the point. Below are some examples. Objections typically fall into the following categories:

Work

Objection: "I have to go to work. I'll lose my job if I don't."

Response: "We've contacted your Employee Assistance Program, and they've informed us that the company has a policy to support your decision to get help. They gave us a number for you to call when you get into treatment, and they will handle everything confidentially."

Objection: "I can't take time off right now, but give me a week to arrange it."

Response: "You don't need to worry. Everything is already arranged. Your job will be waiting for you once you've completed treatment."

Objection: "My boss can't do without me now. We're in the middle of an important project."
Response: "Your boss has written you a letter supporting treatment. She has asked us to read it to you."

Objection: "Work may say they're supportive, but they'll fire me anyway."
Response: "It is against the law for your employer to fire you for getting help for a medical problem."

Objection: "You don't know my boss. He'll find another reason to replace me."
Response: "It sounds like—if your boss has her way—you'll lose this job sooner or later anyway. Saving your life is more important then trying to save this job."

Money

Objection: "I don't have any insurance. I can't afford to go into treatment."
Response: "We have taken care of everything. We've found an excellent low-cost (no-cost) treatment center." Or, "Your life is very important to us. We are taking care of all treatment costs."

Objection: "I'll lose my apartment if I can't pay the rent."
Response: "Your life is more important than your apartment. You can always find another place to live." Or, "We talked to your landlord and she's worked things out with a payment arrangement." Or, "As a family, we've pooled our resources and have enough money to cover your rent and utilities while you're in treatment."

Children

Objection: "I can't go to treatment because I have to take care of my kids."

Response: "Your sister is going to take care of your children while you are in treatment."

Objection: "I couldn't leave my children like that. They need me."

Response: "Your children need a sober mother (father). Your alcohol problem is creating problems for them. Getting treatment is the best thing you can do for your children."

Social Obligation

When an upcoming once-in-a-lifetime event is the objection, such as a wedding, graduation, or baptism, determine if intervening after the event is a better choice. However, if the alcoholic or addict is very sick, in big trouble, or at high risk for imminent danger, it could be too risky to wait. If you are facing this difficult situation, consult with a professional interventionist.

Objection: "I can't go now. I'll miss Jenny and Dave's wedding."

Response: "You need help now. Jenny and Dave are very worried about you. They want you to know that the best wedding gift you can give them is going in for help today."

Practical

Objection: "Who is going to take care of my dog? I can't leave Rusty that long."

Response: "Mom has agreed to take Rusty. You have nothing to worry about. You know how Rusty loves her."

Objection: "I have responsibilities. My house, my bills, my garden. I can't ignore everything for a month."

Response: "Uncle Dave is going to come by weekly to mow your lawn. Aunt Rose is going to take care of the garden. She has the green thumb in the family. Your brother has agreed to sort your bills and either pay them for you or forward them to you in treatment, whichever you'd prefer. He's also going to keep an eye on the house."

Denial

Objection: "I can handle this on my own. I don't need help."

Response: "You've tried to control your drinking before. We now know that this is a disease and willpower doesn't work. We've learned that you need a specific kind of help in order to recover."

Objection: "Joe's been out drinking with me many times. Why is everybody singling me out?"

Response: "Today we're talking about your relationship with alcohol and what is happening to you."

Objection: "I don't drink every night. I mostly drink on weekends."

Response: "It is not just about how much you drink or when you drink, but what happens to you when you drink."

Objection: "I'm not hurting anyone. It's none of your business."

Response: "You may not know it, but we are all very affected by your drinking. The whole family is suffering. Addiction is a family disease."

List objections you expect to hear from your addicted loved one and how you will respond:

_____

_____

_____

_____

_____

_____

_____

_____

_____

Bottom Lines

If you think you don't have a bottom line, go back and review ways you've enabled the addiction. Each of our enabling behaviors can be turned into a bottom line. The following examples will help you brainstorm. We always present our bottom lines as written statements, using love and preserving dignity. See examples in the chapter on bottom lines, page 140.

+ "I will no longer give or lend you money."
+ "I will not pay your mortgage any longer."
+ "If you do not accept help for your drug problem, you can no longer live in my home."
+ "I'm taking the car keys away until you get help for your alcohol problem."
+ "I'm not a liar, so I will no longer lie to people about your addiction problem."
+ "I've pretended not to notice your problem in the past. From now on, if you come over high, you cannot come into the house."
+ "The next time you drive intoxicated, I will have to call the police."
+ "I will no longer listen to your problems until you get help for your primary problem—alcohol and other drugs."

+ "I can no longer ride with you or socialize with you when you are drunk."
+ "Until you get into recovery, I cannot let my children spend time with you."
+ "I will no longer pick up your slack at work. When you don't get your work done, you'll have to explain it to the boss."
+ "I'm not going to tell your boss you have the flu when you have a hangover."
+ "I will not invite you to family get-togethers until you get help for your drug problem."
+ "You can no longer work for the company unless you complete treatment and stay sober."
+ "Your mom and I will quit paying your school expenses until you get help."
+ "I am going to file for a legal separation if you choose alcohol over recovery."
+ "The next time you're in jail, I cannot bail you out or hire an attorney for you."

The bottom line is not a punishment. It's a decision we make *not* to support the addiction and to take care of ourselves. For the alcoholic, the bottom line is a natural consequence of deciding to stay in the disease of addiction. Below, write three of your own bottom lines:

_____

_____

_____

_____

_____

_____

Family and Friends Commitment Statement

Our purpose is to initiate the recovery process. As members of this team, we are asking our addicted loved one to make long-lasting changes. We also agree to make changes in ourselves. Each of us on the team agrees to the following:

1. I will not underestimate the power of the addiction. I agree to educate myself about the disease of addiction and what is required to stay sober.
2. I will no longer enable the addiction. I will identify ways I have enabled in the past and promise to only support recovery in the future.
3. I will support the intervention process. If my loved one refuses treatment, I will adhere to my bottom lines.
4. Once my loved one is in treatment, I will not accept objections to the treatment. I will support the treatment staff's recommendations.
5. I will not allow the addicted person to manipulate me. If I'm being manipulated, I will end the conversation and contact a team member or the counselor for support.
6. I will attend at least one Al-Anon meeting a week.
7. If my loved one relapses, I will reconvene with the rest of the

team to determine our next step. We will follow the relapse
agreement when making decisions.

8. I and the following team members will commit to attending the
family program:

Signatures of all team members:

_____

_____

_____

_____

_____

Date: _____

Self-Quizzes

Assessing a loved one's problem is sometimes tricky for families. The following pages offer five self-quizzes designed to help you think about the possible addiction of a loved one and how it has affected you. These quizzes are not scientific diagnostic tools; they don't prove someone does or doesn't have a problem. Nonetheless, they do provoke thought and may help you determine whether further evaluation may be necessary. You must rely on your discretion and common sense when evaluating the results.

These quizzes are not to be used as "evidence" to present to the chemically dependent person. *Do not bring any of these quizzes to the alcoholic or addict as proof or confirmation of addiction.* This would be an inappropriate way to discuss the problem and may cause angry and resentful reactions from the addict.

Quiz: Is a Family Member Chemically Dependent?

To determine whether or not an alcohol or drug problem is affecting your family, ask yourself the following questions:

[   ]   Does someone in your family undergo personality changes when he or she uses alcohol or other drugs?

[   ]   Are you sometimes anxious before holidays or special occasions because you are worried that he or she may disrupt it by getting high or drunk?

[   ]   Have you ever found it necessary to lie to employers, relatives, or friends to hide his or her alcohol or drug use?

[   ]   Have you ever hidden car keys, thrown out the alcohol or drugs, or used other methods to attempt to control his or her use?

[   ]   Have you ever felt embarrassed or felt the need to apologize for his or her actions?

[   ]   Have you ever asked him or her to stop or cut down on his or her use of alcohol or other drugs?

[   ]   Has he or she ever promised to stop using alcohol or other drugs without success?

[   ]   Has he or she ever failed to remember what occurred during a period of alcohol and/or drug use?

[   ]   Does he or she avoid social situations where alcohol and/or drugs will not be available?

[   ] Does he or she have periods of remorse after periods of use and does he or she apologize for his or her behavior?

[   ] Does he or she justify his or her use by blaming a stressful lifestyle or difficult emotional situations?

[   ] Do other family members fear or avoid this person after he or she has been using alcohol or other drugs?

[   ] Has another person expressed concern about his or her drinking or drug use?

[   ] Has he or she ever made promises that he or she did not keep because of drinking or drug use?

[   ] Has his or her reaction to a given amount of alcohol or other drugs changed?

[   ] Does he or she deny a drinking problem because he or she drinks only wine or beer?

[   ] Do you find yourself avoiding social situations that include alcohol or other drugs?

If you answered "yes" to any of the above questions, there is a possibility that someone in your family is developing a problem with alcohol or other drugs. If you answered "yes" to two or more, chemical use is probably causing serious problems in your family.

Reprinted with permission of Substance Abuse Community Council of Grosse Pointe from the pamphlet How Do I Know? Where Do I Go?

Quiz: Signs of Alcoholism and Drug Abuse in Older People

The signs of alcoholism and drug addiction can be different in adults fifty-five years old and over. For example, they often drink at home so no one notices the severity of the problem. Many older adults are retired, so they don't have work-related problems due to their chemical dependency. They drive less, so there's less opportunity for them to get arrested for driving under the influence.

The following signs of an alcohol or other drug problem are typical in the older adult:

[   ] Prefers attending a lot of events where drinking is accepted, such as luncheons, "happy hours," and parties
[   ] Drinks in solitary, hidden away
[   ] Makes a ritual of having drinks before, with, or after dinner, and becomes annoyed when this ritual is disturbed
[   ] Loses interest in activities and hobbies that used to bring pleasure
[   ] Drinks in spite of warning labels on prescription drugs
[   ] Always has bottles of tranquilizers on hand and takes them at the slightest sign of disturbance
[   ] Is often intoxicated or slightly tipsy, and sometimes has slurred speech

[   ] Disposes of large volumes of empty beer and liquor bottles and seems secretive about it

[   ] Often has the smell of liquor on his or her breath or mouthwash to disguise it

[   ] Is neglecting personal appearance and gaining or losing weight

[   ] Complains of constant sleeplessness, loss of appetite, or chronic health complaints that seem to have no physical cause

[   ] Has unexplained burns or bruises and tries to hide them

[   ] Seems more depressed or hostile than usual

[   ] Can't handle routine chores and paperwork without making mistakes

[   ] Has irrational or undefined fears or delusions, or seems under unusual stress

[   ] Seems to be losing his or her memory

Many of the symptoms listed above are attributed to other diseases or are considered part of the aging process. However, many older people find that once they achieve sobriety, these symptoms disappear.

Reprinted from the pamphlet How to Talk to an Older Person Who Has a Problem with Alcohol or Medications, *published by Hazelden. Reprinted by permission of Hazelden. To obtain copies of the pamphlet, call 800-I-DO-CARE.*

Quiz: Is Our Teen Chemically Dependent?

Many symptoms of teen alcohol and drug abuse are not clear-cut. The signs can be confused with normal adolescent behavior or with health problems. However, it is critical to be alert and to know that a combination of the following characteristics may be cause for concern. Ask yourself these questions:

[　] Has your child's personality changed noticeably? Does he or she have sudden mood swings and unpredictable behavior?

[　] Does your child seem to be losing old friends and spending time with a new group about whom you know little or who are known as a party bunch?

[　] Is your child unable to account for large sums of his or her money, or have you had objects or money mysteriously disappearing from your home?

[　] Does your child defend his or her right to drink?

[　] Is your child reluctant to talk about alcohol or other drugs?

[　] Does your child drive irresponsibly?

[　] Does your child lie about drug and alcohol use as well as other activities?

[　] Have you ever found drug paraphernalia (rolling papers, baggies, small spoons, roach clips, capsules), bottles, or beer cans in his or her room? If so, did your child explain it away when confronted?

[   ] Has your child lost interest in his or her physical appearance?

[   ] Has your child admitted to trying alcohol or other drugs "just once" while denying any regular use?

[   ] Are you hearing rumors about your child's partying, goofing off, or drinking?

[   ] Has your child been cutting classes?

[   ] Do you as parents conceal from each other information about your child's behavior?

[   ] Is your child suddenly less responsive? Is he or she losing interest in schoolwork, athletics, extracurricular activities, family, job, and/or other previous interests? Are grades dropping (not necessarily from As to Ds but from Bs to Cs)?

[   ] Do you detect any of these physical symptoms: excessive fatigue, disturbed sleep patterns, chronic cough, chest pains, "allergy" symptoms, vomiting, loss of appetite, unusual craving for sweets, red eyes, dilation of pupils?

[   ] Have your child's relationships with other family members deteriorated?

[   ] Are there signs of apparent emotional or psychological problems such as depression, loneliness, paranoia, or withdrawal?

If you answered "yes" to any two of the above questions, there is a possibility that your teen is developing a problem with alcohol or other drugs. If you answered "yes" to three or more questions, chemical use is probably causing significant problems.

Quiz: Signs of Inhalant Use in Our Teen

Evaluate the following signs and symptoms of inhalant use based on the number of different signs observed, their frequency, and overall behavior.

[   ] Does the child have a red, runny nose or eyes?

[   ] Have you noticed excessive or inappropriate laughter?

[   ] Are the eyes glassy? Are the pupils dilated or constricted?

[   ] Is the child sweating for no obvious reason?

[   ] Have you noticed paranoia, irritability, excitability, or anxiety?

[   ] Are there times when the child speaks in a nonsensical way?

[   ] Has the child withdrawn from old friends?

[   ] Is the child hanging around a new crowd? Do you have concerns about the child's new friends? Does the child keep them away from the family?

[   ] Is the child exhibiting apathy to things he or she used to care about?

[   ] Have you found plastic bags, rags, or cotton with a chemical odor?

[   ] Have you seen correction fluid, paint, or stains on the child's face, fingers, or clothing?

[   ] Have you found household solvents, cleaners, or adhesives hidden in the child's room?

[   ] Are there spots or sores around the mouth?

[   ] Have you ever detected a chemical odor to the child's breath?

[   ] Has the child appeared dazed or dizzy?

[   ] Has the child's appetite decreased? Does he or she complain of nausea?

If you come upon your child or teen in the act of sniffing inhalants, remain calm. Excitement or outrage may cause someone under the influence of inhalants to become violent, start hallucinating, or suffer heart problems, which can lead to death. Ventilate the room and call 911. If the child stops breathing, administer CPR.

Sudden Sniffing Death Syndrome can happen to first-time users as well as chronic users. Go to the National Inhalant Prevention Coalition's Web site at www.inhalants.org for more information on inhalant abuse.

Adapted from the National Inhalant Prevention Coalition's Web site.

Quiz: Are You Troubled by Someone's Drinking?

This following questionnaire was designed by Al-Anon to help you decide whether Al-Anon is right for you. As you take this quiz, keep in mind that you may have been affected by a parent's drinking when you were a child. Although Al-Anon does not provide guidelines on how to evaluate your answers to this quiz, we suggest you attend Al-Anon if you answer yes to two or more questions.

[ ] Do you worry about how much someone drinks?

[ ] Do you have money problems because of someone else's drinking?

[ ] Do you tell lies to cover up for someone else's drinking?

[ ] Do you feel if the drinker loved you, he or she would stop drinking to please you?

[ ] Do you blame the drinker's behavior on his or her companions?

[ ] Are plans frequently upset or canceled or meals delayed because of the drinker?

[ ] Do you make threats, such as, "If you don't stop drinking, I'll leave you"?

[ ] Do you secretly try to smell the drinker's breath?

[ ] Are you afraid to upset someone for fear it will set off a drinking bout?

[   ] Have you been hurt or embarrassed by a drinker's behavior?

[   ] Are holidays and gatherings spoiled because of drinking?

[   ] Have you considered calling the police for help, for fear of abuse?

[   ] Do you search for hidden alcohol?

[   ] Do you often ride in a car with a driver who has been drinking?

[   ] Have you refused social invitations out of fear or anxiety?

[   ] Do you sometimes feel like a failure when you think of the lengths you have gone to to protect the drinker?

[   ] Do you think that if the drinker stopped drinking, your other problems would be solved?

[   ] Do you ever threaten to hurt yourself to scare the drinker?

[   ] Do you feel angry, confused, or depressed most of the time?

[   ] Do you feel there is no one who understands your problems?

From "Are You Troubled by Someone's Drinking?" copyright 1980, by Al-Anon Family Group Headquarters, Inc. Reprinted by permission of Al-Anon Family Group Headquarters, Inc.

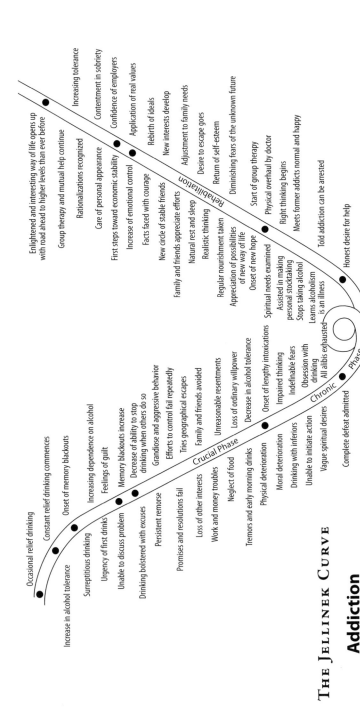

The Jellinek Curve

Addiction and Recovery

Occasional relief drinking

Constant relief drinking commences

Increase in alcohol tolerance

Onset of memory blackouts

Surreptitious drinking

Increasing dependence on alcohol

Urgency of first drinks

Feelings of guilt

Unable to discuss problem

Memory blackouts increase

Decrease of ability to stop drinking when others do so

Drinking bolstered with excuses

Grandiose and aggressive behavior

Persistent remorse

Efforts to control fail repeatedly

Tries geographical escapes

Promises and resolutions fail

Family and friends avoided

Loss of other interests

Unreasonable resentments

Work and money troubles

Loss of ordinary willpower

Neglect of food

Decrease in alcohol tolerance

Tremors and early morning drinks

Onset of lengthy intoxications

Physical deterioration

Impaired thinking

Moral deterioration

Indefinable fears

Drinking with inferiors

Obsession with drinking

Unable to initiate action

Vague spiritual desires

Learns alcoholism is an Illness

All alibis exhausted

Complete defeat admitted

Obsessive drinking continues in vicious circles

Crucial Phase

Chronic Phase

Honest desire for help

Told addiction can be arrested

Stops taking alcohol

Assisted in making personal stocktaking

Spiritual needs examined

Meets former addicts normal and happy

Appreciation of possibilities of new way of life

Onset of new hope

Regular nourishment taken

Right thinking begins

Realistic thinking

Physical overhaul by doctor

Natural rest and sleep

Start of group therapy

Family and friends appreciate efforts

Diminishing fears of the unknown future

New circle of stable friends

Return of self-esteem

Facts faced with courage

Desire to escape goes

Increase of emotional control

Adjustment to family needs

First steps toward economic stability

New interests develop

Care of personal appearance

Rebirth of ideals

Rationalizations recognized

Application of real values

Group therapy and mutual help continue

Confidence of employers

Contentment in sobriety

Enlightened and interesting way of life opens up with road ahead to higher levels than ever before

Increasing tolerance

Rehabilitation

Resources

Addicts and their families may access a wide variety of resources. Following is a partial list of Web sites, treatment programs, books, Twelve Step organizations, and help lines. We hope these resources will help point you in the right direction.

Web Sites

For direct links to these Web sites and more, go to www.lovefirst.net.

> *Alcoholism at About.com:* http://alcoholism.about.com. Offers information on just about any topic related to addiction.
> *Augsburg College, The StepUp Program:* www.augsburg.edu/stepup. Addresses the needs of college students in recovery. This Minneapolis program includes chemical-free housing, weekly individual meetings with staff, a contract calling for standards of behavior, and a weekly community meeting. In the 2006–2007 school year, 90 percent of the 58 participating students remained abstinent.
> *Celebrate Recovery:* www.saddlebackresources.com. A Christian-based program based on the Twelve Steps and the Bible.
> *Free Vibe:* www.freevibe.com. An interactive site that shows kids

how alcohol and other drugs affect their brains. Advice on helping a friend who is taking drugs, coping with stress, and saying no to drugs. Examples of positive role models.

Hazelden Bookstore: www.hazelden.org. Books and gifts to inspire and inform lifelong recovery for both the addicted person and their families.

The Intervention Workshop: www.interventionworkshop.com. An online video workshop with Jeff and Debra Jay. Using the latest video technology, the workshop is comprised of thirty-eight video segments for a total of 4.5 hours. Provides a complete online training program.

Jewish Alcoholics, Chemically Dependent Persons, and Significant Others: www.jacsweb.org. Encourages and assists Jewish alcoholics, chemically dependent persons, and their families to explore recovery in a nurturing Jewish environment by conducting retreats and other events.

Love First: www.lovefirst.net. An information Web site for families interested in intervention. Includes a bookstore of recommended reading as well as links to articles, treatment programs, Twelve Step groups, FAQs, and quizzes.

National Association for Children of Alcoholics: www.nacoa.org. Advocates for the people who are hurt the most by alcohol or other drugs—the children of addicted parents. Check out the "Just for Kids" section.

National Inhalant Prevention Coalition: www.inhalants.org. Referral and information clearinghouse. Excellent source of information for parents and educators.

National Institute on Alcohol Abuse and Alcoholism: www.niaaa.nih.gov. Offers publications, research information, and resources.

National Institute on Drug Abuse: www.nida.gov. Supports and conducts research on drug abuse and addiction. Free publications available, including materials for parents and teachers.

National Organization on Fetal Alcohol Syndrome: www.nofas.org. Building awareness about the consequences of prenatal alcohol exposure. Provides referrals, resources, and information on a broad range of alcohol and pregnancy services.

Parents, The Anti-Drug: www.theantidrug.com. Educates parents on teen drug use. Offers advice, education, and newsletter. Produces television ads, which you can also view online.

Recovery Is Everywhere: www.recoveryiseverywhere.com. Celebrates recovery while working to reduce the stigma associated with the disease of addiction.

Books and Publications

For a more thorough list of recommended books for families, alcoholics, and addicts, go to www.lovefirst.net.

Gorski, Terence T., *Passages through Recovery: An Action Plan for Preventing Relapse* (Center City, MN: Hazelden, 1997).

Jay, Debra, *No More Letting Go: The Spirituality of Taking Action Against Alcoholism and Drug Addiction* (New York: Bantam, 2006). Practical and compassionate, this book offers a course of action for families facing a loved one's addiction. The author argues that the traditional advice of "letting go" too often destroys both addict and family physically, emotionally, and spiritually. www.nomorelettinggo.com.

Jay, Debra, and Carol Colleran, *Aging and Addiction: Helping Older Adults Overcome Alcohol or Medication Dependence* (Center City, MN: Hazelden, 2002). A resource for families, this book provides a respectful, definitive guide for recognizing and addressing substance abuse among older adults. www.agingandaddiction.net.

Jay, Jeff, and Jerry Boriskin, *At Wit's End: What You Need to Know When a Loved One Is Diagnosed with Addiction and Mental Illness* (Center City, MN: Hazelden, 2007). For families seeking answers about a loved one's co-occurring disorder. Learn how psychiatric diagnoses mimic addictive disorders, why chemical use exacerbates psychiatric problems, various treatment approaches, and when intervention is needed. www.dualdiagnosis.info.

Ketcham, Katherine, and Nicholas A. Pace, *Teens Under the Influence: The Truth About Kids, Alcohol, and Other Drugs–How to Recognize the Problem and What to Do About It* (New York: Ballantine Books, 2003). A valuable parenting resource that takes an honest look at the problem of teenage substance abuse including intervention, treatment, and relapse.

Larsen, Earnie, *From Anger to Forgiveness* (Center City, MN: Hazelden, 1992). A practical guide to breaking the negative power of anger and achieving reconciliation.

Moyers, William Cope, and Katherine Ketcham, *Broken: My Story of Addiction and Redemption* (New York: Viking, 2006). The son of broadcast journalist Bill Moyers destroyed a bright career at CNN and deserted his family as a thirty-five-year-old crack addict. The inspiring story of how he turned his life around.

Various authors. Hazelden Meditation Series. Hazelden. The books in this series have guided millions of recovering people, their families, and those looking for spiritual growth. Titles include: *Each Day a New Beginning: Daily Meditations for Women; Days of Healing, Days of Joy; In God's Care: Daily Meditations on Spirituality in Recovery.*

Wegsheider Cruse, Sharon, *Another Chance: Hope and Health for the Alcoholic Family* (Palo Alto, CA: Science and Behavior Books, 1989). Describes the family disease of alcoholism and the roles family members subconsciously adopt to cope with the problem.

Twelve Step Organizations

Al-Anon/Alateen Family Group. www.al-anon.org. Helps families and friends of alcoholics recover from the effects of living with the problem drinking of a relative or friend. Alateen is a similar

program for youth. Call for meetings in the United States and
Canada. Phone: 888-4AL-ANON.

Alcoholics Anonymous. www.alcoholics-anonymous.org. A
fellowship of men and women who want to stay sober. It
is nonprofessional, self-supporting, nondenominational,
multiracial, apolitical, and available most places. Phone:
212-870-3400.

Cocaine Anonymous. www.ca.org. Adapted from the Alcoholics
Anonymous program, the only requirement for membership
is the desire to stop using cocaine and all other mood-altering
substances. Phone: 310-559-5833.

Debtors Anonymous. www.debtorsanonymous.org. The goal of this
program is to live without incurring any unsecured debt and
to help other compulsive debtors achieve solvency. Web site
offers online and telephone meetings. Phone: 800-421-2383 or
781-453-2743.

Families Anonymous. www.familiesanonymous.org. A program for
family members and friends concerned about someone's current,
suspected, or past drug, alcohol, or related behavioral problems.
Call for meetings in the United States and Canada. Phone:
800-736-9805.

Gam-Anon. www.gam-anon.org. Composed of men and women
who are husbands, wives, relatives, or close friends of compulsive gamblers. Phone: 718-352-1671.

Gamblers Anonymous. www.gamblersanonymous.org. A fellowship
of men and women who share their experience, strength, and
hope with each other so that they may solve their common
problem of gambling and help others. Phone: 213-386-8789.

Nar-Anon Family Groups. http://nar-anon.org. Designed to help
relatives and friends of addicts recover from the effects of living
with an addicted relative or friend. Web site lists local meetings.
Phone: 800-477-6291 or 310-534-8188.

Narcotics Anonymous. www.na.org. A program that reaches
out to people addicted to illegal drugs or narcotics. Phone:
818-773-9999.

Nicotine Anonymous. www.nicotine-anonymous.org. Welcomes those seeking freedom from nicotine addiction. Phone: 415-750-0328.

Overeaters Anonymous. www.oa.org. Offers a program of recovery for compulsive overeating. Phone: 505-891-2664.

S-Anon International Family Groups. www.sanon.org. Support for people living with the problem of a friend or relative's sexaholism. Phone: 800-210-8141 or 615-833-3152.

Sex Addicts Anonymous. www.sexaa.org. Reaches out to those who desire to overcome their sexual addiction. Phone: 800-477-8191.

Sexaholics Anonymous. www.sa.org. For those who desire to become sexually sober. Phone: 866-424-8777 or 615-370-6062.

Alcohol and Drug Treatment Centers

We've had positive experiences with the following treatment centers, but please review treatment centers for yourself and decide if they are the best choice for your loved one.

For direct online links to these treatment facilities, go to www.lovefirst.net.

Betty Ford Center. www.bettyfordcenter.org. Adult inpatient treatment program. Special program for licensed professionals. Offers a two- to three-day outpatient evaluation with treatment recommendations. Family program offers a separate program for young children of addicted parents. Rancho Mirage, CA. Phone: 800-434-7365.

Brighton Hospital. www.brightonhospital.org. One of the oldest treatment centers in the country. Adult inpatient and outpatient. Adolescent outpatient. Special track for physicians, lawyers, clergy, and those in law enforcement. Licensed for co-occurring disorders. Holistic healing program. Halfway houses for men and women. Excellent medical team. Located in a rural setting on a lake one hour from Detroit. Moderately priced. Brighton, MI. Phone: 888-215-2700.

Caron Foundation. www.caron.org. Inpatient treatment programs for adults, young adult males, and adolescents. Offers co-dependency and self-development workshops. Outpatient services available. Live help available on the Web site. Main campus in Wernersville, PA. Also, a variety of services are available in Florida, Bermuda, and New York. Phone: 800-678-2332.

Crossroads Centre. www.crossroadsantigua.org. Eric Clapton founded this alcohol and drug treatment center for adults, located on the ocean in the eastern Caribbean. The program is based on a Twelve Step model and incorporates a body, mind, and spirit approach. In addition to traditional approaches to treatment, the center uses holistic methods including massage, yoga, acupuncture, hydrotherapy, nutritional assessment, and fitness training. Offers a family program, renewal center, and scholarship program. Confidentiality of each client is maximized, as records remain out of the country. Antigua, West Indies. Passport required. Phone: 888-452-0091.

Cumberland Heights. www.cumberlandheights.org. Programs for adults and adolescents: inpatient, outpatient, and extended care. Offers a specialized women's program and track for professionals. Relapse prevention program is available for patients with a previous history of relapse. Main campus is located in the rolling hills outside of Nashville, TN. 800-646-9998.

Father Martin's Ashley. www.fathermartinsashley.com. A stately facility situated on forty-five acres overlooking the Chesapeake Bay. Founded by Father Joseph C. Martin, the center offers inpatient treatment for adults. Relapse prevention and DWI program offered. Go to Web site for virtual tour. Harve de Grace, MD (near Baltimore). Phone: 800-799-4673.

Hanley Center. www.hanleycenter.org. Inpatient services include separate programs for men and women, and a specialized program for adults aged fifty-five and older. A new resource center offers intensive outpatient treatment, executive and professional programs, couples therapy, anger management, family program, and a recovery bookstore, lecture hall, and café. Offers an exercise center and outdoor pool. Ask about creative funding. West Palm Beach, FL. 866-4HANLEY.

Hazelden Foundation. www.hazelden.org. Pioneer of modern treatment, founded in 1949. Inpatient treatment programs for adults and for youth between the ages of fourteen and twenty-five. Outpatient and day treatment available. A newly designed treatment facility for women overlooks the lake. Multiple extended care facilities available. Renewal Center offers workshops and recovery retreats. The Lodge offers a relapse prevention program. The main campus is situated lakeside in a rural setting outside of Minneapolis. Other locations include Chicago, New York, and Newberg, Oregon. A special program for impaired physicians and other professionals is available at the Oregon facility. Hazelden is known for book publishing and research. Maintains a database of professional interventionists. Center City, MN. Phone: 800-257-7810.

La Hacienda. www.lahacienda.com. An inpatient program in the beautiful Texas hill country. Offers both adult and collegiate programs. A relapse program is available. Features a Twelve Step foundation with an optional Christian focus. Clinical services include working with co-occurring disorders. Adult treatment is thirty-two to sixty days. The collegiate program is forty-five to sixty days. Hunt, TX. Phone: 800-749-6160.

Mayflower. www.mayflowercenter.com. Specializing in treating men with a history of relapse. A twelve-week program. Offers a halfway house. San Rafael, CA. Phone: 800-376-0033.

Rosecrance. www.rosecrance.org. Adult inpatient, partial hospitalization, and outpatient treatment. Family counseling and an introduction to the Twelve Steps provided. Amenities include a serenity walking path, a chapel, a fitness center, a child care center, and a playground. Rockford, IL. Phone: 815-391-1000.

Sober Living by the Sea. www.soberliving.com. Non-institutional, homelike atmosphere. Offers primary and extended treatment with innovative programs, including a college-accredited program for continued education while in treatment. Geared toward young adults with an emphasis on community-based recovery. Extended care is available. Situated close to the ocean. Newport Beach, CA. Phone: 866-323-5609.

Talbott Recovery Campus. www.talbottcampus.com. Offers a sixty-day and a ninety-day inpatient program for chemical dependency for adults and young adults, with a strong emphasis on co-occurring disorders. Known for their innovative Professionals Program, originally developed for addicted physicians and now open to all professionals. A ninety-six-hour assessment is available. Also offers intensive outpatient treatment. Atlanta, GA. Phone: 800-445-4232.

WeMAC. www.wemac.com. A specialized model of treatment for chemically dependent health professionals and others in helping professions. Length of stay is three to four months. Offers both a three-day and a two-week diagnostic assessment. Intensive outpatient treatment available. Grand Rapids, MI. Phone: 616-365-8800.

Willingway Hospital. www.willingway.com. Family-run alcohol and drug treatment center founded by Dr. John Mooney in the 1960s. Offers detox, inpatient, and outpatient treatment. Length of stay is four to six weeks. Statesboro, GA. Phone: 800-242-9455.

Low-Cost Alcohol and Drug Treatment Centers

Dawn Farm. www.dawnfarm.org. Located on a working farm, a residential program offering a long-term program. Age seventeen and older. Pregnant women are accepted. Treatment is available for up to six months, with a minimum stay of sixty days. Low-cost transitional housing is available, and mothers with small children are accepted. No one is denied treatment

due to lack of funds, but expect waiting lists. Ann Arbor, MI.
Phone: 734-485-8725.

English Mountain Recovery. www.emrecovery.org. Located on a
twenty-seven-acre campus in the Smokey Mountains. Program
includes Twelve Step work, family program, equine therapy,
relapse prevention, nutritional therapy, yoga, acupuncture, and
more. Ninety-day-program for adults. A good choice when you
need long-term care but finances are limited. Sevierville, TN.
Phone: 877-459-8595.

Harmony Foundation. www.harmonyfoundationinc.com. A
residential treatment program for men and women who are
twenty-three years or older. Situated on a forty-acre campus in
a mountain setting. Group therapy and AA meetings are gender
specific. Treatment includes working through the first five steps
of the Twelve Steps of AA. Length of stay is twenty-eight days.
Estes Park, CO. Phone: 970-586-4491.

High Watch Farm. www.highwatchfarm.com. Located on a
200-acre farm; admits people eighteen years and older who
have been drug and alcohol free for seventy-two hours. Medical
services are available seven days a week. Minimum stay is
twenty-one days. Founded by Bill Wilson and Marty Mann.
North Kent, CT. Phone: 860-927-3772.

Long Island Center for Recovery. www.longislandcenterforrecovery.
com. Good, basic inpatient treatment. Offers relapse prevention,
nutritional counseling, and groups for men, women, and young
adults. Payment plans available. Hampton Bays, NY. Phone:
631-728-3100.

New Found Life. www.newfoundlife.com. Highly structured, inpatient treatment. Program includes group counseling, in-house
meetings, meditation, education sessions. Offers long-term
treatment option. Long Beach, CA. Phone: 800-635-9899.

Phoenix Recovery Center. www.phoenixrecoverycenter.com. In-
patient programs at a reasonable price. Length of stay varies.
A discount is offered to those who don't have insurance.
Edgewater, MD. Phone: 800-671-9516 or 410-671-7374.

St. Christopher's. www.stchris-br.com. Residential treatment
program for adult males. Web site provides good overview of
programs. Length of stay is thirty to ninety days. Baton Rouge,
LA. Phone: 877-782-4747.

Safe Harbor. www.safeharborhouse.com. A ninety-day extended
care program for women who've completed primary treatment.
Will accept those who've relapsed. Program is divided into
three phases. Length of stay up to one year. Located in a lovely
home setting, it's designed to nurture the needs of recovering
women. Must be eighteen years old and medically stable. Must
be alcohol and drug free for seventy-two hours or commit to
detox. Payment plan available. Orange County, CA. Phone:
949-645-1026.

Sundown M Ranch. www.sundown.org. Offers inpatient treatment
for adults and youth. Separate tracks for male and female,
pregnant women, elder adults, relapse prevention, and nicotine
cessation. Programs for teen girls include treatment for eating
disorders, self-mutilation, and depression. Certified school
program available. Exercise room and gymnasium. Extended
care programs. Outpatient services. Selah, WA. Phone:
800-326-7444.

The Retreat. www.theretreat.org. One of our favorite low-cost
centers, program is based on the spirituality of the Twelve Steps
of AA. Beautifully appointed 42,000-square-foot facility in a
picturesque wooded setting. Detox required prior to admission.
Private bedrooms. Go to Web site for a virtual tour and sample
of daily schedule. Long-term residential housing is available.
Located in Wayzata, MN, a suburb of Minneapolis. Phone:
866-928-3434.

Valley Hope Association. www.valleyhope.com. Operates inpatient
and outpatient treatment centers in Kansas, Nebraska,
Oklahoma, Missouri, Arizona, Colorado, and Texas. Length of
stay is twenty-one to thirty days. Phone: 800-544-5101.

Veritas Villa. www.veritasvilla.com. Long-standing program for
adults on 105 acres of woodlands in upstate New York, with

an emphasis on Twelve Step–based treatment and alumni involvement. Offers a women's program and an older adult program. Kerhonkson, NY. Phone: 845-626-3555.

Yellowstone. www.yellowstonerecovery.com. Affordable treatment in a sober house environment. Residential treatment is ninety days to twelve months, as is outpatient treatment. Sober living available for up to two years. Costa Mesa, CA. Phone: 888-941-9048.

Alcohol and Drug Treatment Centers for Special Populations

Programs treating co-occurring disorders

Advanced Recovery Center. www.arc-hope.com. Offers an extended care program for men and women with co-occurring disorders who have completed primary treatment. Areas of special focus include PTSD and relapse prevention. Delray Beach, FL. Phone: 877-272-4673.

The Canyon. www.thecyn.com. Treatment facility, in a beautiful setting, for co-occurring disorders. Specializes in chemical dependency, trauma, and PTSD. Offers equine therapy and adventure/ropes therapy. Nutrition program includes organic cuisine and personal food plans. Malibu, CA. Phone: 877-345-3396.

CORE Center of Recovery. www.laprobgam.org/core.php. Residential treatment for problem gambling. Includes group therapy, individual counseling, and financial planning. Shreveport, LA. Phone: 318-424-4357.

Cottonwood de Tucson. www.cottonwooddetucson.com. Dual diagnosis program treating chemical dependency, gambling, depression, codependency, anxiety, PTSD, trauma, domestic violence, food issues, bipolar disorder, anger issues, grief, and sexual issues. Programs for adults, young adults ages eighteen to twenty-three, and adolescent girls. Specialized program for legal professionals. Campus situated on thirty-five acres in the foothills of the Sonoran Desert. Tucson, AZ. Phone: 800-877-4520.

Keystone. www.keystonetreatment.com. Residential and outpatient alcohol, drug, and gambling treatment facility for adults, young adults, and adolescents. Offers both Christian and Native American tracks. Specialty programs for dual diagnosis, methamphetamine addiction, narcotic dependence, and more. Canton, SD. Phone: 877-762-3740.

The Meadows. www.themeadows.org. Located in the Sonora Desert, treatment focus is on addiction, trauma, compulsive disorders, mood disorders, anxiety disorders, sexual addiction, and other co-occurring disorders. Special services include recreational and art therapy, spirituality counseling, cutting-edge workshops, nutritional consultation, yoga, tai chi, and acupuncture. Program runs for five weeks. Wickenburg, AZ. Phone: 800-632-3697.

Menninger Clinic. www.menningerclinic.com. Excellent psychiatric and chemical dependency services for adults, young adults, and adolescents. Specialty programs include eating disorders, obsessive-compulsive disorders, inpatient evaluation programs, and professionals in crisis. Length of stay varies according to need. Houston, TX. Phone: 800-351-9058.

Pine Grove. www.pinegrovetreatment.com. Mississippi's largest treatment facility for psychiatric and addictive diseases. Programs include psychiatric, adolescent, sexual compulsivity, relationship addiction, and eating disorders. Length of stay is ninety days. If you do not have insurance coverage, you receive a 15 percent discount. Hattiesburg, MS. Phone: 888-574-4673.

Ridgeview Institute. www.ridgeviewinstitute.com. Highly individualized, dual-diagnosis treatment center. Offers adult, older adult, young adult, and adolescent services. Specialized women's program: eating disorders, depression, anxiety, addictive disorders, and obsessive disorders. Inpatient, partial hospitalization, and outpatient options available. Relapse track. Online screening tests. Atlanta, GA. Phone: 800-329-9775.

Shades of Hope. www.shadesofhope.com. A residential and outpatient all-addictions treatment center specializing in the intensive treatment of eating disorders. Programs include: alcoholism, drug addiction, eating disorders, nicotine addiction, exercise addiction, sex addiction, and self-mutilation. Offers a forty-two-day program, transitional housing, and halfway house. Weeklong eating disorder workshops. Buffalo Gap, TX. Phone: 800-588-HOPE.

Sierra Tucson. www.sierratucson.com. Chemical dependency and dual diagnosis services, including trauma, eating disorders, mood disorders, anxiety, gambling and sex addiction. Pain Management Program uses holistic approach for those suffering from chronic pain. Offers innovative therapies: adventure therapy, creative expression, equine-assisted therapy, climbing wall, and challenge course. Located at the foot of the Santa Catalina Mountains. Tucson, AZ. Phone: 800-842-4487.

Vanguard Compulsive Gambling Program. www.projectturnabout .com. For adult men and women suffering from gambling addiction. Located in Granite Falls, MN, it is one of the few residential treatment programs available specifically for problem gambling. Phone: 800-862-1453.

The Victorian of Newport Beach. www.eatingdisordertreatment.com. Residential program treating anorexia, bulimia, binge eating, and compulsive over-eating. Associated with Sober Living By the Sea, which treats addictions. Close to the beach in a Victorian-style house. Program director, Dr. Barbara Cole, is author of *The Eating Disorder Solution.* Newport Beach, CA. Phone: 888-268-9182.

Older adult programs

Hanley Center Older Adult Program. www.hanleycenter.org. A one-of-a-kind inpatient program for adults age fifty-five and older. Homelike atmosphere designed for an older population. Includes a serenity garden and chapel, pool and recreation room, bookstore, beauty salon, and medical and nursing staff.

Beautiful campus with lush tropical gardens and fountains.
West Palm Beach, FL. 888-4HANLEY.

Ridgeview Institute. www.ridgeviewinstitute.com. Offers comprehensive evaluations and inpatient care for adults sixty and older
with psychiatric or chemical dependence disorders. Includes
twenty-four-hour nursing care, medication management, individual and group therapies, family therapy, activity therapy, and
educational groups. Atlanta, GA. Phone: 800-329-9775.

Veritas Villa: www.veritasvilla.com. Offers an older adult program.
Recovering seniors can live indefinitely at the Villa—making it
their home—enjoying a productive life interacting with people
of all ages. Kerhonkson, NY. Phone: 845-626-3555.

Youth programs

Caron Adolescent Center. www.caron.org. Designed for youth ages
twelve to nineteen. Situated in a mountain setting. Offers group,
individual, and family therapy. An on-site teaching staff provides
alternative classroom instruction and contact with the patient's
home school district. Caron is a gender-separate program and
offers an extended care program. Wernersville, PA. Phone:
800-678-2332.

Hazelden Center for Youth and Families. www.hazelden.org. Residential and outpatient treatment for youth ages fourteen to
twenty-five. Services include primary care, extended care, parent
education, and outpatient counseling clinic. Parent program.
Also offers *Teen Intervene,* designed to provide education, support, and guidance for teens who have experienced mild to
moderate chemical use. Plymouth, MN. Phone: 800-257-7810.

Ridgeview Institute. www.ridgeviewinstitute.com. Highly
individualized, dual-diagnosis treatment center offering
adolescent services. Online screening tests. Atlanta, GA.
Phone: 800-329-9775.

Rosecrance. www.rosecrance.org. Offers inpatient, partial hospitalization, and outpatient for adolescents ages twelve to eighteen.
Located on fifty acres of woods, ponds, and gardens. Facility was

designed for this age group. Groups are gender-specific. Onsite school. Fitness center. Offers two recovery homes for females, ages fifteen to nineteen, with length of stay six to twelve months. See videos on Web site for tours of programs. Rockford, IL. Phone: 815-391-1000.

Sundown M Youth Treatment Center. www.sundown.org. Accepts male and female youth. Treatment groups and living quarters are gender-specific. School program is staffed by certified teachers. Grades four through twelve are offered. Patients work on assignments from home schools. Treatment includes a two-phase family program. Selah, WA. Phone: 800-326-7444.

Visions. www.visionsteen.com. Serves males and females, ages twelve to seventeen, with drug and alcohol addiction, behavioral problems, and co-occurring disorders. Intensive, structured program situated in a supportive, homelike environment. Meals utilize natural, organic products that are chemical, sugar, and preservative free. Offers a scholastic academy designed for students having a difficult time in conventional classroom settings. Malibu, CA. Phone: 866-889-3665.

Wilderness Treatment Center. www.wildernessaltschool.com. A sixty-day program for young males. Includes a sixteen- to twenty-one-day wilderness experience. Accepts males ages fourteen to twenty-four. Patient-to-counselor ratio is five to one Sample schedule is available on Web site. Marion, MT. Phone: 406-854-2832.

Gay, lesbian, and transgender program

Pride Institute. www.pride-institute.com. Quality treatment for drug and alcohol addiction in the gay, lesbian, bisexual, and transgender community. Offers specialty treatment for sex addiction, anxiety disorders, HIV/AIDS, related stress, and depression. Ask about financing and step-down programs. Located in Minnesota, Texas, and New Jersey. 800-54-PRIDE.

Help Lines

Childhelp National Child Abuse Hotline. 800-422-4453. Call if
you are a child being abused, a parent about to lose control, an
adult survivor of abuse feeling suicidal, or an adult looking for
parenting tips. Provides local telephone numbers for reporting
cases of abuse.

Hazelden Foundation. 800-257-7810. A help line for people seeking
guidance for themselves or loved ones. Maintains a national list
of interventionists and a list of books relevant to specific needs.

National Clearinghouse for Alcohol and Drug Information. English:
800-729-6686. Hablamos Espanol: 877-767-8432. TDD:
800-487-4889. Information specialists are trained to answer
questions about alcohol and substance abuse prevention, intervention, and treatment. They also refer crisis calls to appropriate
sources. Available twenty-four hours.

National Council on Alcoholism and Drug Dependence. 800-NCA-
CALL. Twenty-four-hour referral to local NCADD affiliates
who can provide information and referrals to services in callers'
local areas.

National Runaway Switchboard. 800-621-4000. Call if you are a
teenager who is thinking of running from home, if you have
a friend who has run and is looking for help, or if you are a
runaway ready to go home. For parents whose child has run
away, is threatening to run away, or has run and is returning
home. Program for teachers available.

National Suicide Prevention Hotline. 800-273-TALK (8255). A
twenty-four-hour, toll-free suicide prevention service available
to anyone in suicidal crisis, or family and friends who are
concerned about a loved one who may be experiencing these
feelings.

Twelve Steps of Alcoholics Anonymous*

1. We admitted we were powerless over alcohol—that our lives had become unmanageable.
2. Came to believe that a Power greater than ourselves could restore us to sanity.
3. Made a decision to turn our will and our lives over to the care of God *as we understood Him.*
4. Made a searching and fearless moral inventory of ourselves.
5. Admitted to God, to ourselves, and to another human being the exact nature of our wrongs.
6. Were entirely ready to have God remove all these defects of character.
7. Humbly asked Him to remove our shortcomings.
8. Made a list of all persons we had harmed, and became willing to make amends to them all.
9. Made direct amends to such people wherever possible, except when to do so would injure them or others.
10. Continued to take personal inventory and when we were wrong promptly admitted it.
11. Sought through prayer and meditation to improve our conscious contact with God *as we understood Him,* praying only for knowledge of His will for us and the power to carry that out.
12. Having had a spiritual awakening as the result of these steps, we tried to carry this message to alcoholics, and to practice these principles in all our affairs.

* The Twelve Steps of AA are taken from *Alcoholics Anonymous,* 4th ed., published by AA World Services, Inc., New York, NY, 59–60. Reprinted with permission of AA World Services, Inc. (See author's note on copyright page.)

Index

A

abstinence, 15–17, 55
acceptance, 5
addiction, xx–xxi
  characteristics of, 54–55
  costs of, 31–32
  denial by families of, 38–39,
    40, 41
  dependence vs., 31
  determination of, 56–57
  as disease, 30, 57
    family, 19–23, 31, 39, 132
    power of, 76
    primary, 78–79, 105
  doctors knowledgeable about,
    77–78
  effect on brain, 24–28
  Jellinek Curve, 300
  myths about, 6–8, 29–32
  prevalence of, 38
  professionals with, 92–93
  societal influences promoting,
    57 (*See also* prescription
    drugs)
  switching one for another, 14,
    30, 77
  See also alcoholism

addicts. *See* alcoholics
adolescents
  assessing chemical use by,
    172–73, 294–97
  development of alcoholism in,
    170–71
  effect of alcoholism on brains
    of, 27–28
  forcing into treatment, 143–44
  interventions on, 173–75
  treatment centers for, 175,
    315–16
adoption studies, 21
advertising and adolescents,
  170–71
affirmations in letters, 133
aftercare plans, 217, 221–23
*Aging and Addiction: Helping
  Older Adults Overcome Alcohol
  or Medication Dependence* (Jay
  and Colleran), 179
Al-Anon, 41, 50, 168, 231–34
  detachment and, 200
  focus of, 229
  resources of, 105
alcohol
  effect on brain of, 25, 27–28

Abuse and Alcoholism
(NIAAA), 18, 22, 26, 76, 78,
170
Newcomer Asks, A (Alcoholics
Anonymous), 236
Niebuhr, Reinhold, 51

O

older adults
alcoholism in, 176, 177,
292–93
consideration of generational
differences among, 183
detoxification of, 181
doctors' ability to diagnose
alcoholism in, 76
finding treatment centers for,
314–15
interventions on, 176–79,
180–81, 255–56
prescription drugs and, 177–79
treatment for, 180, 181–82
opiates
chronic pain and, 252–55
dependence vs. addiction on, 31
genetics and, 21
interventions on users of, 109,
253, 254
outpatient treatment vs. inpatient,
121–22
overeating, compulsive, 247–48

P

pain
avoiding as primary goal of
addicts, 47–49
opiates and chronic, 252–55
safe management methods of,
31
using interventionist and, 119
during withdrawal

Passages through Recovery (Gorski),
239
Peale, Norman Vincent, 60–61
peer assistance programs, 92–93
*Physicians' Guide to Helping
Patients with Alcohol Problems,
The*, 78
Power of Positive Thinking, The
(Peale), 61
prescription drugs
chronic pain and, 252–55
myths about using, 31
older adults and, 177–79
professionals with addictions,
92–93

R

recovery
being fired during, 82
families resisting, 226–27
importance of Twelve Step
programs to, 55, 105, 223,
236
Jellinek Curve, 300
relationship problems during,
229
without treatment, 124–25
refeeding syndrome, 248
relapse agreements, 205, 241
relapses
Alcoholics Anonymous and,
205, 237
co-occurring addictions and,
240
family support and, 241
frequency of, 239
interventions after, 119, 204–5,
241–42
preparing for, 205, 241
reasons for, 239–40
treatment after, 122

Jeff Jay is a nationally known lecturer and interventionist. He has been seen on CNN, the *Jane Pauley Show*, and PBS. His work has been featured in *Parade* magazine, *USA Today*, *The Washington Post*, and Forbes Online.

Jeff specializes in family and executive interventions. He is the coauthor of *At Wit's End: What You Need to Know When a Loved One Is Diagnosed with Addiction and Mental Illness*, published by Hazelden. He is a graduate of the University of Minnesota and a certified addictions professional. He is a former clinician for the Hazelden Foundation and former director of program development for Brighton Hospital. His personal recovery from alcohol and drug addiction dates from October 4, 1981.

Debra Jay is the author of *No More Letting Go: The Spirituality of Taking Action Against Alcoholism and Drug Addiction*, published by Bantam. She is the coauthor of *Aging and Addiction: Helping Older Adults Overcome Alcohol or Medication Dependence*.

Debra is a nationally known lecturer and has been writing a newspaper column on alcohol and drugs since 1996. A graduate of the Ohio State University and the Hazelden Addiction Professional Training Program, she worked clinically for the Hazelden Foundation and as a nationally known interventionist. Debra appeared regularly on *The Oprah Winfrey Show* and was featured in *Prevention Magazine*.

Jeff and Debra Jay reside in Grosse Pointe, Michigan, and can be contacted through their Web site at www.lovefirst.net.

Additional Resources for Families:

At Wit's End
What You Need to Know When a Loved One Is Diagnosed with Addiction and Mental Illness

Jeff Jay and Jerry A. Boriskin, Ph.D.

Addiction recovery experts Jay and Boriskin provide vital information and support for families dealing with a loved one's co-occurring psychiatric and addiction problems. *At Wit's End* demystifies complex terms and provides helpful insights about why chemical use exacerbates psychiatric problems and when intervention is needed. Softcover, 280 pp.
Order No. 2450

Aging and Addiction
Helping Older Adults Overcome Alcohol or Medication Dependence

Carol Colleran and Debra Jay

Treatment and intervention experts Colleran and Jay reveal how to recognize and address substance abuse among older adults. Key topics include understanding the relationship between aging and addiction, finding help for a loved one, and recognizing the treatment needs of older adults. Softcover, 232 pp.
Order No. 1961

A Steadfast Companion for Those in Early Addiction Recovery:

A New Day, A New Life
A Guided Journal

William Cope Moyers with Jodie Carter

"One of the most exciting new resources I've seen. If I had a wish, it would be to put this in the hands of all newly recovering alcoholics, addicts, and their families."

—Debra Jay, coauthor of *Love First*

This innovative journal and DVD set serves as an effective guide for people facing the challenges of early sobriety. The DVD features an intimate conversation between best-selling author Moyers and a diverse group of people in recovery. The journal helps readers connect the knowledge that they have drawn from the DVD to their own experiences with addiction and sobriety. Softcover, 440 pp. DVD, 25 min.
Order No. 0636

Hazelden books are available at bookstores everywhere.
To order directly from Hazelden, call 800-328-9000 or visit hazelden.org/bookstore.